Tom Murphy

Plays: 6

The Vicar of Wakefield, The Cherry Orchard, The Drunkard, The Last Days of a Reluctant Tyrant

The Vicar of Wakefield: modelled on Oliver Goldsmith's classic novel, Tom Murphy's comedy is peopled with thieves, pimps, bawds and impostors who prey on innocence unless God – or the ruling class – takes a hand.

The Cherry Orchard: 'shot through with an insightful and colloquial sparkle.' *The Times*

The Drunkard: 'a wonderfully eloquent play. Murphy's ear is finely attuned to the glories and absurdities of melodramatic exclamation, and even while he is wringing out its ludicrous overstatement, he is also making it sing.' *Irish Times*

The Last Days of a Reluctant Tyrant: 'its contemporary Irish resonances are amplified to highlight greed and the hollowness of religious hypocrisy . . . as a morality tale, this is thumping with home truths.' *Guardian*

Tom Murphy was born in Tuam, County Galway and now lives in Dublin. He has received numerous theatre awards and holds honorary degrees from Trinity College Dublin and NUI (Galway). A six-play season celebrating his work was presented by the Irish National Theatre – 'Tom Murphy at The Abbey' – in 2001. He has written for television and film, and a novel, *The Seduction of Morality*. His stage plays include *A Whistle in the Dark*, *On the Outside* (with Noel O'Donoghue), *Famine*, *A Crucial Week in the Life of a Grocer's Assistant*, *The Morning After Optimism*, *The White House*, *On the Inside*, *The Vicar of Wakefield* or *She Stoops to Folly*, *The Sanctuary Lamp*, *Epitaph Under Ether* (a compilation from the works of J. M. Synge), *The Blue Macushla*, *The Informer* (from the novel by Liam O'Flaherty), *The Gigli Concert*, *Conversations on a Homecoming*, *Bailegangaire*, *A Thief of a Christmas*, *Too Late For Logic*, *The Patriot Game*, *The Wake*, *The House*, *The Drunkard*, *The Cherry Orchard*, *Alice Trilogy* and *The Last Days of a Reluctant Tyrant*.

TOM MURPHY

Plays: 6

The Vicar of Wakefield
The Cherry Orchard
The Drunkard
The Last Days of a Reluctant Tyrant

with an introduction by the author

Methuen Drama

METHUEN DRAMA CONTEMPORARY DRAMATISTS

1 3 5 7 9 10 8 6 4 2

This collection first published in Great Britain in 2010 by Methuen Drama

Methuen Drama
A & C Black Publishers Limited
36 Soho Square, London W1D 3QY
www.methuendrama.com

The Vicar of Wakefield originally published as *She Stoops to Folly* in 1996.
Revised in this volume. Copyright © 1996, 2010 by Tom Murphy

The Cherry Orchard first published in 2004. Revised in this volume.
Copyright © 2004, 2010 by Tom Murphy

The Drunkard first published in 2004 by Carysfort Press.
Revised in this volume. Copyright © 2004, 2010 by Tom Murphy

The Last Days of a Reluctant Tyrant first published in 2009.
Revised in this volume. Copyright © 2009, 2010 by Tom Murphy

Introduction © 2010 Tom Murphy

Tom Murphy has asserted his rights under the Copyright, Designs and
Patents Act, 1988, to be identified as the author of these works

ISBN: 978 1 408 12388 1

A CIP catalogue record for this book is available from the British Library

Typeset by Country Setting, Kingsdown, Kent
Printed and bound in Great Britain by Lightning Source UK, Milton Keynes

To
JB

all happiness

Contents

Tom Murphy
Chronology

<table>
<tr><td>1961</td><td>A Whistle in the Dark (Theatre Royal, Stratford East)</td></tr>
<tr><td>1962</td><td>On the Outside (with Noel O'Donoghue), Radio Eireann</td></tr>
<tr><td>1968</td><td>The Orphans (Gate Theatre)
Famine (Peacock Theatre)</td></tr>
<tr><td>1969</td><td>A Crucial Week in the Life of a Grocer's Assistant (Abbey Theatre)</td></tr>
<tr><td>1971</td><td>The Morning After Optimism (Abbey Theatre)</td></tr>
<tr><td>1972</td><td>The White House (Abbey Theatre)</td></tr>
<tr><td>1974</td><td>On the Inside (Peacock Theatre)</td></tr>
<tr><td>1975</td><td>The Vicar of Wakefield (adaptation; Abbey Theatre)</td></tr>
<tr><td>1976</td><td>The Sanctuary Lamp (Abbey Theatre)</td></tr>
<tr><td>1976</td><td>The J. Arthur Maginnis Story (Irish Theatre Company)</td></tr>
<tr><td>1979</td><td>Epitaph Under Ether (compilation from J. M. Synge; Abbey Theatre)</td></tr>
<tr><td>1980</td><td>The Blue Macushla (Abbey Theatre)</td></tr>
<tr><td>1981</td><td>The Informer (adaptation; Olympia Theatre)</td></tr>
<tr><td>1982</td><td>She Stoops to Conquer (Irish setting; Abbey Theatre)</td></tr>
<tr><td>1983</td><td>The Gigli Concert (Abbey Theatre)</td></tr>
<tr><td>1985</td><td>Conversations on a Homecoming (Druid Theatre)</td></tr>
<tr><td>1985</td><td>Bailegangaire (Druid Theatre)</td></tr>
<tr><td>1985</td><td>A Thief of a Christmas (Abbey Theatre)</td></tr>
<tr><td>1989</td><td>Too Late for Logic (Abbey Theatre)</td></tr>
<tr><td>1991</td><td>The Patriot Game (Peacock Theatre)</td></tr>
<tr><td>1994</td><td>The Seduction of Morality (a novel, pub. Little, Brown)</td></tr>
<tr><td>1995</td><td>She Stoops to Folly (South Coast Repertory Theatre, Costa Mesa, California)</td></tr>
<tr><td>1998</td><td>The Wake (Abbey Theatre)</td></tr>
<tr><td>2000</td><td>The House (Abbey Theatre)</td></tr>
<tr><td>2003</td><td>The Drunkard (b*spoke Theatre Company)</td></tr>
<tr><td>2004</td><td>The Cherry Orchard (Abbey Theatre)</td></tr>
<tr><td>2005</td><td>Alice Trilogy (Royal Court Theatre)</td></tr>
<tr><td>2009</td><td>The Last Days of a Reluctant Tyrant (Abbey Theatre)</td></tr>
</table>

Introduction

If chance there is, it is how the commissions to do these adaptations/versions of Goldmsith, Chekhov, W. H. Smith & A Gentleman and Saltykov-Shchedrin came about.

I had wanted for a long time to do a version of a Greek play, and my wish was to be fulfilled, I thought, when the Abbey Theatre came knocking and asked me would I have a look at *Antigone*. Of course I would. It was an invitation, one that relieved me of the business of selecting a particular play, the Abbey would commission a literal translation and, all being well with my part, I had a management and theatre that would put the thing on. Then the caveat: 'Set it in Belfast.' I could see the theatre's point: the play's potential could be worked to overtly represent and relate to the contemporary situation that was happening in Northern Ireland. But it wasn't for me.

I discovered that the word 'contemporary', or indeed 'ancient', did not come into the matter of how I read, recognised, was excited by, loved and was deeply affected by Greek drama; and Greek drama couldn't be local to anywhere – not even to Greece! It was about humankind, alright, in action and at war, looking for order; but I couldn't get away from the abstract: that it was more to do with self-conscious mankind in holy, pure, eternal, existential quest of itself.

So, regrets to the Abbey and to say, honestly, that I did not have the skill to fulfil the requirement. Well, came the reply, would I like to do a stage version of *The Vicar of Wakefield* by Oliver Goldsmith? Flattering: I was considered to be an all-rounder.

I knew of Goldsmith's book from childhood, but I had never read it.

It is delightful. It is a book that makes one happy. The Primrose family: Dr Primrose the vicar – pastor, father, husband, with humanity, humour, wit, moral dignity, innocently not as wise as he thinks he is, but superior to the shrewdest wisdom; Deborah, his loving wife, with her harmless vanities; and six children: all a familiar family gallery; generous, credulous, deluded. And the rogueries waiting outside this bright family circle.

For the best part of a year, prior to this, I was working on an original play and it was giving me a very hard time. I phoned the Abbey, said I'd love to do an adaptation of the book, and added, 'Now if you like.'

Doing the adaptation was not easy, but compared to the writing world I'd been inhabiting it was a honeymoon.

The adaptation of *The Vicar of Wakefield* was presented by the Abbey Theatre in their Christmas slot and it was very successful. The success was due to the fine, stylish direction of Hugh Hunt, to the designers and actors. I wondered about the script. (A honeymoon is not the time for sobriety of judgement.)

I returned to the original work that I had suspended to do the adaptation and it was like going back to conquer a disease. (The work was *The Sanctuary Lamp*, a play that now leaves me happy enough.)

The Vicar, though, continued on my mind, that I hadn't done my best justice by it and twenty years later, like a man wanting to pay conscience money, I revisited the Primrose family.

The revised adaptation (1995) is much shorter than my original effort, the Vicar's patience, like Job's, isn't so limitless, the eccentric character, Mr Burchill, who is really Sir William Thornhill in disguise, becomes more clearly a fallible *deus ex machina*, and so on with other emendations. To distinguish the revised adaptation from the earlier one, I gave it a new title, *She Stoops to Folly*; and though it has been performed under that title and though that title is true to the play's sub-plot, Olivia's story, I feel now that it is a bit too clever of me. Now, in 2010, I revert to calling it *The Vicar of Wakefield*; it is the best title. *She Stoops to Folly*, if wished, may be used as a sub-title.

*

Actors Jane Brennan and Alison McKenna, founders of a new theatre company called b*spoke, assembled a group of actors to read a play with a view towards producing it. It fell out that my living room became the venue for the reading and it fell out that I comprised the audience of one. The piece, a melodrama, an American Temperance play, was *The Drunkard* by W.H. Smith & A Gentleman.

A discussion followed the reading, every *contra* immediately followed by a *pro*. It, the play, would be expensive, it required a large cast, but 'something' could be done about that, like 'doubling up', like 'the usual'. Technical demands would make it difficult to stage and, again, expensive, but the same could be said about 'almost anything'. Minor characters were hogging the piece, their orchestrations threatening the melody, but look at the acting opportunities for the leads, for big playing. Really, objectively, all that was wrong was that the play didn't have a prologue, and it was essential that it have a prologue, and if, as someone said, the play was all over the place, couldn't someone be found to remedy these trifles? What did the audience think? I said, can you not find something better to do with your time than the play you have just read?

Several photocopied scripts of *The Drunkard* by W.H. Smith & A Gentleman were left lying about the place, I observed over the next few days, as were a few fledgling attempts at what were purporting to be a prologue, one of which I picked up in idle curiosity, began to doodle with it, which is how I became involved and the commission came about.

W. H. Smith has nothing to do with our famous bookseller. His real name was William Henry Sedley, who added Smith to become Sedley-Smith, to lessen his parent's embarrassment, it is said, at his going on the stage; he later dropped the Sedley part entirely, or at least for the purpose of writing *The Drunkard*. The identity of A Gentleman has been attributed to half-a-dozen others, none of whom disclaimed the honour, including one Phineas Taylor Barnum of circus fame. Barnum, too, is said to have been something of a temperance reformer.

To become match fit I suppose, I read whatever there was on my shelves of Victorian drama. Later in the process I looked up what plays I could find about drinking, drinkers, inns and bar rooms. The script contained in this volume is indebted to Douglas Jerrold's melodrama of 1828, *Fifteen Years of a Drunkard's Life*.

I worked from the original script, the same as was read by the b*spoke assembly of actors. I assume it is the original script. It is dated 1844, it gives the original cast and the venue is down as Boston Museum.

There is a comic character called Miss Spindle in the original script who isn't very funny any more; she is of minor importance and of little interest, yet she has possibly more lines than anyone else in the play. (Curiously, Miss Spindle is down in the original cast as having been played by 'Mrs ———— ', while the other eighteen specified characters, male and female, are credited with their names in full, as well as their titles. For instance, Edward Middleton, the leading character, was played by Mr W.H. Smith. Perhaps 'Mrs ———— ' was a speciality actress of popular favour and repute with audiences, an improvisator whose embellishments on stage, ad libs and asides, were recorded and printed; though she, for some reason or other, was not one to have her name included with the others.) In the version given in this volume Miss Spindle becomes Widdy Spindle, who appears in one scene only and with a widow's mite of lines.

I moved the setting to this side of the Atlantic, altered characters' names, dropped characters, introduced songs and new material and, as well as the prologue that was said to be essential, I wrote an epilogue.

*

Did I know *The Cherry Orchard* was the greatest play of the twentieth century? I said I believed *Three Sisters* was given that credit. No, *Three Sisters* was *arguably* the best; *The Cherry Orchard was* the best.

That exchange, with an Abbey personage did not prevent my eventually receiving an invitation to do a version of *The Cherry Orchard*, but, arguably, it endangered it and, arguably, it delayed the matter considerably, because when the invitation did come it was four years later, and the literal translation given to me, that the Abbey had commissioned, was dog-eared and dated 1998, the year of the exchange with the Abbey personage on the order of precedence of Chekhov's masterpieces.

I needed second opinions and I asked for a second literal translation. The version of *The Cherry Orchard* contained in this book derives from two literal translations: the 1998 one, which

was done by Chris Heaney, and the second one done by
Patrick Miles. I needed advice. Patrick Miles was also engaged
as my consultant.

The objective of a literal translation – to render in another
language the exact contextual meaning of the original – differs
from the purpose of a version. A version, as I see it, is more
subjective, more interpretatively open, which does not mean
that nonchalance, broadness of approach are allowed to
whoever is doing the version; but it is speculative in its
consideration of the 'spirit' of the original and seeks to translate
that 'spirit' into a language and movement that have their
own dynamic and vibrancy and, hopefully, music. And in the
case of Chekhov: who could faithfully inhabit that sensibility
and exceptional delicacy? And a version, of itself, does not
want to look like the back of a tapestry.

*

1998. I had a meeting with the theatre director Anthony Page
in London. The meeting done, en route to the front door
through a sort of ante-room that had a lot of books, without
stopping he reached to a shelf, withdrew a book from it and
gave it to me. No reason given for the gesture. I'd never
heard of the book nor of its author: *The Golovlyov Family* by
Mikhail Saltykov-Shchedrin.

The book, a novel, first issued in 1880, has classic status in
Russia; its author was a commanding literary figure (more
famous as a satirist than as a novelist) in a time that included
Tolstoy, Lermontov, Dostoyevsky, Turgenev.

There are seven or eight translations into English of the
book. I acquired four of them including the one given to me
by Anthony Page, which was the one I worked from, which
I thought the best. (It is an Everyman's Library publication,
translated by Natalie Duddington, the edition dated 1934.)
I used the other versions in my possession for cross-reference
purposes. And, again, I had the invaluable help of the translator
Patrick Miles.

The book is a very compelling read that chronicles the
degeneration of a provincial family of minor gentry who are
landowners.

Its stage potential, I thought, obvious. The process, though, of adapting it was going to be a long one and difficult. Several times while working on it I tried to recall what it was that made the book so compelling in the first place; whatever it was, wasn't to be recaptured. The book hasn't much by way of plot and development and all the characters are dead at the end, except one – and she is mortally ill. Several times I regretted ever having clapped eyes on it. (I have read that *The Golovlyov Family* can be read as a series of obituaries. I have also read that it is the bleakest or blackest of Russian novels, which is quite a badge when you consider the field.)

Porphyry, also known as Iudushka (little Judas), dominates the book; as such the one to follow one would, and should, think. He is a married man whose wife is dead, he has two sons, one of whom commits suicide, the other, convicted of embezzlement, perishes on his way to Siberia: all down to Porphyry's meanness of character; he is a civil servant of no distinction; he is a consummate hypocrite – but an unconscious one – his hypocrisy innate. (When he first appeared in print he was considered to be a Russian Tartuffe. The author said, no, he isn't, and, in a later edition of the book, Saltykov-Shchedrin wrote that Tartuffe knew what he was doing and why, he was a conscious hypocrite; in France, hypocrisy could be regarded as a 'social habit', he wrote, it could be considered as forming a part of 'good manners, so to speak'. Whereas Porphyry was a hypocrite 'of a purely Russian sort . . .' of the kind that live their lives as naturally 'as nettles grow by a fence'.)

Porphyry dominates the book and in early drafts of the play I made attempts to uphold his precedence, without success. I couldn't make it work. (I'd been down that hypocrites' road before – notably with a character called Tom in *The Wake*, 'who believes utterly everything he himself says' – and maybe I didn't want to go there again so pronouncedly.) Also I had trouble with his final end, as the book gave it, where he is transformed from monster to penitent. Despite the commentaries that I read, supporting and explaining this sudden conversion, I couldn't believe it. And a play, I knew, wouldn't accept such reversal of character. (In a contrary commentary to the supporting ones the opinion was offered that, as Saltykov-Shchedrin and Dostoyevsky were known to be enemies, the conferring at last of redemption on Porphyry was a satire on Dostoyevsky's bestowing deliverance on his characters!) In *The Last Days of a Reluctant Tyrant* he is an unmarried man, an ex-seminarian, a civil servant, a hypocrite and, to make it easy, is called Peter; he is prominent, but his is not the principal role.

I turned to Arina, the character second in importance in the book. I think she was waiting for me. She gave me the title. She is the autocratic matriarch of the family. She is the active one, she is a doer. She has a directness and an earthiness. I recognised her type. She is not gentry, I felt, but marries into it; of severe, hardened, tough, peasant stock. Her acquisitive nature, ruthless energy and unyielding defiance bring great material rewards; yet also emasculate the others. She has a weak husband, three no-good sons, and a daughter who has died, leaving in her care two grand-daughters.

Going into old age she begins to question herself, wonder what she has given her life for. For what, for whom? For something that doesn't exist? She resigns her control, loses her authority and suffers the consequences.

She dies half way through the book. Elected to lead, the play needs her to stay the distance, and she does – to a final defiant apologia. She lives to see the others dead, except one – one of her grand-daughters, who survives it all.

Tom Murphy

The Vicar of Wakefield

Previously published under the title
She Stoops to Folly

To the memory of my friend
Noel O'Donoghue

The Vicar of Wakefield, under the title *She Stoops to Folly*, was first presented at South Coast Repertory, Costa Mesa, California, on 1 September 1995. The cast was as follows:

Vicar	Jim Norton
Mrs Primrose	Jane Carr
George	Scott Denny
Olivia	Devon Raymond
Sophy	Jennifer Parsons
Moses	Christopher DuVal
Dick	Aaron Cohen /
	Anthony Petrozzi
Bill	Andrew Wood /
	Jason Lau
Mr Burchill	Richard Doyle
Mr Thornhill	Douglas Sills
Reverend Jenks	Ron Boussom
Maid/Landlady/Lady Blarney	Lynne Griffin
Miss Wilmot/Miss Skeggs	Emily Chase
Wilmot/Flamborough/Gaoler	Don Took
Landlord/Butler	Art Koustik
Timothy Baster	Todd Fuessel

Directed by Barbara Damashek
Designed by Ralph Funicello
Lighting by Peter Maradudin
Music and sound by Nathan Birnbaum

The Vicar of Wakefield, under the title *She Stoops to Folly*, was subsequently presented at the Abbey Theatre, Dublin, on 4 October 1996. The cast was as follows:

Vicar	Jim Norton
Mrs Primrose	Dierdre Donnelly
George	Michael Devaney
Olivia	Alison McKenna
Sophy	Dawn Bradfield
Moses	Rory Keenan
Dick	Simon Jewell / Sean O'Flanagain
Bill	Darren McCormack / Daniel O'Connor
Reverend Wilmot	Clive Geraghty
Miss Wilmot	Dierdre O'Kane
Landlord	Des Cave
Landlady	Fedelma Cullen
Maid	Derdriu Ring
Mr Burchill	David Herlihy
Mr Thornhill	Frank McCusker
Reverend Jeuks	John Olohan
Butler	Derry Power
Lady Blarney	Barbara Brennan
Miss Skeggs	Fionnuala Murphy
Flamborough	Stephen Blount
Gaoler	Niall O'Brien
Ephraim Jenkinson	Brendan Morrisey

Directed by Patrick Mason
Designed by Francis O'Connor
Lighting by Nick Chelton
Music by Shaun Davey
Choreography by David Bolger

Characters

Vicar
Mrs Primrose
George
Olivia
Sophy
Moses
Dick
Bill
Reverend Wilmot
Miss Wilmot
Landlord
Landlady
Maid
Mr Burchill
Mr Thornhill
Reverend Jenks
Butler
Lady Blarney
Miss Skeggs
Flamborough
Gaoler
Ephraim Jenkinson

The play derives from *The Vicar of Wakefield* by Oliver Goldsmith.

Act One

Hollow clanging of an iron door. A spot comes up on **Vicar, Dr Primrose,** *in abject state in the lower depths of prison. (There is another prisoner beside him – later, Jenks – his back to us, who appears to be writing something.)* **Gaoler** *has arrived to stand on the top step above them.*

Gaoler   Vicar! Your fellow-prisoners be assembled for their daily sermon.

Vicar *does not move.*

Gaoler   But, considering the woeful news you had today, I can disassemble them again. Yea, let them do without.

Vicar   Thank you, Mr Gaoler, but I'll continue to do my duty. Sir, a moment, please.

He needs a moment to think. The lights are changing: we are going into flashback. And he begins his story.

I was ever of the opinion that the honest man who married and brought up a family did more for his country than he who continued single and only talked of population. I chose my wife as she did her wedding gown, not for a fine glossy surface but for such qualities as would wear well. To do her justice, she was a good-natured woman, could read any English book without much spelling, and prided herself upon being an excellent contriver in housekeeping, though I could never find that we grew any the richer for all her contrivances. However, we loved each other tenderly, and our fondness increased as we grew old . . . It would be fruitless to deny exultation when I saw my little ones around me, and the vanity and satisfaction of my wife were even greater than mine.

Lights have come up to show the Primrose family in the former happiness and elegance of their Wakefield home. Centre of attention in this happy scene is **George***, the eldest, nervous and eager, who is being groomed and dressed for an event.* **Olivia***, about nineteen, very beautiful and romantic, is trimming his hair;* **Sophy***, the practical one, is sewing an adornment to his jacket;* **Dick** *and* **Bill***, of an age, say about eight – why not, say, twins? – polishing the buckles on his shoes. And the precocious one,* **Moses***, about sixteen, is reading a book. A* **Maid** *enters and exits later on. And the whole is being supervised by* **Mrs Primrose** *who is entering, who is – fifty?*

Mrs Primrose   Haste, haste, haste! Hasten, boys! Laws, Sophia! Is it necessary to sit so, huddled like a creature over your needle? Hasten, Olivia! What would they have said of Venus if she had developed the stoops? (*Demonstrating her deportment as she exits.*) Heads up, so, my dears!

Moses   Venus, said to be the daughter of Jupiter and Dione, the wife of Vulcan and the mother of Cupid, Harmonia, Hymen and the Graces. (*And he returns to his book as abruptly.*)

Vicar   And that was Moses, who had received a sort of miscellaneous education at home . . . Matrimony was one of my favourite topics. It was probably from hearing it so often recommended that George, our eldest – called after his uncle who left us ten thousand pounds – had fixed his affections on Miss Arabella Wilmot, the daughter of a wealthy clergyman.

Olivia   Sister Sophy, could you bear to marry anyone so unbeautiful, so badly made as our brother here? I know I could never endure such a thing. And how can Arabella Wilmot do it?

Sophy   Likes attract, I expect.

Olivia   Here she comes with her father – Whoa, boy! – to put signature on a document, giving control of all her fortune to her husband-to-be – Steady, George! or there'll be a gap in this thatch for your canary-bird to nest in when she arrives.

Sophy   What a goose!

Olivia   What a goose! I vow it! Because before I should take that step, I'd like to know the audibility of my fiancé's snore. For – declare to heavens – did you hear it last night? I was sure we were invaded by a breed of brontosaurus who was – fortunately for us – at napping time.

Sophy   Perhaps our sister-in-law-to-be has a taste in brontosauruses.

Olivia   I shouldn't be surprised.

Moses   Brontosauri!

George (*pulls away*)   Goose! Geese! Mama!

Sophy   Mama has no time to spare just now, George.

Olivia   Come, George, I'll be good, I promise. (*He resubmits himself to her.*) No, the man that I shall marry shall be – all fiery. But if I tell him to kneel, he shall do so. And if I frown, his heart will ache. And, of course, he shall love me. (*She has completed her work and tied a ribbon in his hair.*) There! (*Then, dreamily.*) Yes, I must be loved.

Vicar (*broken-hearted sigh*)   Livy!

George *completes his costume – jacket, shoes.*

Vicar   But there was a particular tenet of marriage that I made a point of supporting: for I maintained with William Whiston that it was unlawful for a priest of the Church of England, after the death of his first wife, to take a second. And my monogamous principles were displayed over our chimneypiece for all to see.

Mrs Primrose, *who has returned, is now taking down the framed principles in question.*

Mrs Primrose   Come, Moses, and deposit this – object – in a stable for the duration of the Wilmots' visit. It always demands comment and provides the cue for your father's lengthy discourses. Moses, you lump, haste! – The Wilmots are upon us. The subject of monogamy must be avoided on this occasion at all costs.

Moses *is taking the frame away as the* **Vicar**, *now, joins the scene.*

Vicar   Hold, my son! Where to so fast with your mother's epitaph?

Mrs Primrose   It wants dusting, my dear.

Vicar (*examining it*) Nothing in extreme. Conscientious child! (*Dusts it.*) Hey presto cockalorum!

Maid (*entering, announcing*) The Reverend Wilmot and Miss Wilmot.

Rev Wilmot *is in his seventies,* **Miss Wilmot** *is about twenty.*

Vicar   Reverend Sir! My most charming girl!

George   Miss Wilmot!

Miss Wilmot   Mr Primrose!

She and **George** *do not speak further, they continue formal.*

Vicar   Dear friends! Oh! (*The framed 'epitaph' in his hands.*) You are familiar with the works of William Whiston and his monogamous principles for reverend gentlemen? Well, I'm glad to say I have gone a step beyond him –

Mrs Primrose   Come nearer the fire, Reverend Wilmot –

Vicar   As Whiston had engraved on his wife's tomb that she was his *only* wife, I have written a similar epitaph for my Deborah –

Mrs Primrose   Pray be seated, Reverend Wilmot

Vicar   See, here, I extol her virtues. And the last line: 'Here, lies Deborah, the *only* wife of Charles Primrose.'

Mrs Primrose   A chair, sir –

Vicar   'Mourned by her loving and faithful husband.' It wanted dusting.

Wilmot   Sir, I have been prevailed upon to give signature to this document: now it only requires yours to make final the marriage contract and settlement I bequeath with my daughter.

Vicar   Where's my quill?

Maid   Beg pardon, a messenger from town's arrived and wishes to see someone.

Mrs Primrose *goes out with* **Maid**. **Vicar** *forgets his purpose to sign the contract.*

Vicar   Are you familiar with Templar's principles on the same subject?

Wilmot   No, sir, I am not familiar with anyone's principles on the subject.

Vicar   You are in jest.

Wilmot   I assure you I am not.

Vicar   And not Whiston's?

Wilmot   Not Whiston's, Wilson's, Templar's, Paget's nor yours, sir. I do not accept such monogamous extremes.

Vicar   Extremes?

Wilmot   They are not orthodox.

Vicar   No-no. You confuse what the laity might do with what we, the clergy, must never do. The reverend gentleman that would marry a second wife after the death of a first commits a bigamy. I am at this moment writing a tract on the matter. Pray excuse while I fetch it from my study.

Wilmot   Dr Primrose –

Vicar   No trouble.

Mrs Primrose, *returning, meets* **Vicar** *and takes him aside.*

Mrs Primrose   Oh laws!

Vicar   What is it, my dear?

Mrs Primrose   You must give up the dispute at once.

Vicar   How – to give up the dispute?

Mrs Primrose   At least till your son's wedding is over.

Vicar   Do you ask me to relinquish truth?

Mrs Primrose   I ask you to sign the contract at once and secure Miss Wilmot's fortune.

Vicar   As to signing the contract, we shall come to it anon; as to my argument, you might as well advise me to give up my fortune. Why, what is it, Deborah?

Mrs Primrose   Your fortune, sir, is gone!

Vicar   What foolishness —

Mrs Primrose   Somebody's foolishness! We are ruined. The news has just arrived. The merchant in town, into whose hands you lodged everything we have, has gone off.

Vicar   D'you mean dear old honest Cribbins?

Mrs Primrose   Gone, flown, to avoid a statute of bankruptcy and has not left a shilling in the pound. Now, let that news serve to moderate the warmth of your argument on monogamy with someone that is courting a fourth wife.

Vicar   Old Wilmot!

Mrs Primrose   And I'm sure that your prudence will enforce the necessity of secrecy in the matter of our new financial position, at least till after the wedding.

Vicar   If what you tell me is true and I am to be a beggar, then it shall never make me a rascal.

Mrs Primrose   Your son's happiness!

Vicar   It shall never make me disavow my principles, Deborah.

Mrs Primrose   He do love the girl!

Vicar   No, child.

Mrs Primrose   I implore, my dear!

Vicar   No! I must go this moment and inform the company of our new circumstances. And as to my argument: I own I had a tendency towards concession on account of the old gentleman's years, but *a fourth* wife! He has driven the matter beyond the verge of absurdity! (*To his family and the* **Wilmots**.) We are ruined.

Vicar *returns to prison. The others react, suitably shocked.* **Wilmot** *stumps out.*

Wilmot   Daughter, come!

Miss Wilmot (*tearfully*)   Goodbye, Mr Primrose!

George (*tearfully*)   Goodbye, Miss Wilmot!

Now ensues some elegant weeping by the Primrose family as they carry out their furniture and belongings for transportation. (Note: this and the following narration covers the transition to Scene Two. And such is the convention throughout – using narration, songs, openings/closings of scenes – to effect transitions.)

Vicar   The only hope was that the report of our misfortune was malicious, or premature. (*Shakes his head: no such luck.*) My thoughts now had to be employed on some future means of supporting my family because, careless of the temporalities, I'd made over my living to the widows and orphans of the diocese. And the Bishop did not like me: a certain theological issue between us. At last, I was offered a small cure [*curacy*] in a distant neighbourhood that nobody else wanted. But one, I thought, where I could enjoy my monogamous principles without molestation. (*Walking off.*) So, it was goodbye to Wakefield. And to George.

Scene Two

A Crossroads

Moses   Whoa, Blackberry!

The Primroses' belongings on a cart. (The cart perhaps is faced upstage, or, in other words, we do not see Blackberry.) **Mrs Primrose**, *despondent, and* **Olivia** *are seated on top of their belongings in the cart.*

Sophy *is on foot and is looking back to the road they have come. They are waiting for the others to catch up.*

Moses (*coming from top of cart*) . . . Our turning, Mother, for Low Groansbury.

Mrs Primrose (*quietly*) How much further?

Moses Seventy miles.

Mrs Primrose (*with sighs*) Seventy miles. Low Groansbury. To a curacy that offers fifteen pounds a year.

Sophy I'm sure that we shall manage when it's added to the profits of the farm that Papa intends to hire.

Mrs Primrose To be seen to be so poor.

Olivia (*beautifully dressed; climbing down from the cart*) Sure, madam, you do not fear the challenge of frugality?

Mrs Primrose And I told you – *madam* – to dress as befits the challenge of a cart! (*She sees* **Vicar** *approaching.*) You are an impossible, impractical, obstinate creature, Dr Primrose!

Vicar *entering with* **Dick** *and* **Bill** *and* **George**.

Vicar There is yet enough for happiness if we are wise, Deborah.

Mrs Primrose Theory, Dr Primrose, all theory.

Vicar Are we arrived at the crossroads where we must part, George?

Dick *and* **Bill** *give* **George** *handfuls of flowers that they have plucked.* **Mrs Primrose** *begins to weep.*

Mrs Primrose Can there not be a postponement?

George I hope not, Mother. (*He is full of confidence.*)

Vicar It's best for George to go where he can contribute to our support and to his own.

Mrs Primrose But to bide with us until we reach the low place to which your father has committed us!

Vicar   Have no fear, Deborah –

Mrs Primrose   Oh, George, George! (*Embracing him.*)

George   Have no apprehension, Mama, as I have none.

Moses (*tearfully, aside to the tearful* **Olivia** *and* **Sophy**)   At least he don't mope no more.

Vicar   I know he will act a good part, be it victorious or vanquished.

George   I trust victorious, sir. Your blessing, Father.

Vicar   I give it you, my son, with all my heart. You are going to London, George, in the manner Thomas Hooker, your great ancestor, went before you. Take from me the same horse that was given him by his father – (*He gives his staff to* **George**.) And take this book. In it you will find two lines worth a million: 'I have been young and now am old; yet never saw I the righteous man forsaken, nor his seed begging their bread.'

George   Thank you, Father.

Mrs Primrose   And let us see you in six months.

Vicar   Yes, whatever your fortune, let us see you in a six months.

George   And perhaps even sooner.

George *leaves, optimistically, eagerly. Their hands, held up in a silent farewell, become still.* **Vicar** *secretly wipes a tear.* **Sophy** *looks at the darkening sky.*

Sophy   It threatens. We had best proceed and see if we can find some place to shelter for the night.

Mrs Primrose   What is to befall us in that remoteness out there?

Moses (*frightened*)   There is no sin upon us, Father? Mother, cheer up?

Vicar *has seated* **Dick** *and* **Bill** *on the cart.* **Mrs Primrose** *and* **Sophy** *climb on to it too.* **Moses** *to the head of the cart.*

Vicar   Take your guitar, Sophy. Thrum a little. What song, Livy, to raise our spirits?

Olivia   'Death and the Lady'!

Moses   Giddy-up, Blackberry!

And, night falling – lights fading – they move off, singing 'Death and the Lady', **Vicar** *and* **Olivia** *hand in hand.*

> As I walked out one morn in May
> All in the merry month of May
> When thrushes sang and the lambs did play
> I met an old man by the way.
>
> My name is Death, fair maiden, see . . . (*Et cetera.*)

Scene Three

The Inn

The **Landlord** *is lazy, dirty, bleary-eyed; cynical and smiling content; drunk. He sets his chair and belches: 'Aye!'* **Mr Burchill** *comes in pursued by* **Landlady**, *who is both sloven and drudge.* **Burchill** *is, of course, Sir William Thornhill. He is eccentric and erratic in behaviour; he is neurotic. He wants to be loved for himself alone and so he goes about disguised in clothes that once were 'laced'; there is a rent somewhere in his top coat. Yet his manner is imperious.*

Landlady   Mr Burchill, Mr Burchill! How d'you mean, you cannot pay? Stand! And flinging coins away like potato-peelings on gypsies, beggars and vagabonds and keeping us out of our own! Stand, I command you! We want our money! We want our – STAND!

Burchill (*rounds on her, considers it but does not deign to speak beyond*)   Hah! (*And walks off.*)

Landlord (*belches*)   Aye!

Landlady   I vow, Tom Symonds, you use me ill. Sitting there like a lord a-beaming. Cool as a dairy-pan and smiling sweet, and the house a-going up the chimbley.

There is a knocking at the door and **Landlord** *gets up lazily to answer it.*

Landlord   Aye!

Landlady (*mimics*)   'Aye! Aye!' But I'll bear it no longer. (*She follows.*)

Landlord   Thrice welcome, ladies, aye, thrice welcome! Lodgings ye be wanting. Then thrice welcome! Lords in hell, the night out there!

Olivia *and* **Sophy** *come in, carrying the sleeping* **Dick** *and* **Bill***; then* **Landlady** *laden with their luggage: she trudges through, leading them off to the sleeping quarters.*

Landlady   House a-going out the windows but does he care! Three-quarters of the work is left for me to do and the fourth is left unfinished. But I'll bear it no more . . .

Landlord (*returning with* **Mrs Primrose**)   Low Groansbury ye be pointed for then. Aye! Aye! That be young Squire Thornhill's domain.

Olivia *returns for a case or a box.*

Mrs Primrose   Squire Thornhill? Take cup with me, Landlord.

Landlord   You ool be wanting to know something o' the young squire, aye, something o' young Ned Thornhill.

Mrs Primrose   I am merely curious to hear since we're most like to be neighbours.

Landlord   Wanting to know something o' young Bezzelybub. There's a pretty bit o' plumpness. (*Olivia.*) He ool be pleased with this one. (**Sophy** *enters and exits for something.*) He ool be pleased with both.

Mrs Primrose   Olivia, my dear, assist Sophia in having the little ones bedded.

Olivia *goes*.

Landlord   Aye, bedded: every farmer's daughter from twelve miles round and more.

Mrs Primrose   Tut-tut and phoo-phoo! You are talking to a woman of the world, Landlord.

Landlord   Solemn-n-dying! (*Oath*.) Never was man more fond of – (*Winks at her*.) Never had man more eye for fair sex. Why, there be nothing he wants in life but his pleasure. (*Confidentially to her*.) He cannot wait.

Mrs Primrose   What alarms! This eternal rumour of the infernal young squire has a hollow universality. What is his exact age and, since I take him to be unwed, tell me if he is affianced?

Landlord   Why, he cannot be a trifle more than the score, and I'd say the same count'd do for his fiancées.

Mrs Primrose   And how are we so knowledgeable about the intimate tricks of our betters?

Landlord   Oh, we've had the pleasure o' entertaining more than one o' his discards here, for, fair dues to young gent, he never do put off a wench without something in her fist to spend as how she likes.

Vicar *and* **Moses** *are coming in;* **Olivia** *and* **Sophy** *a moment later from the sleeping quarters*. **Olivia** *has a new ribbon in her hair;* **Sophy** *has her needle-box and* **Dick***'s jacket to put a stitch in it*.

Landlord   Aye, thrice welcome! (*Aside to* **Mrs Primrose**.) He cannot wait.

Vicar   Blackberry is at supper and I hope, Landlord, your bill of fare will see us showing as much honest enjoyment shortly. A jug of your wine, sir.

Landlord *going for wine.* **Mr Burchill** *comes in again, pursued by* **Landlady**.

Landlord (*going for wine*)   Aye! Aye!

Landlady   Mr Burchill, stand! How dare you, without money in your pocket, look at me like that!

Burchill   Madam, I have nothing about me presently and I have told it you an unnecessary number of times!

Landlady   You have not!

Burchill   I shall pay what I owe on my return to these parts.

Landlady   You shall not! He shall not! Tom! Tom! he declares he cannot satisfy our reckoning.

Landlord   Wants for money!

Landlady   Cannot pay.

Landlord   But that's unpossible. (*To* **Vicar**.) Why, it were only yesterday he paid out three whole guineas to the beadle to spare an old broken soldier as was to be whipped for dogstealing.

Burchill   I shall settle the account on my return next month, now I bid you good evening!

Landlady   Tom! – He shall not! (*She is wielding a cudgel now.*)

Vicar (*simultaneously, aside to* **Landlord**) How much is it?

And **Landlord** *replies.*

Landlady   Tom! He shall not! We ool have satisfaction now, one way or t'other!

Vicar (*simultaneously*)   Madam! . . . I shall be responsible for the reckoning of this gentleman who showed such charity to an old soldier. And now be so kind as to fetch our jug of wine.

Landlord *and* **Landlady** *retire.*

Vicar   Sir, my purse is at your disposal.

Burchill   I thank you, but I must previously entreat being informed of the name and residence of my benefactor in order to repay him as soon as possible.

Vicar   Charles Primrose, sir. And this is my family. Our destination is Low Groansbury where I have obtained a curacy.

Burchill   This falls out most luckily then, for my journey too takes me into that region.

Mrs Primrose   You are familiar with Low Groansbury, Mr Burchill?

Burchill (*suspiciously*)   I have *some* knowledge of the place.

Mrs Primrose   What knowledge of the young squire there?

Burchill   Why d'you ask *me* about young Thornhill?

Mrs Primrose   Ah! (*You know him.*) Rumours.

Burchill   Very often the product of idle, spiteful minds.

Mrs Primrose   My own sentiments to an 'S'. How vast are his estates?

Olivia   Is he dark, is he fair?

Mrs Primrose   And his wealth? –

Olivia   How tall is he? –

Mrs Primrose   What size fortune does he command?

Burchill   Mr Thornhill is a Thornhill!

Mrs Primrose   I knew it!

Burchill   A gentleman!

Mrs Primrose (*telling herself*)   What did I tell you!

Burchill   He enjoys the *use* of a large fortune, the control of which is entirely dependent on my – dependent on the will of his uncle, Sir William Thornhill.

Vicar   What!

Moses   What!

Vicar   Is my young landlord then a nephew of Sir William Thornhill, Mr Burchill?

Burchill   Yes.

Vicar   Then – oh, my dears! – we have nothing to fear from our landlord if he be one whit like his uncle. For I have heard Sir William represented as one of the most generous, though eccentric, of men.

Burchill   Eccentric? Surely you mean humorous.

Vicar   No. Eccentric. But a man of consummate benevolence.

Burchill   Perhaps too much so.

Vicar   Oh?

Burchill   Well, at least when young, he carried benevolence to an extreme, for his passions were then strong. His soul laboured under a sickly sensibility of the miseries of others. He loved all mankind, and thus disposed to relieve, it is easily conjectured he found numbers disposed to solicit. He began to lose regard for private interest in universal sympathy. And still they drew – crowds! – who showed him only one side of their character – rascals! His profusion began to impair his fortune –

Vicar (*to* **Moses**)   Hark you well, my son –

Burchill   And then, when no longer able to satisfy a request for money, he gave promises!

Vicar   Tck-tck-tck-tck-tck!

Burchill   They were all, now, that he had to bestow! (*He is getting – or he is – out of hand.*)

Sophy   Poor Sir William!

Burchill (*to* **Sophy**)   Madam, he had not the resolution to give pain to any man by a denial! And still they drew! Swarms of dependents whom he wished to relieve but, now, was sure to disappoint. Then, what did they do? . . . They left him!

Sophy   Dear, dear!

Burchill   They did not *merely* leave him! They left him with sneers and reproaches! (*For* **Sophy***'s sympathy.*) Madam? And in proportion as he became contemptible to others, he grew despicable to himself! Now he cannot abide sycophants and their fawning. Now he suspects all and trusts no one. None, that is, except little children, the only part of humanity I have found to be harmless.

Sophy   Poor, poor, *poor* Sir William.

Burchill   How he searches now for respect uncontaminated with flattery. Oh! if he could find *one* honest upright man – or woman.

Vicar   I'm surprised, dear man, that you have not observed a moral to yourself in the story?

Burchill (*pulls himself together*)   Hah! But I have interrupted this young lady in her needlework.

Sophy   'Tis but a stitch to my little brother's jacket.

Moses   If I may be so bold – dear man – how is it with the estimable Sir William these days?

Burchill   He resolved, young sir, to restore himself to fortune and self-esteem abroad and, now, though scarcely thirty – well, some few years beyond it – has returned, his circumstances more affluent than ever.

Sophy   Oh, I am glad! (*She has finished* **Dick***'s jacket and she puts it down.*) And some accident too seems to have befallen your coat, Mr Burchill. Might I, after supper, undertake the renovation?

Landlord   Supper, aye!

Mrs Primrose   Dine with us, sir. We have strayed from our original topic. I would test you on a dozen questions more about the young squire, this wealthy humorist's nephew.

Mrs Primrose, **Olivia** *and* **Moses** *go out to supper.*

Vicar (*moving away; to himself*)   Humorist? I'm sure I heard eccentric.

Burchill   Miss Sophia.

Sophy   Sir?

Burchill (*has been carrying a book throughout*)   For my amusement I put verses of my own composing in this book and set them to music: will you accept them as token recompense for the promised renovation? (*She hesitates.*) They are all that I may bestow at present.

She accepts and they go out to supper.

Landlord (*collects his chair and follows*)   Aye!

Vicar   We set out again on the following day, with Mr Burchill riding along beside us till our ways had to part, and we lightened the fatigues of the road with philosophical discussion. At last, we approached the place of our retreat. A strange anxiety for my children hung about me, a foreboding of the future that I could not then fix. But, whatever its nature, I knew that it did not rest in my new neighbours, for they were farmers.

Farmer Flamborough, *a figure, crossing the background with a hay-fork on his shoulder, waves to* **Vicar**. *And* **Vicar** *waves back.*

(Remote from the polite, they retained a primaeval simplicity, frugal by habit, they scarce knew temperance to be a virtue, and what conversation lacked in wit was made up in laughter.) And it was in emulation of my new neighbour that I began to rule my little republic: indeed, so successfully – at first – all could agree that every situation can bring its own peculiar rewards. (*He moves off.*) It was about the beginning of autumn.

Scene Four

The Meadow

Afternoon. Sunshine. The birds are singing. **Mrs Primrose** *is spreading a cloth and setting plates for a picnic.* **Sophy**, *having assisted her mother, takes up her guitar and the book given her by* **Burchill** *and strums.* **Dick** *and* **Bill** *have come in, racing, with handfuls/baskets of berries.* **Moses** *is reading a book.* **Olivia** *is looking beautiful and dreamy. Now she is singing the song that* **Sophy** *is strumming.* **Sophy** *adds harmony.* **Vicar** *comes in, carrying his jacket, during the song.*

> When lovely lady stoops to folly
> And finds too late that men betray,
> What charms can soothe her melancholy,
> What art can wash her grief away?
> The only art her guilt to cover,
> To hide her shame from every eye,
> To give repentance to her lover,
> And wring his bosom – is to die.

Vicar (*re.* **Sophy**'*s book*)   That poor gentleman. And he has an elegant hand.

Mrs Primrose (*to herself; coming out of reverie*)   Yes, we shall soon hear from George.

Vicar   What book today, my son?

Moses   Epictetus, Father.

Vicar   Dick and Bill, harken to the carolling.

Dick   To Livy and Sophy?

Bill   And the birdies in the trees?

Vicar *enjoys their reply. A blackbird sings.*

Vicar   One for you, Moses: can you name our soloist?

Moses   Why, sir, surely the species *Merula turdus:* is it not the common blackbird, Father?

Vicar   Bravo, my boy! Though nothing common in that sound. Listen.

They listen to the blackbird. Then, the report of a gun, disturbing the scene and silencing the blackbird for ever.

Jenks' Voice   Well done, Ned! Four-and-twenty blackbirds!

Mr Thornhill *comes in, gun in hand, to search for the bird. A timid servant,* **Butler***, arrives with him and is given the gun, stands by et cetera.* **Thornhill** *pulls up on seeing the Primrose family. He is a young man, a bit hysterical, obsessed with sex.*

Thornhill   What the devil! Who are you? (*He sees* **Olivia***.*) Your obedient! Afternoon, good afternoon, howdyehdo, howdyehdo!

Jenks (*coming in*)   Did you get him – (*Reads the situation.*) The hawk that hovered overhead? But who are these charming people?

Thornhill   I'm trying to discover it – howdyehdo! – but the accident with the wretched jackdaw has silenced them. Ladies – sirs – Ned Thornhill, your servant!

Mrs Primrose (*to herself*)   The squire!

Thornhill   The lands that you see all about you are mine.

Vicar   Charles Primrose, Sir. And this is my family. I'm the new Vicar.

Thornhill   T'be sure you are – Howdyehdo! And this is my – chaplain: Reverend Jenks. Let clergymen confer. (*Getting* **Jenks** *to take* **Vicar** *aside.*) Delighted, delightful! (**Dick** *and* **Bill**.) Young sir! (**Moses**.) Dearest madam!

Mrs Primrose   So pleased to make your acquaintance at last, Mr Thornhill.

Thornhill   T'be sure y'are! And this one is?

Mrs Primrose   Sophia.

Thornhill   Sophia!

Sophy   Sir.

Thornhill   And this one?

Mrs Primrose   Olivia.

Thornhill   Olivia.

Takes her hand, holds on to it. **Olivia**, *struck by him, is petrified.*

Mrs Primrose   Olivia – Saints – the squire!

Thornhill   Howdyehdo!

Mrs Primrose (*speaking for* **Olivia**)   'How do you do, Sir.' Olivia!

Olivia   I am well!

Thornhill   I vow to God you are, Madam, extremely well.

Olivia *blushes and withdraws her hand.*

Mrs Primrose   So pleased, Mr Thornhill – Won't you take some refreshment?

Thornhill   Should like nothing better – Extremely well.

Mrs Primrose   Our gooseberry wine, which was famous all over Wakefield, already gains reputation here.

Thornhill (*going for* **Jenks** *and* **Vicar**)   Frank!

Mrs Primrose   'Dearest Madam.' Moses – to your feet! Shut Epictetus and open the wine.

Thornhill   Our charming hostess offers gooseberry wine. Come, take cup.

Jenks (*aside to him*)   And I'd like to take Miss Bandbox into the bargain.

Thornhill   Which one? – Ah, Vicar! – (*Aside.*) It shall be done. (*To* **Vicar**.) Had I known, Sir, you were arrived!

Jenks   I've told Dr Primrose we were away on business – (*To* **Vicar**.) We returned but yesterday with two –

Thornhill   Cousins.

Jenks   Cousins.

Mrs Primrose   Attend Mr Thornhill, Olivia.

Sophy *and* **Olivia** *take wine to* **Jenks** *and* **Thornhill**.

Jenks   Exquisite!

Thornhill   Extremely well.

Jenks   What a pretty instrument! (**Sophy**'s.) Would I could play on it – Eh, Ned?

Mrs Primrose   Does Mr Thornhill play, perhaps?

Jenks   Play?!

Thornhill   But tolerably, Madam. Would Miss Olivia oblige?

Mrs Primrose   Yes, a song for the gentlemen, my dear.

Olivia   I've discovered a throat, Mama.

Thornhill   Then you, Frank. My chaplain's a most melodious baritone with exceptional knowledge of the modern song.

Jenks   Gladly, another time, but –

Thornhill   But yes, now! – Or I'll defrock you.

Jenks   Our cousins approach.

Thornhill   Our?

Two ladies – 'ladies of the town' – **Blarney** *and* **Skeggs**, *have entered. They are laughing over something (a dirty joke). Then:*

Skeggs   Ow!

Blarney   There they are! –

Skeggs   We thought we'd given you the –

Blarney   Clap! – (*Interjecting, meaning 'Shush!'*)

Skeggs   Pox!

Blarney   We thought we'd lost you.

Jenks (*to* **Mrs Primrose**)   Lady Blarney and the
Honourable Carolina Wilemina Amelia Skeggs.

He follows **Thornhill** *to join* **Blarney** *and* **Skeggs** *upstage, and
they confer (conspire).*

Mrs Primrose   Now I'm going to faint. The squire, a
peeress, and an honourable in our meadow! What a chance!
Moses, stop eating – Dick, Bill, run at once for another bottle
of gooseberry wine. (*They go.*) None of you push forward to
the cloth – Eat only what I put on your plate – I shall offer
second helpings, decline them politely –

Moses   But, Mama –

Mrs Primrose   You can eat berries.

The guests approaching. **Blarney** *can affect style,* **Skeggs** *cannot.*

Blarney   I die to meet them, Teddy, but is it not an
intrusion?

Skeggs   A horrid, horrid intrusing, Capting!

Thornhill   The hospitality of this charming family made us
overlook you. May I present Lady Blarney. Dr and Mrs
Primrose.

Jenks   The Honourable Carolina Wilemina Amelia Skeggs.
Miss Sophia Primrose.

Thornhill   Miss Olivia. And-and! (*Clicking his fingers:* **Moses***.*)

Blarney   How do you do!

Skeggs   How do you do!

Olivia   Your ladyship!

Sophy   Miss Skeggs!

Blarney   Charmed!

Skeggs   Charmed!

Mrs Primrose   *Je suis enchanté!*

Skeggs *Je suis!*

Blarney We are recommended the country air, dontcha know. In my case, a tickling of the throat.

Skeggs And in mine, a tickling of the – (*She giggles.*) Dontcha know.

Blarney I always say that air is so – natural.

Skeggs (*to* **Vicar**) Pure laughing gas, Capting!

Vicar Heartily welcome. (*He's polite but he is puzzled by them all.*)

Mrs Primrose Some wine, your ladyships? Olivia, Sophia, attend.

Blarney Now I can see why we were abandoned.

Skeggs There's a shape, your ladyship. (**Olivia**'s.)

Blarney I can see it. Turn round, my dear.

Skeggs Make a leg and show your breeding.

Blarney Such modesty deserves a shrine.

Vicar (*to* **Jenks**) Are both relatives of Mr Thornhill?

Jenks No. She's mine.

Mrs Primrose I can see the family resemblance between Mr Thornhill and Lady Blarney – if you'll pardon the observation.

Vicar Are you his aunt, Lady Blarney?

Blarney Dang me, Vicar! do I look it?

Skeggs Ow-oo-ee!

Blarney Mmmmmmmah!

The last in reaction to tasting the gooseberry wine. They genuinely like it. And they enjoy – eat heartily – everything that is offered them.

Vicar (*aside to* **Mrs Primrose**) 'Dang me!'?

Mrs Primrose   'Tis the fashion – dontcha know.

Dick *and* **Bill** *have returned with another bottle of wine.* **Moses** *opens it.*

Thornhill (*quietly, cueing* **Blarney**)   Ah the countryside.

Blarney   Ah the countryside!

Skeggs   Ah!

Blarney   I'm devoted to it!

Skeggs   We're devoted!

Blarney   But don't you girls need for town, for diversions in refinement?

Skeggs   What do country ladies do?

Blarney   Without Lord Easel's exhibitions –

Skeggs   Easel's exhibitions –

Blarney   Or Shakespeare, Carolina –

Skeggs   Or Shakespeare, your ladyship, and the musical glasses, mum?

Mrs Primrose   Don't I know it, Miss Skeggs, don't I know it, Lady Blarney; but what am I to do?

Lights fading to sunset. **Vicar** *has a word with* **Moses**. **Moses** *leaves, taking* **Dick** *and* **Bill** *and baskets – whatever is appropriate – home.*

Blarney   The sun goes down!

Skeggs   The sons go home!

Jenks   But what sunshine lights the heart unpolluted with guilt!

Thornhill (*cueing/planting thought in* **Mrs Primrose**'*s mind*) What a pity that this day has to end?

Mrs Primrose   What a pity that this day has to end!

Thornhill (*to* **Blarney**)   'Does it?'

Blarney   But does it?

Skeggs   Does it?

Blarney   For my part I'm unwilling to lose the company of these dear girls, Carolina.

Skeggs   Your ladyship, I twig. And speaking of diversions –

Blarney   Speaking of diversions in refinement–

Skeggs   Does a body need to go to the world for it?

Blarney *and* **Skeggs**   When Thornhill-Castle-yonder –

Blarney   Is near at hand.

Skeggs   And where –

Blarney   But there –

Skeggs   Would young ladies find refinement of an evening –

Blarney   Around here? I demand the company of these dear girls home.

Mrs Primrose   Oh!

Skeggs   And so do I.

Mrs Primrose   Charles?

Skeggs   For the night.

Vicar   Too kind.

Thornhill   No!

Vicar   Sudden.

Jenks   I myself would be at all times present.

Olivia (*whispers*)   Papa?

Vicar (*quietly*)   No.

Mrs Primrose (*to* **Vicar**)   There's nothing I more wish for than their polishing and refining.

Vicar   I'd imagine, my dear, that as their breeding is already superior to their fortune, greater polish will only serve to make their poverty more ridiculous. Wisdom at last – sirs, ladies – bids us conform to our humble station.

Mrs Primrose (*a huffed aside*)   Cold water, Dr Primrose.

Thornhill   What wisdom, Sir? –

Blarney (*aside to him*)   Mum, Teddy –

Thornhill   What, do these two lovely girls not deserve?

Blarney (*aside*)   Leave it to us –

Thornhill   What, Sir?

Skeggs   Couple of hours to look at the Capting's musical glasses!

Thornhill   Why, curse me, if a settlement of half my estate could give Miss Olivia or Miss – Miss – (*Clicks his fingers, meaning* '**Sophy**'.) pleasure, it would be theirs.

Vicar   You are most kind, but –

Thornhill   And the only favour I should ask in return is to add myself to the benefit!

Vicar   We have given up splendours, Mr Thornhill. Honour, sir, is our only possession at present. And of that last treasure we must be careful. You are our landlord – (*And to the others:*) You, sir, ladies, were guests to our humble cloth, and for the family which you condescended to favour with your company, I thank you.

Blarney (*kneels*)   Do you have any objection, Vicar, to giving prayers?

Vicar   Our Father, which art in heaven, we thank you for the bounty of this day. For its pleasures and disappointments. Bless all who are gathered here. And, as our faith in you is strong, increase our trust in one another. (*He walks off; narrates.*) For which, for the whole of the following day, I had nothing but sullen looks and short answers from my family.

Mrs Primrose, **Olivia** *and* **Sophy** *go home, disappointed.*

Jenks   Send a haunch of venison tomorrow, Ned?

Blarney   A moonlight ball in front of their house on the following night?

Skeggs (*softly; plaintive; sorry for him*)   Capting?

Thornhill   . . . Amen.

Act Two

Scene One
The Primrose House

Sophy *sorting through a pile of dresses.* **Mrs Primrose** *and* **Olivia**, *in, out, hustle-bustle, with articles of clothing and more dresses.* **Vicar** *comes in and stands in the middle of the excitement. They hardly notice his presence.*

Olivia   Oh no, oh no, this (*dress*) will never do!

Sophy   Try the crinoline –

Mrs Primrose   What would you say to me in this? (*Dress.*)

Olivia   Where is it? – Where? – Please help! – Someone!

Sophy   It's on the bed! –

Mrs Primrose   Or try the taffeta, Olivia!

Vicar *puts away his bible.*

Olivia   Where?! (*Is her taffeta.*) Where?!

Sophy   I left it on the bed – the crinolene!

Mrs Primrose   Open your eyes, my dear!

Vicar   Supper?

Mrs Primrose   Organdie? (*Would* **Vicar** *like her in the organdie dress.*) Your bottom drawer the taffeta, Olivia, I said!

Vicar   What is this?

Olivia   It's all rumpled –

Sophy   I'll iron it –

Vicar   Deborah?

Mrs Primrose   Guess!

Olivia   The roughing's come undone –

Vicar   Can't. (*He can't guess.*)

Sophy   I'll sew it for you –

Mrs Primrose   Mr Thornhill.

Vicar   I'm still in a puzzlement.

Mrs Primrose   The haunch of venison he sent to us this morning?

Vicar   Yes?

Mrs Primrose   Why did he send us a haunch of venison?

Vicar   . . . To eat it?

Sophy   There's going to be a ball, Papa.

Olivia   And I'm going to look awful.

Mrs Primrose   Now he is organising a ball for us, for tomorrow night, Charles, to be held in the moonlight in front of our house. And begging for Olivia's hand in the dancing!

Vicar   A ball?

Mrs Primrose   Begging! (*To* **Olivia**.) Hold it up, my dear. (*The dress.*)

Vicar   A ball in front of this humble house?

Mrs Primrose   On the Green across . . . Well, I have known stranger things to happen.

Vicar   Stranger things than, my dear?

Mrs Primrose   Mr Thornhill and Olivia.

Vicar   Deborah, there is no character more contemptible than a fortune-hunting man, and I see no reason why a fortune-hunting woman should not be contemptible too!

Mrs Primrose   And I see no reason why the two Miss Wrinkles should marry warm fortunes and my girls get none!

Vicar   Nor I, nor I – Nor why Mr Simkins should draw twelve thousand pounds in the lottery while we sat down to a blank!

Mrs Primrose   Cold water, cold water! This is the way you always set out to damp me and my girls when we are in spirits.

Vicar   And whatever your opinion of Mr Thornhill, my children, and notwithstanding his generosity, I think he is perfectly sensible of the social distance between us.

Mrs Primrose   Would you not have us aspire?

Vicar   Let us keep to companions of our own rank.

Mrs Primrose   Where are they – pray tell, Dr Primrose! – the companions of our own rank in Low Groansbury? Not alone would you not have us aspire, *you* are seeking to drop us *another* rung. (*She turns away.*)

Vicar   No prudence on anyone's part – Deborah! – could have prevented our late misfortune! But prudence can do much to disappoint its effects. Supper?

Mrs Primrose (*turns to him, holding up her organdie dress*)   You once told me, Charles, how you liked me in red.

Vicar (*calls*)   Moses! Where's Moses?

Moses (*coming in*)   Father?

Vicar   And you shall prepare the coach.

Moses   The coach?

Vicar   Yes. For tomorrow evening.

Moses   But we have no coach.

Vicar   Bless me! That is so. Then we shall have to hire one or buy one.

Mrs Primrose   What is this – coach – to be for, my dear?

Vicar   To take us to the moonlight ball.

Mrs Primrose   But surely you –

Vicar   No-no! – you mistake, child, I do not jest. For though it's but a step or two across to the Green out there, if we walk to it in this – trim – the very children of the village will hoot after us. These ruffings and pinkings and patchings will make us hated by the wives of our neighbours.

Mrs Primrose   You would not have us neat? You would have us, the guests of your landlord, Lady Blarney, Miss Skeggs and the Reverend Jenks, attend the ball dressed in our – smocks? . . . Or you would not have us attend at all?

Vicar   . . . You may be as neat as you please and I shall love you the better for it. But this is not neatness but frippery. These may be altered to a plainer cut.

Moses   And I have often thought that coat-tails are a vicious superfluity. (*He goes out.*)

Vicar (*narrating*)   My remonstrance to bring down the pride of my family to its circumstances had the proper effect, and they went with composure that very instant about their normal duties.

Mrs Primrose (*clearing things away*)   So much for our attempts at thrift. We shall not be so caught out again. Next time, we shall have bought *new* dresses, elegant and to size and kept hidden till the moment of demand.

Dick (*off*)   Mr Burchill!

Bill (*off*)   Mr Burchill!

Mrs Primrose   Bless me, here comes Mr Burchill, that poor gentleman we met on our journey and that fair run you down in argument!

She goes off with **Olivia** *with the pile of dresses. Both, in and out, through the following, with supper.* **Sophy** *lays the table.* **Burchill** *comes in with* **Dick** *and* **Bill***, and* **Moses***.* **Dick** *and* **Bill** *have whistles, presents from* **Burchill***, made out of reeds.*

Burchill   Hah, Primrose! (*His greeting.*)

Vicar   Mr Burchill, dear friend, welcome!

Burchill   The money I borrowed.

Vicar   Oh, I did not expect it back – so soon.

Burchill   Madam! Madam! (**Olivia** *and* **Mrs Primrose**.) Ah, Miss Sophia!

Vicar (*to* **Moses**)   See that Mr Burchill's horse is given a drink.

Moses   I have already done so, Father, but found no horse.

Vicar   Sure, sir, you're not now on foot!

Burchill   It has become my belief that we have grown too dependent on *Equus caballus* to the detriment of our health and, in experiment, the findings of which I shall publish in a book, I am resolved that, for a year, my sole means of locomotion will be effected by the ambulatory organs, be the journey of one or one hundred miles.

Vicar   (*dubiously*)   Mmm!

Sophy   And I too consider the use of equestrian transport extreme and a denial of our self-sufficiency. I hope, sir, we shall be favoured with a sight of your findings.

Burchill   It is another of my beliefs that a young woman cannot esteem a man that seems poor?

Sophy   . . . Mmm!

Vicar   But come to our table. Let us leave off disputation until we have supped.

Burchill   Happily, but night falls and I have not yet arranged for lodgings.

Mrs Primrose   And in this small house all our beds are occupied.

Dick   Brother Moses, if I offer the part of the bed that I share with Bill to Mr Burchill, will you let me into your bed?

Bill   And Livy and Sophy, if I offer the other part, will you let me in with you?

Vicar   Well done, good children! It's settled. Hospitality is one of the first Christian duties. Deborah, give those boys a lump of sugar each after supper, and let Dick's be the largest because he spoke first.

They sit to supper.

Olivia   You'd never guess whose present this venison is, Mr Burchill. A gift from our friend, Mr Thornhill.

Mrs Primrose   The squire, dontcha know.

Burchill   I did not know you had become acquainted.

Mrs Primrose   *Acquainted?* Oh yes!

Olivia   He dropped in – to our meadow – yesterday.

Sophy   Accompanied by two ladies and his chaplain.

Mrs Primrose   Possessed of such charm and wit. 'Dearest Madam': so respectful and affectionate all at once. And now will have nothing but to organise a ball for us tomorrow night.

Olivia   With music and refreshment.

Mrs Primrose   He has swept us off our feet. And begging for Olivia's hand for the whole of the evening's dancing.

Burchill   I am pleased to hear from your tone of voice that you do not put weight on these attentions as I happen to know that the marriage contract for young Thornhill's betrothal to a wealthy young lady is being drawn up presently.

Mrs Primrose   . . . Where do you glean all your knowledge and information? Mr Burchill, you are a marvel: so full of news, a man without a horse!

Vicar   Ah, feasts of this kind acquire a double relish from sharing.

Mrs Primrose   You might perhaps even know the name of Mr Thornhill's intended?

Burchill   I believe I do. It is a Miss Arabella Wilmot.

Olivia   She be George's fiancée.

Sophy   Was, Livy, was.

Vicar   Another slice of venison, Mr Burchill?

Burchill   Thank you.

Sophy   Can we expect your company at the ball tomorrow evening, Mr Burchill?

Burchill   Is it to be a masked one?

Mrs Primrose   *Masked?* My girls!

Burchill   Then I'm afraid I have some business to attend to elsewhere.

Mrs Primrose (*aside*)   Business indeed! And that young chaplain of Mr Thornhill's, Reverend Jenks: possessed of such good manners, Mr Burchill, and will have nothing but to secure Sophia's hand for the dancing.

Burchill   Perhaps then I can devise a means of attending.

Mrs Primrose   He's a baritone, dontcha know, and has promised us all kinds of modern songs.

Burchill   There is very little genius in the modern song. Indeed, I consider it contributes vastly to false taste. The lines are loaded with epithet, which perhaps improve the sound but do not carry on the sense. Also, we are given combinations of luxuriant images without connection or plot. But perhaps you will give me the opportunity of introducing to the company a ballad of my own composing which, whatever its defects, is, I am sure, free of those I have mentioned. Miss Sophia, would you be so good as to accompany me? 'Turn Gentle Hermit of the Dale'. It was discovered in my musical studies in Italy that *my* voice covers all three ranges: bass, baritone, tenor. Tonight I shall sing baritone. An excellent supper, Madam.

There are thirty-nine verses in the song and **Burchill** (*a boring baritone*) *sings as many of them as are required for transition. Soon, he loses* **Sophy** *too, his accompanist, as she, like the others, must change for the next scene.*

> Turn gentle hermit of the dale,
> And guide my lonely way,
> To where yon taper cheers the vale,
> With hospitable ray.

> For here forlorn and lost I tread . . . (*Et cetera.*)

Scene Two

The Ball

A bowl of punch / mulled wine on a drinks table: **Thornhill, Jenks, Blarney** *and* **Skeggs** *around it, tasting it, doing things to it.*

Skeggs   Ow! it's nice.

Thornhill   It requires more.

Blarney   Steady, Teddy: enough.

Thornhill   No, more, more! Spike it, Frank! Now, remember your purpose: full tubs every time for the old dowds, half-measures for the young dotes.

Blarney   Too much haste, Teddy, and –

Thornhill   It has to be tonight!

Skeggs   Yikes! –

Blarney   Yeeks!

The last in reaction to **Mrs Primrose**, *who is entering in her party dress and who, they fear, may have seen them doctoring the drink.*

Thornhill (*to himself*)   Damme!

Blarney   What fashion! How enchanting!

Skeggs   *Je suis!*

Mrs Primrose   This? (*Old thing.*) No! But I was never a stranger to fashion, your ladies. At Wakefield I was everywhere imitated in it no less than in wit.

Thornhill   Dearest Madam!

Mrs Primrose   Mr Thornhill! My *bon mots*, dontcha know.

Jenks   A warming cup, Madam? (*Offering her a drink.*) Not as individual as your gooseberry wine, but – interesting.

Mrs Primrose   I wil-mot.

Jenks   Beg pardon?

Mrs Primrose   Wilmot, Mr Thornhill? A little bird has twittered a tale: the glad tidings, Mr Thornhill, of your engagement to a beauteous Miss Arabella Wilmot?

Thornhill   Miss – ? Dang me!

Blarney   Every little chit in the country, my dear, would link her name with cousin Teddy's.

Skeggs   Every little horrid little chit and scrub.

Thornhill *takes drink from* **Jenks**, *puts it in* **Mrs Primrose**'s *hand, taking her aside to reassure her.*

Thornhill   And strike me ugly – and may you eat this cup – if anyone can call that fright a beauty . . .

The others arriving: **Vicar** *and* **Olivia** – *beautiful and nervous* – **Sophy**, **Moses**, **Dick** *and* **Bill** *and* **Farmer Flamborough**. **Mrs Primrose** – *now laughing, reassured* – *and* **Thornhill** *joining them. Spiked drink being handed around as greetings are exchanged.*

Vicar *blinking after drinking; his glass is being filled up again.*

Flamborough   Oh, right, rare, good rum it be, Vicar!

Skeggs   Who that?

Mrs Primrose   A *native.*

Blarney   Let him approach!

Vicar   Our nearest neighbour, Lady Blarney, Farmer Flamborough.

Blarney   These last two days, Thornhill Castle is become quite unbearable for ladies-in-residence as a compliment can be had only for two young ladies out-of-residence.

Skeggs   Who shall be nameless.

Vicar (*narrating*)   The ball. Ahm . . . (*His memory of the ball seems peculiarly poor – and he would like to cover the fact. He retires to get / receive another drink.*)

Blarney   But we're saying all the wrong things, Carolina: the dear boys' blushes are no less than the ladies.

Skeggs   Who shall be nameless.

Blarney   Run along, my dears, be happy!

Thornhill   Miss Primrose.

Olivia   Sir.

Thornhill   May I have the honour?

They go to the dancing area – as do **Sophy** *and* **Jenks***, a moment later. The music starts up and they dance.*

Burchill *enters background, briefly, being careful not to be seen, and leaves again.*

Flamborough   Livy's feet be as pat to the music as its echo.

Blarney   Surely they were made for each other.

Mrs Primrose   Yes, my girls do it very cleverly, but all those steps were stolen from me, Lady Blarney.

Flamborough   Let's see them then in their ancient origins.

He does not give **Mrs Primrose** *a chance to refuse and they join in the dance.*

Vicar *(narrating)*   Yes, the ball. Ahm . . . And I was glad to see that Deborah was not too old to join in the fun. But, ever mindful of my calling, and with my customary vigilance, I –

Skeggs   Ow, come on, Vicar!

And **Vicar** *dances – a spirited dance – with* **Skeggs***. The following exchanges during the dance:*

Olivia   Oh, Mr Thornhill –

Thornhill   Miss Primrose –

Olivia   You are being precipitate –

Thornhill   Oh, may I have the intimacy? –

Olivia   You are being too hasty –

Thornhill   Olivia, Olivia –

Olivia   Oh, Mr Thornhill –

Thornhill   Oh, may I call you Olivia?

Olivia   Yes.

Thornhill   Oh, thank you, Miss Primrose!

Jenks *(a moment later)*   May I call you –

Sophy   No!

Butler *–* **Thornhill***'s servant – comes in, an air of timid urgency. He can't get* **Thornhill***'s attention and he confides a message to* **Blarney***.*

The dance continues.

Olivia   I cannot, Mr Thornhill –

Thornhill   You can –

Olivia   Oh, I cannot –

Thornhill   You can –

Olivia   Oh, Mr –

Thornhill   Call me Ned –

Olivia   Oh, Mr –

Thornhill   Call me Ned and make me happy.

Olivia   Ned.

Jenks (*a moment later*)   Call me Frank and –

Sophy   No!

The dance ends.

Skeggs   By the living jingo, I'm in a muck of sweat!

Vicar   There's a shortage of chairs.

Thornhill   'Tis easy resolved, Vicar: let every gentleman sit in his lady's lap.

Vicar   Tut, we cannot . . .

But the others are laughing at **Thornhill***'s wit. And* **Vicar** *laughs too.*

Blarney (*calling him*)   Teddy!

Thornhill (*aside to* **Olivia**)   Don't move.

Olivia   I won't.

Thornhill, *highly pleased with himself, to* **Blarney** *for the message brought by his servant, Butler.*

Vicar (*brushing the air in front of his face*)   See – feel – hear a mist, anybody? (*And has another drink.*)

Thornhill   Blast him! (*Returns to Primroses.*) Sirs, ladies, I am summoned to the Castle. My uncle is to arrive at any moment and I am to be there to receive him. (*Returns to others.*) My entire financial circumstances – present and future – are dependent on him. (*He is walking in circles. To his servant,* **Butler**, *the messenger.*) Out of my way or I'll lash you like a hound! (*To* **Olivia**.) I could cry.

Olivia   Beg – ? (*'Pardon'. But he's gone again.*)

Jenks   Bad luck, Ned –

Thornhill   *You're* coming with me!

Skeggs   Oh, Capting! (*She's sad for him.*) And look, the old ones are full cut already!

Blarney (*calls*)   Let the music continue! (*She has been working out an alternative plan.*) Get them to London.

Jenks   Like we always do, Ned.

Thornhill   Then look to that chance and your craft will have a bonus on the head of its usual recompense.

Blarney, **Skeggs** *and* **Jenks** *confer/conspire.* **Thornhill** *to Primroses.*

Vicar   Does he mean his – *uncle?!*

Thornhill   My esteemed, sir.

Vicar   Come to these parts – Sir William Thornhill?!

Moses   Whom senates listen to with applause and parties hear with conviction?!

Vicar   Oh my dear young sir, do not apologise for having to leave.

Thornhill *bows and returns to his friends.*

Blarney   It means a postponement, Teddy, but leave it to us.

Thornhill (*grimly*)   How can I support this delay? I desire the lovely girl so much I already want her sister.

And he is gone with **Jenks**.

Olivia*'s disappointment.* **Vicar** *and* **Moses** *looking off reverently in the direction of Thornhill Castle. And* **Burchill** *now enters. And* **Sophy***, finding* **Burchill** *suddenly beside her – he has taken out a whistle and is playing it – gets a fright.*

Sophy   Oh, Sir!

Blarney (*cueing* **Skeggs**)   How agreeable you –

Skeggs ('*Oh yes!*')   How agreeable you make the countryside, mum. Did we ever think it was possible, your ladyship?

Blarney   And how sad we are to be leaving.

Mrs Primrose   Your ladyships are returning to London?

Blarney   Alas, Madam, the day after tomorrow. (*A cue.*) And oh –

Skeggs   And oh, if there was some way to make more lasting acquaintanceship!

Blarney   We shall have to do with Sir Tomkyn's company, Carolina, Countess Burdock and that lot in Hanover Square.

Skeggs   Horrid!

Burchill   Fudge!

Skeggs   But then your ladyship has her compositions and verses to keep her amused.

Blarney   But did I not tell you?

Skeggs   No!

Blarney   I've had to forgo them.

Skeggs   Your compositions!

Blarney   Since my reader and companion, Miss Quill, left me to run off with – you-know-who.

Skeggs   Capting Roach? Now you're up against it!

Blarney   And I have for some time been looking for a replacement.

Burchill   Fudge!

Blarney   Who he?

Mrs Primrose *rolls her eyes.*

Skeggs   Let him approach!

Burchill   Fudge! (*And leaves.*)

Skeggs   How horrid ungenteel!

Blarney   And I have for some time been looking for a replacement, Carolina.

Skeggs   And your ladyship is not going to find it no easy matter to find the proper person.

Blarney   Don't I know it, my dear! And, to be sure, thirty pounds is a small stipend for a well-bred girl that can read and write and behave in company.

Skeggs   And where are you going to find those qualities in those little – those little –

Blarney   Chits –

Skeggs   Those little chits about the town? – For of the last three companions I had, one refused to do plain work for a single hour a day, another thought twenty-five guineas too small a salary, and – and! – I was obliged to send the third packing because I suspected an intrigue with – you-know-who.

Blarney   Capting Roach?

Skeggs   The chapling.

Blarney   Virtue, my dear!

Skeggs   Is it not worth – any price?

Blarney   But where is it to be found?

Skeggs   Where?

Olivia *and* **Sophy**, *as well as* **Mrs Primrose**, *have been attending the above.* **Mrs Primrose**, **Vicar**, **Flamborough** *and* **Moses** *are drunk at this stage.*

Mrs Primrose   I hope your ladyships will pardon my present presumption and allow me to speak. (*Calls.*) Dr

Primrose! Well, to say that my girls have a pretty good
education. At least, the whole country cannot show better.
Girls.

Sophy   We apply ourselves with diligence to what we pursue.

Olivia   Oh, London!

Skeggs   D'you hear, Lady

Blarney   Shh! Continue.

Mrs Primrose   You are vastly kind. They can read and
write and cast accounts. They understand their needle,
broadstitch, cross and change, and *all* manner of plain work.
They can pink, point and frill, they know something of music,
they can do small clothes and work upon catgut, Sophia can
cut paper and – both – have a very pretty manner of telling
fortunes in teacups.

Skeggs (*to* **Blarney**)   Hmmm?

Blarney   Mmmmmm!

Skeggs   It strikes me, Lady Blarney, that the young ladies
are not unfit for –

Blarney (*sharply*)   I am very much aware of it, Hon Skeggs!
But a thing of this kind requires a more perfect knowledge of
each other. Not that we suspect the young ladies' virtue,
prudence and discretion, but there is a form to these matters,
Madam, there is a form.

Mrs Primrose   Oh, we understand and if I were in your
position – if you will pardon another presumption on my
part – I too would be suspicious. But I suggest – pardon,
presumption – you refer to any member of Dr Primrose's
flock for the character of my girls.

Blarney   Not necessary, mum. I shall refer the matter to one
person only, Carolina, and be guided by his recommendation
of my Olivia.

Skeggs   And who is that?

Blarney   Why, my cousin, Squire Thornhill.

Skeggs   'Pon my word, if I shan't do the same for my Sophia!

Lights fading. The others go off, leaving **Blarney** *and* **Skeggs** *who call:*

Blarney   Adieu! We shall call in the morning with our decision!

Skeggs   Adieu!

Blarney   We have them at the edge of the pit.

Skeggs   D'you think it's right? I mean, to push them in.

Blarney   Push.

Skeggs   What fun!

Blarney   Yeeks!

Skeggs   Yikes!

Suddenly, they have jumped back in alarm. Out of the ground, as it were, has risen a figure, **Burchill**. *He flashes open his overcoat, produces a letter and hands it to them. And he is gone. They read the letter with trembling hands, drop it and run off for their coach.*

Scene Three

A Bed

A candle. **Vicar** *and* **Mrs Primrose** *in bed.*

Vicar *(vaguely; brushing the air in front of his face)*   Still a little of that mist . . . (*About the place.*)

Mrs Primrose   Well, I think we made a good day's work of it.

Vicar   Pretty good.

Mrs Primrose   Only pretty good? I think very good. London. My girls. And I'm told it is the only place for all manner of husbands.

Vicar   But don't we hang on young Thornhill's reference? You see! You're running ahead again, my dear.

Mrs Primrose   A formality. Mr Thornhill will be more than eager to forward the plan. What could be better for him than the training Olivia will acquire to qualify her for his fortune?

Vicar   Then what advantage London and its open market in husbands if, as you continue to suggest, Olivia is already fixed? You see!

Mrs Primrose   The London market is for Sophia. And not a moment too soon, Charles. I'm growing alarmed at these repeated visits of Mr Burchill and the attentions he is paying Sophia.

Vicar   Mr Burchill I confess has had me in a puzzlement.

Mrs Primrose   Witness that rudeness tonight.

Vicar   But I've hit on it at last.

Mrs Primrose   'Fudge!' While Lady Blarney was speaking.

Vicar   'Hah, Primrose!' (*That's how he addresses me.*)

Mrs Primrose   I tell you, my dear, there's something queer.

Vicar   Mmm.

Mrs Primrose   Hmm?

He nods.

Do you mean?

Vicar   There can be no two ways about it.

Mrs Primrose   That he is deranged?

Vicar   The poor dear man.

Mrs Primrose   And would he ever turn violent, do you think?

Vicar   No . . . No.

Mrs Primrose   Then I am not sure I find your explanation adequate. No, Charles, you shall speak to both Sophia and Mr Burchill tomorrow. And, meanwhile, to raise a little money, we'll be getting on with selling Blackberry.

Vicar   How, child? What is this now? To sell Blackberry! give me your reasons.

Mrs Primrose   A dozen. He just gets fat. He has a wall-eye and a spavin. Without a companion he's useless, single, at the plough –

Vicar   Deborah –

Mrs Primrose   And now that we're about to hold our heads a little higher, it is not proper to own such an animal.

Vicar   We shall not sell Blackberry.

Mrs Primrose   Later on we'll buy a horse.

Vicar   But he is a horse!

Mrs Primrose   Phoo! A horse as is suitable for riding on, to carry single, or double if it should make a pretty picture.

Vicar   Deborah, my dear –

Mrs Primrose   We can discuss it in the morning. Thirty pounds and twenty-five guineas a year going a-begging.

Vicar   And so is my wife.

The last is the kind of remark that usually causes a row but, this time, when they look at each other they start to giggle, without knowing why.

Mrs Primrose   Pray, total, Charles.

Vicar   Makes . . . fifty-six pounds and five shillings.

Mrs Primrose   English money. Goodnight, my dearest.

They kiss.

Vicar (*blows out the candle*)   Goodnight, my dear.

Mrs Primrose   Don't you think I did well by my children?

He gets out of bed and removes his night-shirt – under which is his usual dress.

Vicar   Well, as the journey of my daughters to the town seemed resolved upon, and as it was thought that their appearance should begin to equal the greatness of their expectations, a way had to be found of raising some extra money. And, as Blackberry was useless single at the plough, on the following morning I took him to the fair in the neighbouring town. Well, truth to tell, I was tired of being always wise.

He walks off.

Scene Four

Outdoors

Morning. **Dick** *and* **Bill** *run across to call and wave.*

Dick   Bye, Papa, goodbye, Blackberry!

Bill   Bye, Blackberry, goodbye, Papa!

Dick*, first, returns the way he came, picking chestnuts and putting them in his pockets. He picks up a paper. What interests him in the paper – we assume from his delicate manoeuvring of it – is a ladybird which he is endeavouring to transfer from the paper to the back of his hand.*

Bill*'s disposition is a sadder one than* **Dick***'s and he has continued to look off in the other direction.*

Bill   Bye, Blackberry . . . bye . . .

He wipes a tear from his eye and, now, returns to follow **Dick** *off.*

Scene Five

Primrose House

Mrs Primrose *and* **Olivia** *coming in.*

Mrs Primrose   Calmly, my dear. You must take stock of all your garments – just as Sophia is doing – list what you will need in complement, commence packing and, indeed, not look all bloused and red like the winner of a smock race when our dear friends, Lady Blarney and Miss Skeggs, arrive.

Olivia   Mr Thornhill!

Mrs Primrose   Mr Thornhill? . . . Mr Thornhill, we were not expecting you!

Thornhill (*arriving in a state*)   They are not coming to visit, Blarney or Skeggs! They have gone, flown, back to London! I do not understand it! (*To himself.*) I really don't!

Mrs Primrose   What is it you say, Mr Thornhill?

Thornhill   That the trip to town is over! Butler, my servant, who was to return them to the Castle last night, informs me that they jabbered on about a letter – a report was handed them by *someone* in the area, and its contents had such effect, they ordered that he take them to the London Road, stop the London coach, and then got on it.

Mrs Primrose   Then it was a malicious report from a malicious person!

Thornhill   I shook my servant, I thrashed him within an inch of his life, but I can discover nothing further, neither the tendency nor the author. (*He sits heavily.*) Oh, Madam!

Mrs Primrose   You'll take morning tea with us, Mr Thornhill, and taste my girdle cakes.

Thornhill   No tea. The only thing I crave is to be of service to you and, with your permission, have a word with your daughter.

Mrs Primrose (*going out*)   Who could have writ such a thing?

Thornhill (*to himself*)   Cannot understand it!

Olivia   Do not o'er upset yourself, Mr Thornhill, I beg you.

Thornhill   Ned.

Olivia   Oh, Mr –

Thornhill   Ned-Ned!

Olivia   Ned.

Thornhill   Olivia – Olivia! I could scream – I *could faint* at this very moment!

Olivia   Oh, Ned, it was good of you to –

Thornhill (*not listening*) What shall I do? . . . Yes?

Olivia   But . . . if the ladies did not return to the Castle last night, how did you discover it was proposed that we go to London?

Thornhill   Shall I make a confession? Shall I? Shall I tell you it was all my plan that you should go there? Shall I tell you that?

Olivia   To Lady Blarney's?

Thornhill   To Lady Blarney's, to the dickens, to the town! Isn't that honest of me? To where the ardour of my love, unmolested by convention, would be outpouring!

Olivia   I do not understand the half of what you say.

Thornhill   You do.

Olivia   Oh, Mr –

Thornhill   Ned-Ned!

Olivia   Ned.

Thornhill   You do – you do – you do – you do – you do! But all is not lost – What is lost?

Olivia   Pray, desist from speaking further –

Thornhill   Nothing is lost if you will come away with me today – this evening – At what time do you take the airs?

Olivia   I beg you! This is most improper.

Thornhill   But if I love you, what can hold you back?

Olivia   But *do* you, *do* you?

Thornhill   Hah! Yes, yes-yes, yes-yes! Come to the Three-Acre Copse tonight when you hear the sound of the horn. A servant will be waiting with a coach and –

Olivia   *You* will not be there?

Thornhill   How can I?! My uncle! But I shall follow you to London at the crack of dawn.

Olivia   Three-Acre Copse, sound of the horn, nightfall, and alone? I am overwhelmed with confusion. No, speak to my father, Ned.

Thornhill   Yes, by heaven! – No, it's useless! Without drink on him, he suspects – misjudges me too much. Time alone – Olivia-Olivia – can overcome his prejudice.

Olivia   We shall both go to him and –

Thornhill   I haven't got the time! Even now I risk the displeasure of my uncle in not being at the Castle to attend him. I risk a fortune for you – *Our* fortune. Oh, curst if I shan't be throwing up the whites of my own eyes next! I have not come to hear your pretty speeches or to see how charmingly you look: I have come for love – my love – for my right – for my wife! Tck! here she comes again. (*He sees* **Mrs Primrose** *returning.*) Do you want me or not? We can part now, for ever, or tonight, if you come alone at the sound of the horn, you shall be blessed for eternity. (*To* **Mrs Primrose**.) Madam!

Mrs Primrose *has come in, followed by* **Sophy** *and* **Moses**.
Sophy *carries the book* **Burchill** *gave her.*

Mrs Primrose   I have been through every name in the village ten times o'er and I cannot find the label for such malice.

Thornhill   Whoever it be and whatever was writ, be assured of my continued friendship. Madam, ladies, young sir, permit me to take my leave. (*He goes.*)

Sophy   What obnoxious ingrate could it have been?

Moses   Who could be so base as to asperse the character of a family so harmless as ours, too inoffensive to create disgust, too humble to excite envy?

Mrs Primrose (*sighs*)   Laws!

And **Olivia** *retires or goes out, nervous with her own problem and the decision she must make.*

Lights have been changing during the above. Now it is afternoon. **Dick** *and* **Bill** *come in. Chestnuts from their pockets on to the table.*

Moses   What have you here?

Bill   Chestnuts.

Moses   What is this? (*The paper* **Dick** *found earlier.*)

Dick   I found it.

Dick *and* **Bill** *run out again.*

Moses   It's a letter.

Mrs Primrose (*without interest*)   An elegant hand: I've seen it before.

Moses (*reads*)   'To the Two Ladies at Thornhill Castle.'

Their suspicions are alerted.

Sophy *looks at the handwriting: it is the same as in her book.*

Sophy   I am confident that of all men, Mr Burchill would not be guilty of such baseness.

Mrs Primrose   I knew it!

Sophy   I insist on its being read.

Moses (*reads*) 'Ladies, I am acquainted of your intention of bringing two young ladies to town under the character of companions. As I would neither have simplicity imposed upon, nor virtue contaminated, I must offer it as my opinion, the impropriety of such a step will be attended with dangerous consequences. Take, therefore, the advice of a friend and reflect on the consequences of introducing infamy and vice into retreats where peace and innocence have hitherto resided.'

Mrs Primrose   Is the mystery solved?

Moses   But it occurs to me –

Mrs Primrose   But did Mr Burchill not say that he too would call on us today and is that not . . . (*His step?*) Who are the children calling to?

Dick *and* **Bill** (*off*) Papa! Papa!

Olivia *comes hurrying down to greet her father, but stops, and retires again with guilty thoughts.*

Vicar (*coming in with* **Dick** *and* **Bill**)   Ah, my dears, I'm home again and poor Blackberry is no longer a member of the family! But his new master is a gentleman, who was familiar with my work on the monogamy principles, and who gave me – look! – this draft for three pounds and five shillings which I am to claim from our honest neighbour, Farmer Flamborough, on sight. But let me tell the day's adventures from the beginning. What is it, child?

Olivia *has approached but only to retire again in tears.*

Moses   The trip to London is over, Father.

Mrs Primrose   Read this malicious piece of Mr Burchill's composing.

Vicar   Mr – ? I perceived him on the hill, approaching.

Dick *and* **Bill** *run out.*

Mrs Primrose   See how he has so aspersed us to the ladies – calls us 'infamous', 'vicious' – they want nothing further to do with us.

Dick *and* **Bill** (*off*)   Mr Burchill! Mr Burchill!

Moses   But it occurs to me –

Mrs Primrose   Now we shall be revenged. What would be the most cutting way to deal with him? I shall be witty. And, then, in the flattering calm, confront him with the evidence of his perfidy. Ah, Mr Burchill, come in, come in!

Sophy, *too – like* **Olivia** *– retires, approaches, retires through this scene.*

Burchill   Hah! A fine day.

Mrs Primrose   A fine day, indeed, for some, Mr Burchill!

Burchill   Though I fancy we shall have rain by the shooting of my corns.

Mrs Primrose (*a guffaw*)   The shooting of your horns! Beg pardon – Sir! – but I'm over-fond of jokes.

Burchill   I pardon you – but I protest I should not have thought it a joke had you not told me.

Mrs Primrose   Perhaps not, Sir – (*she winks at the others*) – as I dare say you can tell how many jokes go to the ounce?

Burchill   I fancy, Madam, you have been reading a jest book this afternoon – that ounce of jokes is such a good conceit. Yet, I'd rather see half an ounce of understanding.

Mrs Primrose   I believe you might. And yet I've seen some men pretend to understanding that have very little.

Burchill   And no doubt you've seen ladies set up for wits that have none?

Vicar   Both wit and understanding, sir, are trifles without integrity. The honest man, sir, is the noblest work of God.

Burchill   Is that not a hackneyed maxim of Pope's? My belief, of late, is that as the reputation of books is raised, not by their freedom from defect but by the greatness of their beauties, so should that of man be raised.

Vicar   Your present observation, Sir, is just when there are shining virtues and minute defects. But when great vices and great virtues are opposed in the same mind, such a character deserves contempt.

Burchill   Perhaps some monsters, as you describe, exist, but I have never found one instance of them in my wide progress through life.

Vicar   And yet it would be easy, at this very moment, to point out a man whose head and heart form a detestable contrast.

Burchill   Impossible.

Mrs Primrose   How would you describe this, Mr Burchill?

Burchill   Hah! That is a letter.

Vicar   And do you recognise the hand it is written in? Nay, never falter, man, but look me in the face. . .

Burchill   Mine own.

Vicar   And how could you presume to write such a letter?

Mrs Primrose   He would prevent my girls going to town that he might have the company of Sophia here at home.

Burchill   I would advise, Madam –

Vicar   Do not advise, Mr Burchill –

Mrs Primrose   When we come to ask advice, we shall apply to persons who seem to have made use of it themselves.

Vicar   How-came-you-so-basely-to-write-this-letter, Sir?

Burchill   And how came you so basely to read what is clearly addressed to another?

Vicar   What?!

Burchill   Don't you know I could hang you all for this!

Vicar   Ungrateful – !

Burchill   What – !

Mrs Primrose   Wretch!

Vicar   Begone!

Mrs Primrose   Begone!

Vicar   And no longer pollute my dwelling!

Mrs Primrose   Never let us see you again!

Vicar   Go, sir, instantly!

Burchill   Hah! (*Then composed.*) I bid you good evening. (*Leaves.*)

Vicar (*calls after him*)   And the only punishment I wish you is an alarmed conscience which will be sufficient tormentor! . . . Are we surprised that bad men want for shame? No, they only blush at being detected in doing good.

Moses   But it occurs to me, Sir, that the censures in the letter might as well be referring to those to whom it is written as to us.

Vicar *is about to consider this, but* **Mrs Primrose***'s remarks keep distracting him.*

Mrs Primrose   What censures could be applied to a peeress and an honourable, you dull and heavy blockhead!

Vicar   Deborah, it is Moses you address, your son!

Mrs Primrose   And is he not your son also? (*To* **Sophy**, *who is now, also, in tears.*) There-there! You are well rid of him and free of all his embarrassing and secret attentions.

Vicar   And were there instances of secret and embarrassing attentions?

Sophy   No, Sir. His conversations with me were always sensible and pleasing. The only remark of his that caused me pain was the recurring one in which he expressed the philosophy that a woman cannot esteem a man that seems poor.

Mrs Primrose   The common cant of the unfortunate and the idle.

Vicar   And what encouragement did you give in reply to his observation?

Sophy   None, Papa. As I believe it to be true in the general rule, fearing to depress him by agreement to it, I remained silent. (*She weeps again.*)

Vicar (*to himself*)   Is it possible we may have misused a poor stranger?

Mrs Primrose   There, there! No matter how our plans are thwarted, we shall find better choice for you than that low cunning thing. Perhaps the Reverend Jenks: it was plain for all to see how taken he was by you. Why, what is it now, my dear?

Olivia (*also in tears*)   She don't love the Reverend Jenks.

Mrs Primrose   And how does she know she won't love him tomorrow?

Vicar (*to himself*)   But if he is not a lunatic, what is he? (**Burchill**.)

Mrs Primrose   There, there! We shall find someone else for you, then, someone as good as your sister's fiancée.

Vicar (*his thoughts disturbed*)   Deborah, could we, once for all, have the matter of Olivia's engagement cleared? Can you tell me, my dear, the exact date she became betrothed? And why I, her father, though not consulted on the matter, was not informed in order that I might congratulate her? And would you be good as to tell me if my son-in-law-to-be is our young free-thinking landlord?

Mrs Primrose   I have every confidence in Olivia's ability to make the conversion.

Vicar   What conversion?

Mrs Primrose   To convert her husband from free-thought. Olivia is very skilled in controversy.

Vicar   What controversy?

Mrs Primrose   The controversy she learns in her books.

Vicar   What books?

Olivia   Indeed, Papa, I've read a great deal of controversy.

Vicar   Beg pardon?

Olivia   I have read the disputes between Thwackum and Square, the controversy between Robinson Crusoe and Friday the savage, and I am now employed in reading the controversy on Religious Courtship.

Vicar   Very good, that's a good girl, and now that I find you perfectly qualified in making converts, go with your sister and make the supper!

Olivia, **Sophy** *and* **Mrs Primrose**, *all, are now in tears. And* **Bill**, *too, puts his thumb in his mouth and takes* **Dick**'*s hand.*

Mrs Primrose   Why are you so down on us?

Vicar   I cannot keep up!

He feels inadequate to deal with the tears of the three weeping women. He ushers out **Dick** *and* **Bill**, *and they run off to his instruction. It is dusk now.*

Vicar   Boys, run, fetch more roasting chestnuts. (*Narrating.*) I could not keep up. I now decided to call on our honest neighbour, Farmer Flamborough, and draw the money I had against him.

He stands outside with the money draft in his hands. In the background, **Mrs Primrose**, **Olivia**, **Sophy** *and* **Moses** *have retired, gone* *off. Now we hear the sound of the hunting horn. And* **Olivia** *appears. The sound of the hunting horn once more.*

Vicar   But somehow I knew my disappointments were not yet completed for the day.

Olivia (*whispers*)   Farewell, Papa! (*And she steals away, drawing her cloak about her.*)

Vicar   And even as I strolled from the house my heart was sinking, as I reflected that I should not have accepted a draft from a stranger.

Flamborough *comes in.* **Vicar** *gives the draft to him.*

Vicar   You can read the name, I suppose?

Flamborough   Oh, it be nicely writ.

Vicar   Ephraim Jenkinson.

Flamborough   Aye, Ephraim Jenkinson.

Vicar   'If you know Solomon Flamborough,' said he, 'I believe we can deal. And you shall have a draft on Solomon' – three pounds, five shillings? – 'payable on sight. And let me tell you,' said he, 'Solomon Flamborough is as warm a man as any within five miles round him' . . . Ephraim Jenkinson.

Flamborough   Was he a long-legged man?

Vicar   That, certainly, he was.

Flamborough   And did he talk about Greek, cosmogony and the Book of Job?

Vicar   And monogamy.

Flamborough   Egypt?

Vicar *nods.*

Flamborough   I don't know him. But I know of him. And I fear that you've been duped. (*He leaves.*)

Vicar   . . . Poor Blackberry . . . And the very next thing – (*He sets off home.*) Could anyone have guessed the further misfortune awaited me?

Dick *and* **Bill** *come running home.*

Dick   Papa, Papa!

Bill   Mama, Mama!

Dick *and* **Bill**   Our sister Livy is gone for ever!

Vicar   Speak clearly, boys.

Dick   We were in the wood.

Bill   Gathering more roasting chestnuts for us all.

Dick   When up ran Mr Burchill.

Mrs Primrose   Ah, Burchill again!

Bill   Carry the word to the vicar, he said, that his daughter is gone.

Dick   And tell your mother it was Burchill sent you.

Vicar   While feigning interest in our younger, in reality he was pursuing our eldest daughter.

Mrs Primrose   What did I tell you!

Vicar   My sweet innocence that I was leading up to heaven!

Mrs Primrose   No, she is a strumpet!

Vicar   To rob me of my child!

Mrs Primrose   She has deserted us without provocation!

Vicar   Go, my children! Our earthly happiness is over!

Mrs Primrose   She has vilely deceived us!

Vicar   Go, be miserable and infamous!

Moses   Father! –

Sophy   Mother! –

Moses   Is this your fortitude?

Vicar   Yes, he shall see that I have fortitude –

Mrs Primrose   The ungrateful creature never had the least constraint put upon her!

Vicar   Fetch me out my old pistol –

Sophy   Father!

Moses   Mother! –

Vicar   Old as I am he shall find that I can sting him yet!

Moses (*to both parents*)   Your rage is too violent and unbecoming! –

Sophy   You should be my mother's comforter and you increase her pain!

Vicar   . . . Heaven forgive me for my rage. Thus to bring your grey hairs, Deborah, prematurely to the grave . . . But, yes, I'll pursue them. I must go and find her and bring her back.

Mrs Primrose   She has brought us to shame but she will never more deceive us.

Vicar (*leaving the scene*)   No, my dear. (*Returns to prison – to how he was at the top of the play.*) But thus continued the misfortunes, that started out by leaving me no better off than a beggar, to sever the love-knot that was my family. And they would continue, to leave me the incumbent of these offices (*prison*), and to bring death to . . . to my family's fairest member. But I'll continue to do my duty . . . No, my dear, I said. My son, fetch me my staff; daughter, hand me my Bible. We shall hearken to the music of Livy's voice again. I will find her wherever she is and, though I cannot save her from shame, I may prevent the continuance of her iniquity.

Act Three

Scene One

The Road / Promenade

Vicar, *walking. Walking, walking, walking . . . But first, perhaps, we see* **George**, *begging, singing 'An Elegy on the Death of a Mad Dog'.*

Good people all, of every sort,
Give ear unto my song;
And if you find it wond'rous short,
It cannot hold you long.

In Islington there was a man . . .

Vicar   I walked earnestly to the town of Welbridge, thinking that if I did not find them there, I would take the road to London. There I was met by someone who had seen the pair twenty miles further on, and twenty miles further on there was always someone else to direct me to a greater remove.

Figures now, meant to be a crowd engaged in some kind of revelry. Perhaps they are lit behind a gauze and they grow light and dark, their sounds rising and falling: **Vicar**'s *mind is growing feverish.* **George** *is among them, continuing his song.*

George
And in that town a dog was found,
As many dogs there be
Both mongrel, puppy, whelp and hound,
And curs of low degree . . .

Vicar   Then, one evening, I came upon a place. The company made a brilliant appearance, all engaged in one pursuit, that of pleasure. At one moment I thought I perceived . . . Lady Blarney? . . . At another, I fancied I saw my eldest son, George, actually singing for his supper.

George (*and* **Crowd**)
The dog and man at first were friends,
But when a pique began,

> The dog to gain some private ends,
> Went mad and bit the man . . .

Vicar   The agitation of my mind and the fatigues I had undergone were inducing . . . inducing a fever . . . Dear old Blackberry, and the long-legged rogue that . . . My most charming Miss Wilmot? And her heterodox . . . heterodox father who had . . . So many familiar faces, none of them my darling Livy's.

He collapses in a faint. **George** *from one direction, from another* **Miss Wilmot** *– and her father,* **Reverend Wilmot***, a moment later – to* **Vicar***'s aid.*

George   Father!

Miss Wilmot   Sir!

George   Miss Wilmot!

Miss Wilmot   Mr Primrose! To what happy accident do I owe the pleasure of your visit to my home town?

George   I was on my way to Welbridge, seeking to enlist in – But my father is unwell.

Wilmot   This man has fainted! He must be taken to my house at once!

The **Crowd** *complete the song as* **Vicar** *is helped / carried off.*

Crowd
> But soon a wonder came to light,
> That showed the rogues they lied:
> The man recover'd of the bite,
> The dog it was that died.

Scene Two

Wilmots' House

George *and* **Miss Wilmot** *sit by a couch on which the* **Vicar** *is sleeping.*

Miss Wilmot   Shall we ever again see such pleasing hours as were once spent round your father's fireside at Wakefield, Mr Primrose?

George   How remote they seem now, Miss Wilmot.

Miss Wilmot   Shall we ever see them again?

Vicar   But we'll see better ones yet.

He has awoken. And **Wilmot** *is coming in.*

Wilmot   I fancy, young sir, you have seen a great deal of the world and I have no doubt that an account of your adventures would be most amusing. (*He looks at his watch.*)

George   I promise, Sir, the pleasure you have in hearing will not be half so great as my vanity in repeating them. I –

Vicar   My son's account was lengthy. No other child of mine had such a knack of hoping and of failing. Since leaving us, he had been an usher, a sailor, a musician of sorts, a street vendor, a serious writer, and a drama critic. However, it was the account of his next profession that held most interest. Yes, my son?

George   Then, one day, whilst reflecting that whichever way the new revolution of the wheel, it could only lift and not depress, I met Ned Thornhill and was employed by him.

Miss Wilmot (*as surprised as the others*)   Mr Thornhill?

Wilmot   We have been waiting Mr Thornhill's visit for two weeks. He was to arrive to sign in my presence a marriage contract drawn up by his uncle. Some unforeseen business has been detaining him but he has promised again for today. What did your position with Mr Thornhill entail?

George   My position with Mr Thornhill entailed that I attend him at auctions, keep him in spirits when he sat for his picture, carry the corkscrew and stand godfather to the butler's children.

Wilmot   How long were you in this-this-this – ?

George   In this honourable position I was not without a rival. There was another that was better formed for it, having early acquired a taste for pimping and pedigree, and having a talent for impersonation: the role of cleric being a favourite of his. Thus opposed in my patron's affections, I was going to give up the field when my good employer found another use for me.

Miss Wilmot   Oh, what was that?

George   This was to fight a duel for him, Miss Wilmot, with a gentleman, whose sister Mr Thornhill had used ill.

Wilmot   What a good report, and now –

George   I undertook the affair and disarmed my antagonist, but soon had the pleasure of discovering that the lady was only a woman of the town.

Wilmot   What an interesting career! And now –

George   And then –

Wilmot   Is it not time for Dr Primrose's broth?

Vicar   I've had it: there's the – (*Bowl*).

George   Then, Mr Thornhill and his companion left for the country with two more ladies of the town –

Wilmot   Horses! (*He hears horses in the yard and goes out.*)

George   But not before Mr Thornhill had given me a token of his gratitude. This was a letter of recommendation to his uncle.

Vicar   Do you mean Sir William Thornhill, George – that you have met him?!

George   'I will have nothing to do with you,' said Sir William, for he guessed I'd fought a duel for his nephew. 'And I wish, sincerely wish,' said he, 'that Sir William Thornhill's refusal to have anything to do with you will be punishment for your guilt.' (*His eyes brim with tears: the unfairness of it all.*)

Vicar   But the rebuke was just, my son.

George *retires with tear-filled eyes.*

Vicar   His hope will buoy him up anon

Thornhill (*off*)   Hulloo-hulloo! Mr Wilmot, Miss Wilmot, Ned Thornhill's here! (*Coming in.*) Your servant, everybody! Miss Wilmot, your obedient! (*Sees* **Vicar**.) By the powders!

Vicar   Mr Thornhill, how nice to see you!

Miss Wilmot   Pray excuse while I get my father. (*And she goes out.*)

Thornhill   What're you doing here, Vicar?

Vicar   We're old friends. Miss Wilmot was once affianced to my eldest son.

Thornhill   Was she indeed! And what of your enquiries about your daughter?

Vicar   I fear I've drawn a blank so far.

Thornhill   Excellent. But have you told them of her misfortune?

Vicar   Why blight the Wilmots with the news?

Thornhill   I approve your caution, for to make it known is at best a divulging of one's own infamy. Which, by the way, I called on your family.

Vicar   Oh, how are my dear ones?

Thornhill   Excellent. Your younger daughter is extremely so.

Miss Wilmot, *looking at her father, is returning to the room.* **Wilmot** *has the marriage contract in his hand.*

Miss Wilmot   But, Father –

Wilmot   Young Primrose's reports are the product of a mind crazed with jealousy! The young man, like his father, is raving.

70   The Vicar of Wakefield

Miss Wilmot   But, Father –

Wilmot   Daughter! do you suggest renaging on a match
with *Thornhill* money? On a contract drawn up by Sir William
Thornhill himself?

Thornhill   Ah, sir, howdyehdo, howdyehdo! And, again,
most humble apologies for being unable to attend you sooner.

Wilmot (*coolly*)   We were not greatly inconvenienced, sir.

Thornhill   Then think nothing of it. (*He sees* **George**.) Ah!
How are you, Giles, how are you!

Miss Wilmot   George, sir. (*Coldly.*)

Thornhill   George, Sir, t'be sure! I have always called him
Giles and he has always called me Willie. What're you doing
here, George?

George   I was on my way to Welbridge, seeking to enlist as
a volunteer when I met –

Thornhill   You haven't a moment to lose. The Queen's
Own Seconds are embarking for the West Indies on the
weekend and if you take a note to my old friend, Captain
Lovelady, at the regimental barracks, it will procure for you
an ensign's commission. I happen to know that the going rate
for a commission is three hundred pounds – you haven't got it,
I suppose? Then here's another note to guarantee that sum –
what d'you say? You want a moment to think. Then, in the
meantime – is that the marriage contract, sir? – as I have quill
in hand –

Wilmot, *yielding to a glance/gesture from* **Miss Wilmot**,
withholds the contract for a moment, while **George** *confers with*
Vicar.

George   There is no way to contest a courtship with honour,
is there, Father? I thought not, Sir. Had I but distinguished
myself in profession, for she has, I know, more than enough
for two. Permission, Father, to go to the West Indies.

Thornhill   Yes, let him go! –

Vicar   Your quill, sir. (*Writes an IOU for* **Thornhill**.)

Thornhill   'Twill make a man of him!

Vicar   And here is my bond, Mr Thornhill, for the three hundred pounds you give my son. And I thank you.

Thornhill (*pockets the 'bond'*)   Think nothing of it. And now the marriage contract. (*He signs it.*)

George (*tearfully*)   Goodbye, Miss Wilmot.

Miss Wilmot (*tearfully*)   Goodbye, Mr Primrose.

Thornhill   There! (*Signed. Pockets marriage contract.*) I hope that you'll be very happy, Miss Wilmot. (*He leaves.*)

All leave – various directions.

Vicar   And the next morning I too took my leave to resume the search for my daughter. In all, I was a month away from home.

He walks off.

Scene Three

Outside / Inside the Inn

Landlady, *outside, presumably coming from a well because she is carrying two buckets of water, muttering, to go into the inn. The inn as in Act One, Scene Three. Drunken, belching, smiling* **Landlord**, *immobile throughout, and his sloven-drudge wife. Both are drunk on this occasion. It is night.*

Landlady   Toiling, moiling, out in hail, rain, snow, house agoing up the chimbley, out the windows and all he does: sits-n-soaks, sits-n-soaks. 'Aye!' (*And a belch / hiccup of her own.*) Oh, Tom Symonds, you use me ill, you use me sore!

Landlord (*his belch*)   Aye!

Landlady (*her belch / hiccup*)   And whereas if two drops of liquor were to cure me of a famine, fever, pox or plague, I'd only ever bide the one to cross my lips. (*Through the following, she sits, drinking from a tankard.*) But, no, I ool bear it no longer. He'd as lief eat that glass he holds as budge as see to her is lodged upstairs right now and mind her o' her reckoning. Sittin' there, smiling sweeter than the babes in stone a-top the tombs in chapel. Well, as all can see, there's others too can sit relaxed and take their ease.

Landlord   Aye!

Landlady   'Aye!' (*And a belch of her own.*)

Olivia – *frightened, frail* – *enters background, stealthily, mug in hand, to steal a drink of water from one of the buckets.*

Landlady   But does he care? . . . And I tell thee, Tom, for all her airs and o'er-civility she dunna got a rap. She up there, a-swimming round her room like a marigold in broth.

Landlord   We ool have it in a lump.

Landlady   But does he care, does he . . . We ool have it in a – ? (*Rage.*) We ool have it now whichever way! We ool have it now or out she tramps! (*Rage subsiding.*) All falls down on my back, all – (*A belch.*) Always falls on me to do the dunning . . . . Blood-n-oons! . . . Stand!

She has seen **Olivia** *– 'Blood-n-oons!' One hand is raised, commanding* **Olivia** *to wait while she drains her tankard.*

Olivia (*petrified. 'It is but'*)   Water. (*'For my'.*) Thirst.

Landlord (*completely unperturbed*)   But consider, dear Floss, she be a gentlewoman, deserves a deal o' more respect from likes o' you.

Landlady   Likes o'?!

Landlord   Aye!

Landlady   Gentle – ?! She be a trollop! 'N' a strumpet-n-a harlot-n-a hussy-n-a-jade! And out o' here she's going with a sassarara!

Olivia   Pity, madam –

Landlady   Likes o' me! Come along, I say! Five nights here and not once yet seen sight or light o' money!

Olivia   Only for one night more, let me –

Landlady   Out, you scrub! Tramp, you baggage! Pack at once and – No! you'll leave your pack behind. Out, this *now* or I'll leave you with a mark to last you a three-month!

She has ejected **Olivia**. *Now, returning, muttering again, collecting her buckets, taking them off.*

Landlady   'Pity, madam'! What trumpery! To take up lodgings in a Christian house without cross or coin to bless herself . . .

Landlord   Aye! (*Retiring, presumably to get more drink.*) Aye!

We are outside the inn again. There is no sign of **Olivia**. **Vicar** *comes along the road. He's tired – perhaps even bewildered. He sees the inn. Stops, feels his pockets (no money); goes on; stops, considers a tree (shelter); about to go on.*

Olivia's Voice (*a whisper*)   Papa.

He reacts but, then, thinks it's his imagination and is setting off again.

Olivia's Voice   Papa.

Vicar (*silently*)   Livy.

Olivia *appears out of the darkness.*

Vicar (*a whisper*)   Olivia? . . . Livy? . . . Oh, child! (*She turns her head away: shame.*) Oh no, child. No. (*He goes to her, embraces her, holds her.*) Welcome, welcome, my lost one, my dearest, dearest Livy.

Olivia   Oh, Papa, I am forsaken.

Vicar   No. No. You are not foresaken. You are safe now and all is forgiven.

Olivia   Oh, Papa.

Vicar   No. And if you had ten thousand crimes to offer, I would forget them all. Come, shelter here beside me.

They sit on a log/stone under a tree. He has half of his coat – like a wing – around her.

Olivia   Oh, Papa, Papa.

Vicar   Rest, my fondling. Sleep.

Olivia   Oh, Papa.

Vicar   Sleep, my princess.

Olivia   Oh, Papa. (*She is falling asleep.*) Oh, Papa.

Vicar   My treasure. My beloved child. You will never see a change in my affections. Yes, sleep. And tomorrow I shall take you home. We shall yet be happy. (*He looks up at the heavens, wondering will they yet be happy.*) I'm convinced of it. (*Then he sighs and stares out at the night.*)

Scene Four

The Road

Morning through to night. **Vicar** *and* **Olivia** *are walking fast. She is animated; she has so much to tell him.*

Olivia   And on my very first day in town – oh, that villain! – he introduced me to another unhappy woman he had deceived but who lived in contented prostitution. I loved him too tenderly to bear such rivals in his affections. Oh! and the gentlemen who visited there: they told me every moment – every moment! – of my charms, and then, one day, the monster had the assurance to offer me to one of them.

Vicar   Tck! . . . But what surprises me is that a person such as Mr Burchill – even granting him mixed senses – could have the imagination!

Olivia   Mr – ? You labour under some mistake, Papa. Mr Burchill never attempted to deceive me. It was Ned. It

was Mr Thornhill. (*They stop.*) Yes! And Lady Blarney and
Miss Skeggs? They were two abandoned women more,
without pity or breeding, decoys being used by Mr Thornhill
to get Sophy and me to London. And when that plan did not
work –

Vicar (*off, briskly again*)   Ah, Thornhill! My first suspicions
were only too well grounded. (*Stops.*) But what surprises me is
that the impressions of the education I gave you could be so
swiftly – obliterated?

This seems to surprise **Olivia** *too, for all she can do is shrug her
incomprehension of it.*

Olivia (*off again*)   And I strove to forget myself, Papa. I
danced, I sang, dressed, I talked – a tumult of pleasures! But
still I was unhappy, because I knew that the ceremony which
was privately performed was in no way binding and I had
nothing to trust to but his honour.

Vicar   What! (*Stops.*) But were you married – and by a priest
– a priest in Orders?

Olivia   By Mr Jenks, Mr Thornhill's companion.

Vicar   But, my child, you are a thousand times more
welcome for you are his wife and therefore sinless! You have
been joined in the great institution of matrimony. No law of
man – though it be written on tables of adamant! – can lessen
that sacred and holy estate.

Olivia (*walking again, this time, slowly*)   Ah, Papa, you are too
little acquainted with the world. I was his mistress, not his
wife.

Vicar   No.

Olivia   Ned, Mr Thornhill, cares little for the sacredness of
matrimony or the principles of monogamy. Mr Thornhill has
been married to several others like me.

Vicar (*off, briskly again*)   No! (*He's stubborn on the matter.*)

Olivia (*hangs back*)   The design was to seduce me under the *pretext* of marriage. A mock licence, a mock priest.

Vicar (*returns to her*)   Reverend Jenks?

Olivia   He is counterfeit too.

Vicar   Then we must hang him tomorrow!

A sound escapes, a laugh as at his sudden pique, but it slides into tears. Night is gathering around them.

Vicar (*gently*)   There is but a mile or so to go.

The reality for her of arriving home, again the shame.

They proceed, arm in arm – their steps are now much slower in the dark.

Vicar   Let us keep a good spirit, Livy.

Olivia   And then one day I told him I was leaving.

A shrug of her shoulder: **Thornhill**'s *reply.*

Vicar   Let us hold to what is right.

Olivia   He gave me a purse.

Vicar   And fortune will at last . . .

Olivia   I flung it in his face.

Vicar   And fortune will at last . . . we hope . . . change in our favour.

He has not been listening to her last remarks. His eyes searching the distance, straining; his frown. He sees something. A light? He quickens his step.

Scene Five

The Fire

Flamborough (*giving the alarm*)   Fire! Fire! The vicar's house be on fire! (*Runs for buckets.*)

The Primroses in their night clothes escaping from the burning house with a few of their possessions. Just as they are breaking the last sheet of flame, **Mrs Primrose**, *overcome, is collapsing.* **Moses** *and* **Sophy** *rescue her. But in this action,* **Dick** *and* **Bill** *are forgotten. We see them, frightened of coming through the flames, retreating and being lost in the greater danger behind them.*

Flamborough (*fire-fighting*)   It's no good, we'll never put her out!

Sophy   Oh, Mama, Mama, come to your senses!

Mrs Primrose (*recovering*)   Where are Dick and Bill?

Sophy   Where are Dick and Bill?

Dick *and* **Bill**'s **Voices**   Mama! Mama!

The flames driving **Moses** *back.*

Flamborough   You can't get through!

Mrs Primrose   Burned in the flames and I'll die with them.

Flamborough   You cannot, Ma'am, you cannot go into that fire.

They restrain her. They are helpless.

Vicar *comes in and goes into the burning house.*

Flamborough   Vicar!

Moses   Father!

Sophy   Papa!

Mrs Primrose   Charles!

Flamborough   He's gone for sure.

Vicar *emerges from the flames with* **Dick** *and* **Bill**. *He has received a bad burn on his arm.*

Vicar (*shouting*)   Burn, burn, now let it burn! And let our possessions perish! I have saved our treasures!

Mrs Primrose, *laughing and crying, holding* **Dick** *and* **Bill**.

Vicar (*defiantly*) Burn on! (*And he looks at the sky, perplexed as to why these unending misfortunes. Shouts defiantly.*) We shall yet be happy!

There is an understandable hysteria about them. They huddle together in a common embrace. Then they watch the house burn down.
Flamborough *has gone off and, now, returns with blankets.*

Moses   Father, our neighbours recommend the outhouse. It is tolerably dry and the roof can be mended tomorrow.

Vicar *thanks* **Flamborough** *and shakes hands with him.*
Flamborough *leaves.*

Vicar   Let us give thanks that we are all safe.

Mrs Primrose   I cannot. (*Quietly.*)

Vicar   Deborah.

Mrs Primrose   Let us curse Heaven for these misfortunes!

Vicar   Foolish – ! (*About to shout at her 'Foolish woman!' But his faith, too, is shaken. Glances at Heaven.*)

Moses (*frightened*)   We are in the grip of guilt.

Mrs Primrose   I cannot give thanks. (*Quietly.*)

Vicar   Be patient. We are being tested . . . for a time, my dear. Our Father, which art in heaven, we thank Thee for these trials. We should like to understand Thee. We thank Thee for our deliverance. And, though we have nothing but wretchedness now to impart, grant us too the revival of our tenderness to welcome the return of our poor deluded wanderer, our dearest Livy. Amen.

Sophy   Livy?

Vicar (*calls*)   Livy!

Olivia *comes out of the shadows. She does not have the courage to look at them. She continues isolated.*

Vicar   Our daughter awaits your greeting, Deborah.

Mrs Primrose   I have only one daughter.

Vicar   The real hardships are now come fast upon us. Let us not increase them by dissension among ourselves.

Mrs Primrose   Ah, Madam, this is a poor place – an outhouse with mouldering walls, a humid floor, a bed of straw – you are come to after so much finery and high living!

Vicar   Heaven forgives!

Mrs Primrose   And I do not!

Vicar   (*narrates*) And no instruction of mine could persuade to a perfect reconciliation, for women have a stronger sense of female error than men.

The family has gone into what is meant to be the outhouse and prepare to bed down there.

But, over the days, I strove in other ways to restore us to countenance. The tears we shed might as well be ones of love. (*He joins them in the outhouse.*) Sophy, I have wept so much of late: take your guitar, play us a tune to raise us.

Sophy *strums her guitar. She finds the air of 'When Lovely Lady'.* **Dick** *and* **Bill** *too want to help and* **Vicar** *nods to them, to sing.*

Dick *and* **Bill**
When lovely lady stoops to folly
And finds too late that men betray . . .

Olivia *is weeping. And* **Mrs Primrose** *goes to* **Olivia** *and holds her in an embrace, and they weep together. And the others, now, too, are congregating around* **Olivia** *to welcome her home and comfort her.*

Scene Six

Inside / Outside Outhouse

Morning. The sound of a hunting horn.

Thornhill   Hulloo-hulloo! Ned Thornhill's here!

Thornhill *has arrived – his timid servant,* **Butler***, in attendance – waking up the* **Vicar** *and his family.*

Mrs Primrose   Shut – bar – the door!

Vicar   No.

Mrs Primrose   Sure he don't mean to dog us to the death!

Vicar *goes out. The others cower in the outhouse.*

Thornhill   Ah, Vicar! Lovely weather for the time of year! How are you, how are you? – Good! Shall I tell you why I'm here? To ask you to my wedding. It is even at the request of Miss Wilmot. Though I still can't understand how anyone can call that fright a beauty; she don't move me. What d'you say?

Vicar   Sir, there was a time when I would have chastised you. I am descended from a family that would not have borne this. But you are safe. Age and this disablement – *(his burnt arm)* – have cooled my passions and my calling restrains them.

Thornhill   Most amazed – I vow it – God's truth!

Vicar   Sir, you are a wretch!

Thornhill   Ah! *(The explanation of* **Vicar's** *anger.)* Your house is burned to a cinder.

Vicar   Are you not already married, and to my daughter?

Thornhill   And to six others!

Vicar   No! – No, sir! – You are not! For something inside – some deep monogamous instinct – tells me you are only married to her. But, go, you are a pitiful wretch and every way a liar!

Thornhill   Oh, 'Go – wretch – viper! You are only married to my Bess, Lil, Lizzie, Kate' – You're all the same!

Vicar   Avoid my sight you-you –

Thornhill   Viper –

Vicar Viper!

Thornhill 'Viper', I told you! (*That's what they all say.*)

Vicar Were my brave son, my George, at home he would not suffer this –

Thornhill Vicar-Vicar! If you or your daughter are resolved to be miserable, what can I do about it?! But, still, I would try to make you both happy. We can marry your daughter to another in a short time, just in case she is – y'know? And, what is more, she can keep her lover into the bargain for, God's truth, I continue to have a regard for her. Yes!

Vicar Avoid my sight, you-you –

Thornhill 'Reptile'!

Vicar But no. I'll defeat your purpose. I'll myself today – sick as I am – to the Wilmots and inform them –

Thornhill Vicar! –

Vicar – of your conduct to my family!

Thornhill You won't. You are bent on obliging me to speak in harsher manner. Hear me.

Mrs Primrose. *frightened, comes out and joins* **Vicar**.

Thornhill I have shown what can be hoped from my friendship, now hear what may be the consequences of my resentment. My attorney, to whom your late bond for three hundred pounds was sent, threatens hard; my steward – and it is certain he knows his business – wants to drive for your rent – Hold, Vicar! All this means the rest of your days in prison for you and the road for your family. But still I would serve you if, in return, you attend my wedding. It is, as I've said, at Miss Wilmot's request, who, for reasons best known to her own silly head, has demanded it. I hope, therefore, you will not refuse.

Mrs Primrose Give in.

Vicar   Mr Thornhill –

Mrs Primrose   Do what he asks.

Vicar   I will not attend your wedding – (*To* **Mrs Primrose**, *sharply.*) No! And though your friendship could raise me to a throne, or your resentment sink me to the grave, yet would I despise both. So, go. And though you have my forgiveness, you shall ever have my contempt.

Thornhill   Depend on it, before the day is out, you shall feel the effects of this insolence. We shall see which is the fittest object of scorn, you or me. (*A lash of his crop to his timid servant,* **Butler**, *as he goes out.*)

Vicar *walks off, hands out as if for chains. His family carry their few belongings and follow.* **Olivia** *sways on her feet. She continues, requiring assistance.*

Act Four

Scene One
Prison

> In London's fair city there once was a maid,
> Fair for a shilling, a fair tune she played,
> Played it for Tom, Dick and Harry,
> And though she were my sweetheart,
> Not once played for me – fol-dah-dee.

A prisoner with quill and paper – the paper resting on a Bible – singing the above. We come to recognise him as the **Reverend Jenks**.

The prison is below ground; steps lead up from it to a gate of iron bars. (The gate may be off.)

Clanking of keys: **Gaoler** *arrives outside iron door to unlock it.*

Gaoler Devil and his henchmen button thee, Frank Jenks!

Jenks Damme, Mr Gaoler, that were a piece of my own composing.

Gaoler Then damn thee again if I'll not take your custom from the hangman (and strangle you myself with your own poxicated entrails) if we're to hear any more. Go wake up Vicar Primrose: his family is a-come to visit. (*He goes off for family.*)

Jenks (*singing quietly, to a corner where* **Vicar** *is sleeping*) So I takes out my penknife, cuts her in three, and buries her body beneath the blue . . . Dr Primrose! Vicar! (*He helps* **Vicar** *to his feet; returns Bible to* **Vicar**.)

Vicar Have you been meditating the passage I marked for you? And you'll remember your promise?

Jenks I'm a man of my word, Vicar, I promise anything.

Vicar Repent your sins and leave this life for an honester.

Jenks Your family, Vicar.

Gaoler *lets in* **Mrs Primrose**, **Sophy** *and* **Moses**.

Vicar   Tears, my dear? No-no. I assure you I have never slept with greater tranquility. And the gaoler is humane.

Mrs Primrose   But – ! (*She indicates the grim surroundings.*) And the gaoler's just informed us that you now preach daily, here – to common criminals, Charles.

Vicar   They are still men, Deborah. And you are reacquainted with Mr Jenks, once a boon companion of depravity: his heart remained open to the shafts of reproof.

Moses   And even should Father's preaching fail, Mother, good counsel, the ancients say, returns to enrich the giver's bosom.

Vicar (*smiles on* **Moses**)   Where is Livy?

Sophy   The uneasiness of our situation, Papa, a feeling of guilt and a general fatigue have all conspired to produce a fever.

Vicar   Then we are in need of a plan.

Mrs Primrose   And that is why we have come, my dear.

Sophy   Some practical action is required, Papa, productive and materially advantageous to us.

Vicar   What thanks therefore that we have prayer.

Sophy   Yes, we have prayer, Father, but –

Mrs Primrose   Have you not considered, that we also have George?

Vicar   George? No. George must not be told. In all our miseries, it's our single blessing that one of the family is exempted from what we suffer.

Mrs Primrose (*aside*)   Oh, what have I done!

Vicar   Deborah? Sure nothing ill has befallen my boy?

Moses   Nothing indeed, sir. He is perfectly gay, cheerful and happy. In a letter he informs us that his regiment is countermanded and has not left the country, that he is a great favourite of his colonel and expects the very next lieutenancy that becomes vacant.

Vicar   What happiness that brings me!

During the above, **Jenks** *has a private word in* **Sophy***'s ear.*

Sophy   There is but one remedy for us, Papa.

Vicar   Child?

Sophy   Make proper submission to Mr Thornhill and achieve your freedom.

Vicar *shakes his head.*

Mrs Primrose   What is to become of us?!

Sophy   It will induce him to pity –

Vicar   No –

Mrs Primrose   We implore –

Sophy   As does Livy –

Vicar   Would you have me sit down with him and flatter?! No, I have other means. I can – I can – I can write to his uncle, Sir William Thornhill. A submission to the nephew is not possible as to approve his forthcoming match is to approve adultery.

Mrs Primrose   But is the rest of your family to be sacrificed to the peace of one child – and she the only one who has offended you?

Vicar   I will never be brought to acknowledge my daughter a prostitute! The world may look upon her offence with scorn, but let it be mine to regard it as a mark of her credulity. While my daughter lives, no other marriage of Mr Thornhill's shall be legal in my eyes!

Jenks   Then, if your daughter died?

Vicar   Then, indeed, I should be the basest if, from any personal resentment, I attempted putting asunder those of the *laity* that wish for a second union.

Jenks   Write to Sir William. (*Then, conferring aside with* **Mrs Primrose** *and* **Sophy**.) I do not have the skill to avoid a jail myself, but maybe I can extricate a friend . . .

Gaoler *lets the Primrose family out.*

Vicar   I wrote to Sir William. At last, news came. Not from Sir William. The complaints of a stranger against a favourite nephew were no way likely to succeed. An alarming account of a decline in my daughter's health. A further message: my daughter was speechless. And another: Livy was expiring. My soul was bursting forth from its prison to be near her, to comfort, to strengthen and receive her last wishes. I greatly longed to see her. Then my fellow-prisoner, who had befriended me throughout, gave me the last account.

Jenks (*with quill and paper*)   Can anyone explain the unequal dealings of Providence to the rich and the poor here below? Then be patient, Dr Primrose, your daughter's dead.

Vicar (*broken-hearted sigh*)   Livy!

Jenks   And now, Sir, since you once said you should be the basest of men not to agree to Mr Thornhill's second union were your daughter removed, it is time to sacrifice your pride to the welfare of others.

Vicar   My arm. (*His arm aches; he cannot write.*) Write it down that I am now willing to approve his marriage to another. And, if this further submission can do him pleasure, say that if I have done him any injury, I am sorry for it.

We are now returned to the moment that opened the play: hollow clanging of an iron door; **Gaoler** *is standing on the top step above* **Vicar** *and* **Jenks***; the lights are changing, returning us to present time.*

Gaoler   Vicar! Your fellow-prisoners be assembled for their daily sermon. But, considering the woeful news you had today, I can disassemble them again. Yea, let them do without.

Vicar Thank you, Mr Gaoler, but I'll continue to do my duty. (*We are in present time.*) But there is nothing more that can befall me now.

He signs the letter for **Jenks** *and moves off to preach to the prisoners.*

Scene Two

Prison

Vicar *addresses the prisoners (the audience). In the manner of clerics, he looks at his fob-watch at the beginning and conclusion of his sermon.*

Vicar My fellow-prisoners, when we reflect upon the distribution of good and evil here below, we find that much has been given man to enjoy, yet still more to suffer. Though we should examine the whole world, we shall not find one man so happy as to have nothing left to wish for, but we daily see thousands, who by suicide alone, show us they have nothing left to hope. In this life then, it appears that we cannot be entirely blest, but yet we may be completely miserable.

In this situation, man has called in the friendly assistance of philosophy: and Heaven, seeing the incapacity of that to console, has given us religion. And it is here that we, the unhappy, the sick, the naked, the homeless, the heavy-laden and the prisoner, come to the real motives of consolation. For, though Heaven is kind to all men, it has promised peculiar rewards to the wretched.

To the happy, eternity is but a single blessing since, it but increases what they already possess. But to the unhappy it is a double advantage, for its promise diminishes their pain here and rewards them with heavenly bliss hereafter. And he that has known what it is to be miserable now feels what it is to be glad. And should this be decried as a small advantage, the answer is remembering that it is an eternal one.

And Providence, in another respect, is kinder to the poor man. For, as the wretched have a long familiarity with every face of terror, the man of sorrow lays himself quietly down, with no possessions to regret, and but few ties to stop his departure. Thus, we, the poor, are given these two advantages over the rich. Greater felicity in dying and, in Heaven, all that superiority of pleasure which arises from contrasted enjoyment.

And when I think of these things, my brethren, my friends, Death becomes the messenger of glad tidings – oh yes! When I think of these things His sharpest arrow becomes the staff of my support – when I think of these things, what is there in life worth having! – What?! What is there that should not be spurned away? Kings in their palaces should – groan! . . . groan, for such advantages.

And when I look around these walls, made to terrify as well as to confine us, oh what glorious exchange would Heaven be for these! To fly through regions unconfined as air. To bask in the sunshine of eternal bliss. To carol over endless hymns of praise. To have no master to threaten or insult us but the form of Goodness Himself forever in our eyes.

Then let us take comfort. For each one of us here – and shortly too – will arrive at journey's end. Soon, each one of us will lay down the heavy burden placed by Heaven upon us and cease from our toil. We shall remember our sufferings below. We shall think of them with pleasure. We shall be surrounded by our friends. Our dear, dear departed ones. Our bliss shall be unutterable and, still, to crown it all, unending.

Gaoler   And now, gentlemen, pray return to your cells.

He is moved and he embraces **Vicar**.

Gaoler   That be most comforting, Vicar.

Vicar *returns to his cell.*

Gaoler   The hand of Heaven be indeed sore upon that man.

And we see him pocket the **Vicar**'s *fob-watch which he has stolen.*

Scene Three

Prison

Mrs Primrose, *a distraught woman, waiting, pacing, whatever.*
Jenks *is coming in.*

Mrs Primrose (*to herself*)   Laws, oh laws!

Jenks   Madam, I have procured the conciliatory note for
Mr Thornhill!

Mrs Primrose   Too late!

Vicar (*coming in*)   What is it, child?

Mrs Primrose   He will have no notes, wants no
approbation of his marriage. He has somehow obtained Miss
Wilmot's agreement to go ahead without you. But that is not
all. Oh, Charles!

Vicar   Speak at once!

Mrs Primrose   The member of our family you thought
exempted from our misfortunes?

Vicar   D'you mean our George?

Mrs Primrose   He is now to be its greatest victim.

Vicar   Speak! – How! – Tell!

Mrs Primrose   I must now, my dear, confess to a letter
I wrote to my son in the bitterness of my anger, desiring him
upon my blessing to avenge our cause.

Vicar   What have you done?!

Mrs Primrose   I have broken my heart and forfeited the
life of my first-born! That is what I have done.

Clanking of chains and keys: **George**, *ragged, bloodied and in chains
is brought in by* **Gaoler**.

Vicar   . . . George. Do I behold you thus? – Support that
woman nor let her fall! I own I'd made allowance to see your
return uncrowned with laurels, but . . . ('*Wounded and fettered!*')

George   Give me the courage to drink the bitterness that must shortly be mine.

Jenks   But is there no hope?

Mrs Primrose   There can be no pardon.

George (*crying*)   Let them take my life. They can have it, so they can.

Jenks   Not so hasty, George. Tell us the circumstances.

George (*produces letter, which* **Vicar** *takes*)   When I received Mama's letter, I straightaway came up from Welbridge, determined to punish the betrayer of our honour. I sent him an order to meet me.

Jenks   In writing?

George (*'yes'*)   Which he answered by despatching four of his domestics to seize and beat me. I wounded one but the rest made me captive. Then *he* arrived.

Jenks   Mr Thornhill?

George   Yes. To taunt me with the news of the imminence of his marriage – it occurs tomorrow – to the charming Miss Wilmot. Then – and in all ways suggestive – to add gross insult to his contempt, he said that as fitting celebration for wedding's eve, he was coming here to town, first, to get drunk, then seek my younger sister out.

Mrs Primrose *mouths the word (or whispers it),* 'Sophia'. *Hurrying footsteps, clanking keys:* **Gaoler** *appears with* **Moses** *and lets him in. Their dread.*

Moses   Sophy is gone!

Gaoler   I hope it won't displease you, Vicar, but it be my duty now to remove your son to a stronger cell.

George *is taken away.*

Silence.

Vicar (*quietly*)   Too much.

Moses   Full calamity has come upon us . . . and perhaps we deserve it.

Mrs Primrose   Charles?

Vicar (*continues to ignore them; to himself*)   Stunned.

Moses   Are there perhaps some private matters, some hidden sins, Father, between you and God?

Vicar (*to himself*)   Exhausted.

Jenks (*offering Bible*)   For my part, I'd appeal to Heaven that you might lie down at last unafraid.

Vicar (*to himself*)   From Wakefield to this. My fortune gone. Livy, Livy.

Mrs Primrose (*concerned for him*)   Think how strong you used to be, my dear, when all was going well.

Vicar (*continuing to himself*)   House burned down, Blackberry. My health in ruins, George for the hangman, Sophy gone. Exhausted.

Moses   You have often charmed us, sir, with lessons in fortitude: let us hear them now.

Mrs Primrose   Yes, let us kneel, that your piety may once again, my dear, reassure us.

Vicar   May all the curses that ever sunk a soul fall heavily upon the murderer of my children! May he live like me to see –

Moses   Father –

Mrs Primrose   Dearest

Vicar   I have been patient!

Jenks   Take your Bible, Vicar, and –

Vicar   Oh, that my heart would break at once and let me die!

Moses   Sir, your fortitude! –

Mrs Primrose   Hold, dear one, do not speak so –

Vicar   Oh, that today I might find God and ask His reply to this!

Moses   Father! –

Vicar   No! –

Moses   We blush for you! –

Vicar   I will not hold longer from complaint!

Mrs Primrose   Dearest –

Vicar   Yes, I'm afraid of Him! But will I be a hypocrite and not cry out? God has dealt unfairly with me.

Moses   You are declaring, Sir, the orthodox teaching of the Church to be inadequate!

Vicar   A test is a test!

Moses   For shame!

Mrs Primrose   Forebear – oh my dearest – lest He take you too from us in a stroke.

Vicar   I-will-not-hold! Am I a stone, a whale, the sea?

Moses   The root of the matter, the ancients say – Mother! Mr Jenks! (*Speak up!*) – is in our sins – and now you add rebellion to them!

Vicar   I am innocent! (*To Heaven.*) What is the charge against me? (*To the others.*) What are my faults? I speak no falsehoods, I do no wrong. My heart does not reproach me. Errors (*Yes.*) – little lapses: what harm can they do Him? What are they to Him? – the Almighty! Am I one of His enemies that he launches this onslaught on me? Does it not matter that a man lives an upright life?

Moses   Will you teach God knowledge, Sir?

Vicar   He is in control, He must take the blame.

Moses   Will you claim that any man is just in Heaven's eye?

Vicar   Will I be false to my experience? What am I left but my integrity?!

Moses   Mr Jenks! Mother! (*Speak up.*) – Will you make demand of the Almighty?

Vicar   I will. And I do! I now ask God for explanation of all this. Or! That He attend our cry for help. (*They open their mouths.*) No! (*A glance heavenward.*) Whichever is the most convenient for Him.

Burchill   Hah, Primrose!

There has been a moment's pause / beat / whatever and **Burchill** *is on the top step. Now the* **Gaoler** *comes hurrying with clanking keys to catch up. And* **Sophy**.

Sophy   Papa, Mama!

Burchill   I should have been here sooner had I not to attend this young lady.

Sophy   I was abducted!

Burchill   Am I right in thinking that is a burn you are nursing, Sir? I thought so.

Sophy   Oh, Mama, I was carried off! While out walking, a ruffian came suddenly upon me from behind and forced me into a post-chaise . . .

Sophy, *aside with her mother, telling her story, while* **Burchill** *writes a prescription and sends* **Moses** *off with it. (And from his outburst, through almost to the end,* **Vicar** *holds a dignified remove.)*

Burchill   Boy, take this note at once to the apothecary!

Sophy   . . . I cried out for assistance but my entreaties went disregarded. Then whom should I perceive, out walking with his usual briskness, but Mr Burchill.

Burchill   I was actually on my way to visit you here, Sir.
Miss Sophia:

Sophy   Never ever shall Mr Burchill be able to overtake us,
I thought, but in less than a minute he came running up by
the side of the coach and in a loud voice bid the postillion to
halt. The postillion now endeavoured to drive on at greater
speed but with one dangerous blow of his stick to the side of
the head, Mr Burchill knocked him senseless to the ground.
Now the ruffian who'd abducted me, jumping out with oaths
and menaces, with drawn sword, ordered Mr Burchill at his
peril to retire, but Mr Burchill, springing at him, shivered the
sword to pieces with another single blow. Now the ruffian,
seeing that he was outmatched, turned tail and fled, to make
his escape, with Mr Burchill in pursuit for quarter of a mile.
Oh Mama, oh Papa!

Vicar   Welcome, my child. And you, Mr Burchill, her
deliverer. I have long discovered and repented my error
about you. I hope you will forgive me.

Mrs Primrose   And me. (*But she still retains her reservations
about* **Burchill**.) We were deceived by a wretch who, under
the mask of friendship, has undone the lot of us. Otherwise
I should have seen through everything.

Burchill   But what angers me: the ruffian's still at large.
Would you recognise him again, Miss Sophia, so as to
describe him in an advertisement?

Sophy   Now that I recollect, he had a scar over one
eyebrow.

Jenks   The left one? – Beg pardon, your honour.

Sophy   I think so.

Jenks   And did your honour notice the length of his legs?

Burchill   He outran me, which I considered few in the
kingdom could do over any distance.

Jenks   Please, sir, he is my cousin! I know his very hiding place at this moment. He is the best runner in all England and has beaten Pinwire of Newcastle.

Burchill   And his name?

Jenks   Ephraim Jenkinson.

Burchill (*eye to eye*)   You know who I am?

Jenks   I know who you are.

Burchill   And you, Gaoler: my request is that you permit this fellow to go with two of my servants who are waiting upstairs upon an errand.

Gaoler   If your honour sees fit, your honour can send him and all the other criminals in here all over England.

Gaoler *and* **Jenks** *go out.* **Moses** *is coming in.*

Mrs Primrose (*to* **Sophy**)   Who? What is he? (**Burchill**.)

Moses   The dressing you prescribed, dear man.

Burchill (*calls*)   And – Gaoler! – fetch me in the boy. (*He dresses* **Vicar**'s *arm.*) In my young days I made the study of physic my amusement and, though I say it myself, was considered more than moderately skilled in the profession.

Mrs Primrose   Sure to God he cannot be . . . ?

Sophy   Oh no! For if he is, I have lost him in the unbridgeable gap between our stations.

Gaoler *brings* **George** *in.*

Burchill   And so, *again*, unthinking boy, you –

Gaoler   Beg, beg, beg pardon, your honour, but another gentleman's arrived upstairs as says you summoned here, and begs to know when –

Burchill   Bid him wait my leisure!

Gaoler *leaves.*

Burchill   And so, *again*, unthinking boy, you imagine that a contempt for your own life gives you the right to take that of another!

Vicar   Alas, Mr Burchill – Sir – whoever you are, pity my misguided son, for what he has done was in obedience to a deluded mother. Here, sir, her letter. It will serve to convince you of her imprudence and perhaps lessen his guilt.

Burchill   This is a palliative of his fault, but not a perfect excuse. A decision must be postponed. I see, young sir, you are surprised at finding me here. I have come in God's stead to see justice done and, may I say without boasting, none ever taxed the injustice of Sir William Thornhill.

He removes his long drab overcoat, revealing an elegant costume.

Mrs Primrose   I knew it!

And **Sophy** *turns away in tears.*

Burchill   Gaoler! Fetch Mr Thornhill down here.

Mrs Primrose   Ah, Sir William, the slights you received from me the last time I had the honour of seeing you! My jokes, and the bite of my witticisms! I fear I can never be forgiven.

Burchill   It is not possible to forgive. I saw through your delusion then and, as it was not in my power to restrain, I could only pity it.

Thornhill, *with his timid servant,* **Butler**, *in attendance, are shown in by* **Gaoler**.

Thornhill   Uncle William! (*Coming to embrace him.*)

Burchill   No fawning, sir, at present! I am here to conduct an examination. I know the Primrose side of the case. To enable me to judge on all the evidence, your statement, sir.

Thornhill   Is it necessary for me, Uncle, a Thornhill, to have to justify my actions in the eyes of another member of that noble family?

Burchill   Refrain from addressing me as uncle in the present circumstances. You will address me simply as 'Sir William' or as 'Your Honour'. Now, how is it that this man and his family, for whom you professed friendship, are used thus hardly?

Thornhill   If used thus hardly it is because they deserve it.

Mrs Primrose   Monster! He has vilely –

Burchill   Silence! How is it, Sir, that a vicar is thrown into prison, his daughter seduced as a recompense for his hospitality, his son, whom you feared to face as a man, his –

Thornhill   Uncle – Your Honour – Sir William! I protest! Is it possible that my judge, the esteemed Sir William Thornhill, is putting forward as one of my crimes my refusal to fight a duel?

Burchill   Your protestation, Sir, is –

Thornhill   And that the motive for my refusal is fear?!

Burchill   In this instance, you –

Thornhill   Rather than imputing my conduct to my strictest adherence to your own repeated-and-repeated instructions on the subject of duelling?

Burchill   In this instance you acted prudently and you have my approbation.

Thornhill (*emotionally*)   I find this . . . I find this most upsetting.

Burchill   The rest of your statement, Sir.

Thornhill   Very well then. I appeared, Your Honour, with the vicar's daughter at a few places of public amusement. What was levity is now called by harsher name and it is reported that I debauched the girl. I waited upon her father, *in person* – did I not? – willing to settle the matter to his satisfaction. I invited him as guest of my wedding! The conduct of a guilty man, the action of a debauchee? And he received me, sir, a Thornhill and his landlord, with insult and abuse – with *threats*! 'Were my brave son, my George, at home he would – !' Ask him can he contradict. As to his being here in prison: he owes me money. He is a debtor. Will Your Honour, here, too, censure and call it injustice my pursuing the normal and the legal means of address, which you yourself counsel and practise? Indeed, Your Honour, since the management of my financial affairs rests entirely in Your Honour's hands, it is every bit Your Honour's business, as much as mine, to proceed in the matter.

Burchill   . . . Hah! (*He's stumped.*)

Thornhill   And he cannot contradict a single particular. Ask him.

Burchill   Dr Primrose?

Thornhill   There! Nothing! While I can produce a dozen witnesses to anything I say. Here, you, Butler, do you attest to everything I say? Speak up, you – you –

Butler   I attest!

Thornhill   There! There! And thus! Thus! My innocence is vindicated. And though I should be ready to forgive this old gentleman in every other offence, I cannot-cannot-cannot forgive his attempts to lessen me in the eyes of someone I venerate – you, Your Honour. His very meanness here excites in me a resentment I cannot govern. And this, too, when his son, an *experienced* duellist, was preparing to take my life. And even though Sir William Thornhill himself should dissuade – which I now know he will not – I shall see justice done and you and you (**George** *and* **Vicar**) shall suffer, you shall suffer, you shall suffer! As I have suffered.

Burchill   Can you offer dispute, Sir?

Vicar   I *will* not offer dispute, Sir.

Thornhill   There!

Mrs Primrose (*in tears*)   Sir William!

Sophy (*in tears*)   Sir William!

Burchill   But if there is no further evidence –

Thornhill   There is none! –

Burchill   If my nephew – if Mr Thornhill insists –

Thornhill   I *do* insist – I will persist! –

George (*in tears, to* **Moses**)   What shall I do?

Thornhill   And I shall have justice! –

Sophy   My father and my brother are innocent!

Thornhill   And you and you shall suffer! –

Mrs Primrose   Then, take *my* life! –

Burchill   Silence! –

Thornhill   You *all* shall suffer! –

Moses   It strikes me, George, you should not swing for nothing.

And **George** *goes for* **Thornhill***. A fracas ensues – all shouting:* **Thornhill** *for protection,* **Burchill** *for the* **Gaoler***, et cetera. The* **Gaoler** *comes in and attempts to restore order: he leaves the gate open.*

And **Jenks** *returns with* **Ephraim Jenkinson***, who is a man with long legs: they go unobserved by the others as yet . . .*

Burchill   Silence! Am I to hang you all! Remove this rash young person. (**George**.) And should he be called again, see that he appears in my presence more properly clad!

Thornhill (*hissing*)   You *all* shall suffer! You *all* shall . . .

But now – **George** *is being removed – they become aware of* **Jenks***' and* **Ephraim Jenkinson***'s presence and they become silent.*

Jenks   Ephraim Jenkinson. He has confessed all. It was resolved that he should carry off that young lady, (**Sophy**) that Mr Thornhill should then arrive as if by accident and rescue her, by which means he would have better opportunity of gaining her confidence, then her affections.

Burchill   Gaoler! Lock the gate!

Thornhill   Do you take the word of this – criminal? Mr Jenks is the practising imposter of all professions – why is he here? I had to have him flogged, then dismissed from my service when I discovered his dishonesty – the depth of his depravity. His motives here against me are malicious. Ask any of my trusted servants for testimony. As for this person – (**Ephraim Jenkinson**.) I never saw him before in my life. (*Aside to* **Butler**.) Attest.

Butler   I attest.

Thornhill (*aside, again, to* **Butler**)   Speak up, you-you – ('*ugly useless, little toad!*' *Confidently, strutting, his back to* **Butler**.) Have you once – *ever* – seen me in the company of this long-legged person? . . . Speak up!

Butler   Yes. Yes, I've seen you together. Yes, I've seen you a thousand times together!

Thornhill   How! This to my face?

Butler   Or to any man's face. For I have never loved you, Sir.

Burchill   Address your remarks to me, my man.

Butler   Please, Your Honour, Sir, I was present when the plans were laid to carry off the vicar's daughters, sir. He (**Ephraim Jenkinson**) was the man always brought my master his ladies and the bogus priest that pretended to marry them.

Jenks   Except *one* night, Mr Butler.

Butler   'Cept in the case of the vicar's older daughter, Miss Olivia, Sir. The bogus priest that night had overdone the claret and couldn't stand.

Jenks   And who undertook to marry them?

Butler   Why, you did.

Burchill   Who did?

Butler   He did – Mr Jenks.

Miss Wilmot's Voice   Oh, let me in, let me in!

Burchill   This grows complicated.

Jenks   Begging your leave, Your Honour, in a little I shall set the affair in its proper light. While on release I sent message to Miss Wilmot and to one other witness more . . . (*He continues his private word to* **Burchill**.)

Miss Wilmot (*has come in during the above*)   Sirs, ladies – my dear Mr Thornhill! But I take it a little unkindly that, in what must have been your haste to get here, you neglected to inform me of the situation of a family dear to us both. I find that like your uncle you take most pleasure in doing good in secret.

Mrs Primrose   Hymph! His good is as base as he is!

Miss Wilmot   Goodness! (*How is she to understand it all.*)

Burchill (*to* **Gaoler**)   Remove him (**Ephraim Jenkinson**.) And return the prisoner, George Primrose.

Miss Wilmot ('*Goodness!*')   Mr Thornhill informed me that Dr Primrose's eldest son, Mr George Primrose, had married in London and that his hastened escape to the West Indian Islands was in order to abandon his wife and the child she bore him!

Moses   I have heard my brother say he would die a bachelor for your sake, Miss Wilmot.

Mrs Primrose   My son would wait for ever while you engage so quickly to another. You are too quick off your marks, my dear.

Burchill   And you, Sir, who are so fond of justice, what further before I give judgement?

Thornhill   You should now know – *Uncle* – that my financial situation no longer depends on your whim, for I have secured another fortune which no one can take from me. Yes, the charming Miss Wilmot's, which, thanks to her father's assiduity, is pretty warm and which, thanks to you, is mine whether she marries me or not.

Miss Wilmot   Oh, is this true, Sir William?

Burchill   By heaven! The legality is on his side: I drew up the articles in the contract myself.

Miss Wilmot   Then never shall I be able to renew my warmest vows to Mr Primrose. I have only my hand to give.

George   And that is all you ever had to give, Miss Wilmot. (**George**, *in regimentals, being let in by* **Gaoler**.) At least, all I thought was worth accepting. I now protest by all that's happy, your want of fortune this moment increases my pleasure as it serves to convince you of my sincerity. He can have it, Miss Wilmot, so he can!

Jenks   Not so hasty, George. Sir William, can a gentleman have one lady's fortune if he be married to another?

Burchill   How do you make such simple demand? Undoubtedly he cannot.

Jenks   Then your marriage contract for Miss Wilmot's fortune is not worth a tobacco-stopper to you, Capting. There is one other witness more, Sir William.

Burchill   Gaoler!

Gaoler *opens the gate and stands back.* **Olivia** *comes in. She descends the steps with* **Dick** *and* **Bill** *flanking her, like page-boys.*

Vicar (*whispers*)   Livy . . . Olivia?

Olivia   Oh, Papa.

Vicar   Livy? Do I behold thee? Yes, it is. And my boys. My life, my happiness.

Olivia   Oh, Papa.

Vicar   Are you returned to me?

Jenks   That she is, Vicar, and make much of her for she is as honest a woman as any in the room.

Burchill   Sir!

Jenks   Then a final word will explain the difficulty. You see me, as great a sinner as ever a member of the laity: but I am not, as Mr Thornhill asserted, all counterfeit. No man is. One of my disguises was not fake. (*Aside to* **Thornhill**.) You treated me rotten, Ned! (*Produces a document.*) My ordination papers. (*A second document.*) And this is the marriage licence that joined those two together. I kept it with the purpose of getting money on it from Mr Thornhill at an opportune moment, and should have used it, but, my vocation, refired by the example of this upright man (**Vicar**) now craves to take up the trade of cleric once again. (*Presents documents to* **Burchill**.) Sir William.

Burchill   You shall not find my leniency wanting, Reverend Jenks. I shall see that you continue the good work, so ably begun by the Vicar, *here*.

He gives the marriage licence to **Olivia**.

Madam, I restore you to reputation. And as for you – (**Thornhill**) your vices and crimes of ingratitude deserve no pity. A bare competence of what you presently receive shall be supplied to support the wants of life, but not its follies. In the future, it will be from the tenderness and intercession of your wife that you will receive any extraordinary supplies.

Thornhill   Oh, my dearest wife!

Moses   His repentance is too sudden!

Burchill   Do not aggravate your meanness, Sir, with hypocrisy!

Thornhill   My dearest Uncle –

Burchill   Depart from me and from England for a period of ten years and seek reformation. From all your former servants, choose one – Not Mr Butler, sir! This decent domestic, who only wanted a master to love, is to be accommodated into my own employ.

Olivia   Papa, *ten* years.

Vicar   Sir William. Forgiveness. Heaven has blessed me this night and forgiven my pride. Might we allow the wife, now grown prudent, to be sure, to decide the term?

The decision is given to **Olivia**.

Olivia   Then, if severance there has to be (*she touches her stomach*) let it be for six months.

Thornhill   Olivia, Olivia! –

Olivia (*tears*) Oh, Ned!

Burchill   Leave, sir – Depart!

Thornhill   I shall long for you till then – (*To the others.*) I really shall. My dearest wife, farewell – six months – adieu . . . (*He's gone.*)

Vicar   But how could you add to my miseries by telling me that my darling girl was dead?

Mrs Primrose   To save you, dearest. And you are dearer than all else to me.

Vicar   But it matters not, my pleasure at finding her again is more than compensation for the pain.

Olivia   And allow me to increase your joy, Papa, with the news that arrived an hour ago, to say that the merchant from Wakefield who absconded with your fortune was arrested at Antwerp and, far from being bankrupt, gave up effects to a much greater amount than was due to his creditors.

Burchill   And now that I have sorted out your problems, I think we are ready to go to supper.

Mrs Primrose (*drawing* **Sophy** *forward*)   Some little matters yet, Sir William, to be tied?

Burchill   Some little matters? Yes! What, Bill, you chubby rogue! You remember your old friend Burchill, dontcha? And Dick too, my honest veteran! Well, you shall find I've not forgotten you. Your favourite gingerbread!

Mrs Primrose   But, is there not *one* little matter more?

Sophy (*coyly*)   Mama.

Burchill   You are sensible, Dr Primrose, of an obligation we both owe the Reverend Jenks?

Vicar   Indeed.

Burchill   Then if I pledge five hundred pounds as fortune to enable him find a wife, will you give him your younger daughter?

Mrs Primrose   Laws!

Burchill   Will you have him, Miss Sophia?

Mrs Primrose   What d'you say, Sir William? – She cannot!

Burchill (*to* **Sophy**)   Mr Jenks, who is to be chaplain to this prison – (*To himself.*) I must be really certain – and a handsome enough young fella with five hundred pounds?

Mrs Primrose (*speaking for / cueing* **Sophy**)   'No, sir, never!'

Burchill   Ay?

Sophy   No, sir, never; I would sooner die.

Burchill   Can this young lady have taken a shine to the cut of my jaw? Ah, how I have searched for a wife – striven even among the pert and the ugly – who, a stranger to my birth and fortune, would love me! How great then is my rapture to find that woman! Miss Sophia, will you become Lady Thornhill?

Sophy   Yes, oh yes.

George   And, Miss Wilmot – Arabella – will you become my wife?

Miss Wilmot   Yes, dearest Mr Primrose – George.

Moses   The world goes on very well.

Mrs Primrose   I haven't done too badly by my children, Dr Primrose?

Vicar   Yes, child.

George   Give us your blessing, Father.

Vicar   I give it from my heart. May you be happy as I, and glory in the mystery of being alive. Once have I objected, spoken of things I do not understand, things too wonderful for me to know. But I'll proceed no more in complaint. I believe in good, I believe in the power of forgiveness, I believe in life. My pleasure is unspeakable when I look at you. And it only remains that my gratitude in good fortune shall exceed my former submission in adversity. God's blessing on us all.

The Cherry Orchard

This adaptation of *The Cherry Orchard* received its premiere at the Abbey Theatre, Dublin, on 17 February 2004. The cast was as follows:

Ranyevskaya	Donna Dent
Lopakhin	Lorcan Cranitch
Anya	Gemma Reeves
Petya Trofimov	Michael Colgan
Yepikhodov	Phelim Drew
Firs	Tom Hickey
Gayev	Nick Dunning
Varya	Alison McKenna
Dunyasha	Janet Moran
Yasha	Dylan Tighe
Charlotta	Clara Simpson
Boris Pishchik	Des Cave
Vagrant	Simon O'Gorman
Post Office Clerk	Peter Daly
Stationmaster	Des Nealon
Guests/Servants	Peter Daly
	Ruth McGill
	Conor Ryan

Director Patrick Mason
Designer Joe Vanek
Lighting Designer Paul Keogan

Characters

Lyubov Andreyevna Ranyevskaya, *owner of the estate*
Anya, *her daughter, aged 17*
Varya, *her adopted daughter, aged 24*
Leonid Gayev, *her brother, aged 51*
Yermolay Lopakhin, *a businessman*
Petya Trofimov, *a student*
Boris Borisovich Simeonov-Pishchik, *a landowner*
Charlotta Ivanovna, *a governess*
Simon Panteleyevich Yepikhodov, *a young estate office clerk*
Dunyasha, *a young housemaid*
Firs, *manservant, aged 87*
Yasha, *a young manservant*
Vagrant
Stationmaster
Post Office Clerk
Guests *and* **Servants**

The action takes place on Ranyevskaya's estate.

Act One

A room which is still called the nursery. One of the doors leads to **Anya**'s *bedroom. The windows are shut. Daybreak: the sun will soon be up. May.*

Dunyasha *comes in carrying a candle with* **Lopakhin** *who is holding a book.*

Lopakhin   Well, it's in.

Dunyasha   Thank God.

Lopakhin   What time is it?

Dunyasha   Nearly two.

Lopakhin   So how late does that make the train?

Dunyasha *blows out the candle.*

Lopakhin   Two hours at least.

Dunyasha   . . . It's nearly light already.

Lopakhin   But I'm a fine one: I fall asleep. And I came here specially to meet her at the station. You might have given me a shout.

Dunyasha   I thought you'd gone to the station with the others.

Lopakhin   What? No. Suddenly I'm asleep sitting down with this. (*Book.*) A pleb.

Dunyasha (*listening*)   I think they're . . . ['*coming*'] Are they?

Lopakhin (*listens*)   No. Their luggage, bags, one thing and another to be collected . . . What will she be like after her five years abroad? She won't have changed . . . The eyes, you know: the kindness in them. Always . . . I'll never forget it for her: I was fifteen, and my father – oh, he'd 'progressed' to having the little shop over in the village then.

And we'd come here, to the yard out there, for something or other, and he hit me. Drunk, of course, what else. Smack, here in the face with his fist, and the blood started to pour. And Lyubov Andreyevna, so young then, *so* – slender – took me in. I mean into here, the house, to this room, the washbasin that was over there. 'Do not cry, little peasant, it will get better before you are married' . . . Now: little peasant . . . And I still am, despite my waistcoat and yellow boots. And everything else. A pig's snout in a pastry shop. (*The book*:) Trying to make head or tail of this and couldn't understand a blessed word of it, I fall asleep.

Dunyasha (*whispering*)   The dogs can sense it. (**Dunyasha** *is a little given to the dramatic.*)

Lopakhin (*absently*)   What?

Dunyasha   That the mistress is returning. They have been awake too all night, and trembling.

Lopakhin   What's the matter with you?

Dunyasha *holds out her hands to show him they are trembling.*

Lopakhin   What? (*Silently.*)

Dunyasha   I think I'm going to faint.

Lopakhin   Well, aren't you the lady! Your clothes and hairdo too. That's not the way, Dunyasha. Remember who you are. (*He sees/hears someone coming in and moves aside with a little impatience.*)

Yepikhodov *comes in. He is the young estate office clerk; jacket and highly polished boots that squeak; innocently pretentious; awkward, accident-prone. He has a bunch of flowers behind his back that he would gallantly present to* **Dunyasha**; *now he produces them with a flourish*:

Yepikhodov   Tra-la! (*The nosegay comes apart, the flowers fly, scatter. His smile is one of both disbelief and conviction at this demonstration of his accident-proneness.*) You see!

Lopakhin   Tck!

Yepikhodov   I mean to say, the gardener sent them. (*Gathers the flowers, gives them to* **Dunyasha**.) They're to go in the dining room, he said.

Lopakhin   And bring me a glass of something, Dunyasha.

Dunyasha (*going out*)   Sir.

Yepikhodov   . . . A morning frost of three degrees again this morning? And the cherry is in blossom. Dear sir, I cannot approve this climate. The climate, I regret to say, does not facilitate the requirement. In no way whatsoever is it equal to the occasion. Further, Yermolay Alekseich, if I may append, I purchased these boots two days ago and they squeak so excessively I have little hope in them. In your opinion what should I oil them with?

Lopakhin (*undertone: containing himself*)   Stop.

Yepikhodov   Each day something falls out. Do I complain? I've grown used to it.

Lopakhin   Stop.

Yepikhodov   One thing after another.

Lopakhin   Buzz, clear off!

Yepikhodov *lingers.* **Dunyasha** *returns: a glass of kvass to* **Lopakhin**.

Yepikhodov   . . . I'll be going, then. (*And he walks into a chair – or some accident. Triumph:*) You see! The concatenation? It's even rather remarkable! (*He's gone.*)

Dunyasha   He proposed to me . . . Yermolay Alekseich?

Lopakhin   Aah!

Dunyasha   I don't know, though . . . He's nice. But when he opens his mouth – Do *you* understand what he says? . . . It sounds right, *really* sophisticated, but . . . I *think* I like him. He loves me. Madly. But when they tease him, and call him 'Two-and-Twenty Troubles'?

Lopakhin   Shh! (*Listening.*)

Dunyasha   I don't know, though. Heigh-ho!

Lopakhin   There!

Dunyasha   Are they coming?

Lopakhin   They're here.

Dunyasha   I'm shaking again.

Lopakhin   Will she recognise me? (*Going out.*)

Dunyasha   I'm going to faint. (*Following him.*)

The stage is empty.

Two carriages have been heard drawing up. (And voices off, indistinctly, of the kind: 'Whoa!', 'Welcome home!' 'Where's the luggage to go?', 'Those to the other door, those in here!')

Now, noise of people in rooms off, and **Firs** *comes in, hurrying across the room as best he can, leaning on a stick. He is wearing old-fashioned livery and a top-hat for the occasion: he has been to the station. He's talking to himself, words no one can make out.*

Voice   This way, this way.

Anya *comes in, then* **Lyubov Andreyevna** *and* **Charlotta** *with a little dog on a lead. They are in travelling clothes.*

Anya   Mama, mama, in here, come through here! Do you remember what this room is?

Lyubov *smiles, silenced by it, tears coming to her eyes. They are followed by* **Varya** (*full-length coat and a headscarf*), **Gayev**, **Pishchik**, **Lopakhin**, **Dunyasha** (*carrying a bundle and an umbrella*) *and* **Servants** *carrying luggage. All are on their way through the room.*

Varya   It's so cold, it's so cold.

Lyubov   The nursery.

Varya   My hands are numb.

Lyubov   Sweet, darling, beautiful, *angel* of a room.

Varya   Mamochka, we've left your rooms exactly as they were, the white one and the mauve.

Lyubov   The nursery. I used to sleep here when I was little. (*She's tearful.*) And now I'm a little girl again. Leonid – (*She kisses her brother,* **Gayev**, *then* **Varya**.) My Varya too, the same as ever, like a little nun. (*Kisses her brother again.*) Oh, Leonid! And Dunyasha: how you've grown, but I recognised you straight off! (*Kisses her.*)

Gayev   Train, two hours late: how's that for efficiency?

Varya (*leading them off*)   This way, this way . . .

Pishchik (*asking* **Charlotta** *what her dog eats, making sounds like a dog eating*)   He?

Charlotta   He is very fond of nuts.

Pishchik (*astonished*)   Well I never! Nuts?! . . .

All have gone out except **Anya** *and* **Dunyasha**. **Dunyasha** *helps* **Anya** *out of her things – gloves, coat, hat.*

Dunyasha   Now. My *little* darling. Oh, I'm so, oh! ['*excited*'] We've worn ourselves out waiting for you.

Anya   I didn't sleep for the whole four nights of the journey.

Dunyasha   Pet.

Anya   *Freez*ing.

Dunyasha   *Freez*ing when you left in Holy Week, but now! *Long*ing to see you – My *little* flower! But I can't wait to tell you, wait'll I tell you!

Anya   Oh, Dunyasha –

Dunyasha   No! You'll never guess what.

Anya (*listless*)   What this time?

Dunyasha   Yepikhodov has proposed to me. The clerk.

Anya   Oh, Dunyasha –

Dunyasha   No! At *Easter*!

Anya   ['*You're*'] Still at it. I've lost all my hairpins. (*Then a half-swoon: tiredness.*)

Dunyasha   I don't know, though. But he does, does, really love me.

Anya (*looking into her room*)   Aaaaa! My room. As though I had never been away. I'm *home*! Tomorrow when I wake up I shall be *here*. And I shall get up and I shall *run* out and into and through the orchard. (*Tiredness again.*) But, oooh, if only I could get to sleep! I didn't sleep all the way because of worries.

Dunyasha   Peter Sergeich has arrived.

Anya (*pleased*)   Petya!

Dunyasha   Two days ago.

Anya (*a new thought, silently to herself*)   Oh. (*A worry.*)

Dunyasha   He's sleeping in the bath-house, he's living there. I don't want to put anyone out, he said – Should I wake him up? Varvara said don't: 'Don't-you-Dunyasha-wake him!' But should I, for you?

Varya *comes in, a bunch of keys at her belt.* (*She is superstitiously religious, sentimental, well-intentioned and sexually frustrated.*)

Varya   Coffee, Dunyasha, quickly. Mamochka wants coffee.

Dunyasha   Varvara Mikhaylovna, at once. (*And she's gone.*)

Varya   Well! Let me look at you. You've arrived, and safely, thank God, thank God. (*Stroking* **Anya**'*s hair.*) My beautiful one is back!

Anya   And what a business.

Varya   I can imagine.

Anya   Snow and ice when I left, Charlotta talking the
whole way there and doing her conjuring tricks – What did
I do to deserve Charlotta's company?

Varya   But you could hardly have gone on your own – at
seventeen?!

Anya   But we got there – at *last*. Paris. *More* snow, *more*
cold – and my French is *terrible*. Mama is living on a fourth
floor of this place. She has Frenchmen there, *des dames*,
dressed up, drinks, a little old priest, a little black book in his
hand all the time, cigarette smoke all over. So – messy.
Messy. Unreal. And suddenly I felt sad. I felt so sorry for
her. I took her face in my hands, I felt so sad. Then she
started to cry, and I held her. Mama.

Varya   Don't tell me, Anya, you're only upsetting
yourself. (**Varya** *is the one who's upset.*)

Anya   The house she bought in Monaco? That's gone.
She'd already sold that. We had barely enough to get back
here. I had nothing. She doesn't *grasp* the situation. We get
out at a station to eat and the most expensive things are
ordered: then *all* the waiters have to be tipped. She doesn't
understand. Charlotta behaving the same. And Yasha –
Yasha? She has him for a manservant now. He orders for
himself, whatever he wants. We brought him back with us.

Varya Yes, I've seen *him*.

Anya   Heigh-ho!

Varya   Heigh-ho. (*And blows her nose.*)

Anya   And how are 'tricks' here? Have you managed to
pay off anything?

Varya   With what? The estate will be sold in August.

Anya   ('*My God!*'), *Ho*-heigh!

Lopakhin *comes in, was considering joining them, does a circle
instead / an about-turn, goes out again, talking to himself*:

118 The Cherry Orchard

Lopakhin Moo-oo – Baaa – Wuff-wuff – Miaow!

Varya Oh, that! (*With her fist – she could hit him.*)

Anya Has he said anything? (**Varya** *shakes her head.*) Why don't you – explain – yourself to him, to each other. Everyone says – knows – he loves you.

Varya He's too busy to pay any attention to me.

Anya No-o-o-o. (*Silently.*)

Varya And that's fine by me. Honestly, Anya, I'd prefer it if he kept away from here entirely, honestly I would! Bless him, but it annoys me to see him – Yes-it-does – And good riddance. Everyone is on about a wedding day, everyone congratulates him, congratulates me, and it's all about – *nothing.* It's all someone's dream! (*New tone.*) Your broach is like a little . . . bee?

Anya Mama. (*Meaning 'Mama bought it'. Going off to her room.*) I went up in a balloon in Paris.

Varya (*follows to* **Anya**'s *room door*) My beautiful one is back.

Dunyasha *has returned with coffee pot and coffee things.*

Varya (*at* **Anya**'s *door*) . . . I never stop dreaming. I run the house, I go about my work, all day long, and d'you know what I dream? If only we could get you married. I'd be at peace then. I'd go off to a retreat then. To Kiev. Then Moscow. I'd walk to the monasteries, to all of Russia's holy places. I'd walk, I'd walk, and walk. And it would be bliss.

Anya (*off*) The birds are starting to sing.

Varya Yes, it's time for you to sleep. It would be bliss. (*She has gone into* **Anya**'s *room.*)

Yasha, *an affected young manservant, comes in carrying a rug and a travelling bag.*

Yasha Mamzelle? May one come through here?

Dunyasha   Yasha?!

Yasha   Hmm.

Dunyasha   I hardly recognise you: You've changed so much abroad.

Yasha   And? . . . You may be – *Who?*

Dunyasha   Me, Dunyasha! Fyodor Kozoyedov's daughter.

Yasha   Aaaa!

Dunyasha   When you left I was only . . . ['*about that size*']

Yasha   The cucumber. (*A quick look round before he grabs her in an embrace.*) A cuke!

She shrieks, drops a saucer. He leaves quickly.

Varya   Now what?! What is going on in here? (*She comes in.*)

Dunyasha   Broke [*a*] saucer, miss.

Anya (*off*)   Varya?

Varya   Well, a broken saucer brings luck.

Anya (*coming in*)   Mama ought to be warned Petya's here.

Varya   I've given instructions that he shouldn't be woken.

Anya   My beautiful little brother, Grisha, drowned in the river. Petya was his tutor. It was a terrible time for her. Papa died only a month before that. She went away without once looking back. If only she knew how I understand things. Petya may bring it all back of a sudden . . . Varya?

Varya *is in tears again.* **Firs** *comes in, short jacket and white waistcoat. He is putting on white gloves.*

Firs   The mistress will take coffee in here now. (*Inspecting things.*) Is the coffee prepared? (*To himself.*) Shit! You! Simpleton! Where is the *cream?*!

Dunyasha   Oh, my God! (*Hurrying out.*)

Firs   Bungle-arse! (*Fussing over the coffee things, talking to himself.*) The old master, too, you know, went to Paris once, in a carriage. Horses in those days . . . (*And he's laughing to himself.*)

Varya   Firs, what is it?

Firs (*joyfully*)   My mistress has returned, you know. I've lived to see it. Now I can die.

Dunyasha *returns with the cream and stands by.* **Lyubov**, **Gayev**, **Lopakhin** *and* **Pishchik** *are coming in (the latter wearing the traditional – older form of dress).* **Gayev** *is miming billiard shots.*

Gayev (*off*)   Declare that shot for me, sister.

Lyubov   Red into the corner –

Gayev   Yellow! – Yellow first – screw-shot! –

Lyubov   Double back for the red? –

Gayev   Two cushions –

Lyubov   And into the middle! (*They are laughing.*)

Gayev   . . . Isn't it strange: once upon a time, sister, you and I slept in this room. Now I'm fifty-one.

Lopakhin   Time flies.

Gayev   Wha-oo? (*His own form of 'What?', a sound that is part of his vagueness.*)

Lopakhin   Time flies.

Gayev   Smell of – hmm? (*Sniffing the air.*) Mint, patchouli?

Anya   I'm going to bed. (*Kiss.*) Mama.

Lyubov   Goodnight, my precious. Are you happy to be home? I'm not come to my senses yet.

Anya   Goodnight, uncle.

Gayev (*kisses her*)   God bless you. So like your mother. You were, Lulu, exactly like this at her age.

Anya *shakes hands with* **Lopakhin** *and* **Pishchik** *and goes to her room.*

Lyubov   She's very tired.

Pishchik   Journey: Five days, what, four nights!

Varya   Well, gentlemen, it's nearly three. (*Time to call it a day.*)

Lyubov   Oh, Varya, my little nun! ['*The same as ever*'] I'll drink my coffee, then we'll all go. (**Firs** *places a cushion at her feet.*) Thank you, thank you. I've got used to coffee. I drink it in the morning, I drink it in the night.

Varya   I'll check that everything's brought in. (*She goes.*)

Lyubov   Is this really me sitting here? (*Laughs.*) I want to leap about and shout. (*Hands to her face.*) Horrors! What if I'm dreaming it? (*Becoming emotional.*) I love my country, God knows I do. I love my homeland so much. In the train I couldn't look out of the window, I kept crying. But, I must-have-my-coffee! Thank you, Firs, dear little old friend, I'm so glad you are still alive.

Firs   The day before yesterday.

Gayev   His hearing's bad.

Lopakhin   Lyubov Andreyevna, you're looking awfully well, splendid! Those eyes! I wanted to sit down and have a good look at you, have a good talk but – It's a nuisance: I have to set off for Kharkov at –

Pishchik   Awfully well!

Lopakhin   Yes! At five o'clock ['*this morning*'], if you please, and –

Pishchik   Dressed like a Parisian, what!

Lopakhin   Yes! And –

Pishchik   Head over heels, I am, I am!

Lopakhin   But! Your brother here – he calls me a boor, a grabber, a jumped-up bumpkin. Water off my back, he can say what he likes. It's you I want to listen to me and look at me with those amazing eyes and trust my advice. Merciful hour! my father was one of your father's and grandfather's serfs, but you, you once did something for me – did so much for me – I've forgotten all that and I love you – care for you – like a relative – *more* than a relative.

Lyubov   I can't sit down. (*She's up, walking about.*) I can't sit still. This – joy! – is too much for me. Laugh at me: I know I'm a silly! (*Emotionally.*) My little table, bookcase – everything! My little table. (*She kisses it.*)

Gayev   Nanny died while you were away.

Lyubov   God rest her. Someone wrote to me. (*Sits again with her coffee.*)

Gayev   Anastasiy too. (*She nods.*) . . . Petrushka? Cross-eyed one? He left. Some kind of work in town now with the police. (*He takes a box of fruit-drops from his pocket and sucks one.*)

Pishchik   Dashenka? My daughter? . . . Sends her regards.

Lopakhin (*looks at his watch*)   I want to say something pleasant, something that will cheer us all up. I haven't much time now – Well, in a nutshell. Cherry orchard, your estate, is going to be sold by public auction to pay off your debts – No, wait a minute! There's a way out – You can sleep soundly, my dear Lyubov Andreyevna. Here's the plan. Attention please! Divide up the whole estate into plots and lease the plots for holiday cottages.

Gayev   I'm sorry, what-is-this?! ['*rubbish*']

Lopakhin   You'll have – at the very least – a yearly income of twenty-five thousand roubles.

Lyubov   I don't understand, Yermolay.

Lopakhin   You'll get – at the very least – twenty-five roubles per acre per year and if you advertise *now*, I'll bet you anything you like, by autumn you won't have a single plot left, they'll be snapped up. The location is perfect: thirteen miles from the town – the railway now is laid on there – the river is deep: bathing! Wonderful! In a word, congratulations, you're saved. Some preliminary stuff of course, cleaning up a bit – (*Gestures: 'nothing to it'.*) Those old buildings, demolish them, this house for a start – what earthly use is it now? – and cut down the trees.

Lyubov   Cut down the? Excuse me, my dear.

Gayev   Yes, ex-cuse-me!

Lyubov   I'm sorry, but you don't understand anything.

Lopakhin   But you know the place is going to be sold, you know that, don't you?

Lyubov   If there's an interesting or remarkable thing in the whole province it's the orchard.

Lopakhin   The only remarkable thing about Cherryorchard is that it's very large.

Gayev   Tck!

Lopakhin   And it fruits only once every two years, and even at that you can hardly give the cherries away.

Gayev   The orchard is mentioned in the *Encyclopaedia Russica*.

Lopakhin (*looks at his watch*)   Well, unless there's another way, at the auction on the 22nd of August, your – Cherrylands – are gone . . . There-is-absolutely-no-other-way!

Gayev   Is there not!

Lopakhin   I swear to you. So, make up your minds about it.

Firs   In the old days, you know, they dried the cherries, and they used to soak them, put them in jars, made jam. And they used to –

Gayev   Be quiet, Firs.

Firs   Yes. Send them to Moscow and Kharkov. Wagonloads. (*Laughs.*) They fetched some money! The dried cherries in those days were soft, juicy, sweet, fragrant. They knew the recipe then.

Lyubov   And where is the recipe now?

Firs   Forgotten.

Pishchik   What about Paris? Did you eat frogs? Let's hear.

Lyubov   I ate a crocodile.

Pishchik (*credulous*)   You actually?! (*They laugh.*)

Lopakhin   But, you know, it's interesting to watch. Up to now only the gentry and the peasants lived in the country. Now these summer visitors have started appearing all over. All the towns, even the small ones, are becoming surrounded by these holiday cottages, and they're going to go on multiplying?

Gayev   Tck!

Lopakhin   At the moment your holiday-maker just sits around on his verandah drinking tea, but it's going to happen that he'll start to grow things on his hectare and then see all the land all about – the provinces! – here! – flourishing, become rich, thriving, happy.

Gayev   What nonsense!

Varya *returns with* **Yasha**.

Varya   Mamochka, two telegrams arrived for you. (*She unlocks the bookcase.*)

Lyubov   From where?

Varya   Paris. Here they are.

Lyubov   I've finished with Paris. (*She tears them up without reading them.*)

Gayev   Lyubov, d'you know how old that bookcase is? Last week I pulled out the bottom drawer and there, branded in the wood, was the date. (*He has risen.*) This bookcase was made exactly one hundred years ago. How's that for you?

Pishchik   One hundred?!

Gayev   One hundred. Eh? We should be celebrating its centenary. It may be an inanimate object but, whichever way you look at it, it's a bookcase.

Pishchik   Fancy that!

Gayev   What a piece of work! (*He strokes the bookcase.*) Dear Venerable and Most Respected! we salute your custodial existence, which for a century now has been directed to the noblest ideals of man. Your silent call to fruitful labour has not weakened over time – (*Emotional.*) Nor has that call to labour fallen on deaf ears – instilling in generations of this family a cheerful faith in a better future and a dedication to the shining ideals of goodness, social self-awareness and justice for all.

Pause.

Lopakhin   Yes. Well.

Lyubov   Oh Leo, Leo! ['*You haven't changed*']

Gayev (*to cover his embarrassment*)   In-off, right-hand corner, screw-shot back for red, middle pocket!

Yasha   Would you care to take your pills now, madam?

Lopakhin   I must be going.

Pishchik (*comes to*)   What's that! (*He has been nodding off – and on – during the above.*) Pills? They do you no good – Show them here, give them here. (*He takes the box of pills, shakes them* *out into his hand and blows on them.*) Do you no good, do you no bad. Watch this. (*He swallows them, washing them down with kvass.*)

Lyubov   Boris Borisovich!

Pishchik   There!

Lyubov   Are you mad?!

Pishchik   I've taken the lot!

Lopakhin   What a stomach!

They laugh.

Firs   He was here too at Easter and ate half-a-bucket of pickles. (*And continues muttering.*)

Lyubov   What does he say?

Varya   He's been rambling like that for three years now.

Yasha   Cuckoo.

Charlotta *comes in, crossing the room.* (*A white dress, tightly laced, lorgnette on her belt; thin.*)

Lopakhin   Charlotta Ivanovna! I haven't said hello to you. (*He goes to take her hand.*)

Charlotta   *Nein!* If I allow you to kiss my hand, you will want to kiss my elbow, then my other elbow, then . . . ?

Lopakhin   Today is not my lucky day. (*They laugh.*) Do us a trick then.

Charlotta   No.

Lyubov   Do, Charlotta, show us a trick!

Charlotta   But I must go to my . . . (*Unsmiling, po-faced.*) Who is that knocking out there? (*A knock on a door, as from outside.*) Who is that knocking at my door, who wants to come in? (*More knocking, a 'special' knocking.*) Ah, it is m'sieur, my fiancé. (*She goes.*) I'm called to bed!

They laugh.

Lopakhin   Well, it's time for me to go. We'll see one another in three weeks. (*Bows to* **Lyubov**.) Till then, *madame?* (*To* **Gayev**.) Sir! Far-thee-well. (*Kisses* **Pishchik**.) And far-*thee*-well too, my friend. (*Shakes hands with* **Varya**.) Goodbye. (*And with* **Firs** *and* **Yasha**.) I wish I didn't have to go, but! (*He flaps his hands. To* **Lyubov**.) If you make your mind up – you know, about what I was saying – let me know. I can organise the money for the preliminary work and – and so forth. So. Well . . . Give it some serious thought.

Varya   I thought you said you were going?!

Lopakhin   Going! I'm gone. (*He's gone.*)

Gayev   Businessman: a boor. (*Silently.*) Oh! Beg pardon. Varya's going to marry him, he's Varya's fiancé.

Varya   *Please*, uncle. All this joking!

Lyubov   Well, Varya, I shall be very happy about it.

Varya   About *what?*

Lyubov   He's a good man.

Pishchik   True, true, worthy fellow. And my daughter, daughter, Dashenka says . . . you've got to, got to hand it to him. She says . . . various things. (*He nods off with a snort, the same snort immediately waking him up.*) By the by: lend me two hundred and forty roubles. The interest's got to be paid on the mortgage tomorrow.

Varya   She can't!

Pishchik   What's that?!

Varya   We haven't got it!

Lyubov   I really don't think I do! (*She laughs.*)

Pishchik   It'll turn up! (*He laughs.*) Never lose hope. *I* don't! I thought 'I'm done for!', and what happens? They come along and build a railway through my land.

They laugh with him through the above and the following. **Firs**,
perhaps, too. And **Dunyasha** *is happy because they are laughing.
And* **Varya** *does her best.*

Actually gave me money! . . . If it don't happen today it'll
happen tomorrow, what! . . . Dashenka'll win two hundred
thousand. She has a ticket, you know!

Lyubov   . . . Well, that's the coffee done, now we can
retire.

Firs (*brushing* **Gayev**'s *trouser-legs*)   The wrong trousers on
again! What am I to do with you?

Varya   Anya's sleeping at last. (*She quietly opens a window.*)
The sun's up, it's not cold now. (*She smiles. Whispers.*) Look at
the trees. My God! . . . Mamochka, look . . . The air. The
starlings are singing.

Gayev (*opens the other window*)   You haven't forgotten the
whiteness, Lyubov? The orchard is all white. The avenue:
look how far that ribbon stretches . . . And it sparkles on
moonlit nights . . . Do you remember? You haven't
forgotten.

Lyubov (*now looking out at the orchard*)   Oh my childhood,
when I was pure and good . . . I woke each morning and
looked out on this. Happiness woke me . . . (*A dawning.*) It's
still the same. (*And laughs for joy.*) Nothing has changed. It has
forgotten the shrivelling of autumn – Oh, my white orchard!
– the cold of winter . . . Young again, white, and full of
happiness. The heavenly angels have not deserted you . . . If
only I too could forget.

Gayev   Yes, and that's to be sold to pay – debts. Seems
odd 'business' to me.

Lyubov   Look! (*She points.*)

Gayev   Wha-oo?

Lyubov   Mama. Mama, walking, in her white dress.

Gayev (*a whisper*)   Where?

Lyubov   Look! It is her. (*Laughs for joy.*)

Varya (*frightened, superstitious*)   Bless us, mamochka, don't.

Lyubov   No. Nobody. See: at the turn that leads to the summerhouse, the outline of that tree, like a woman.

Petya Trofimov *has come in, unnoticed.* (*Shabby student-type uniform; spectacles.*)

Lyubov   White banks of flowers, blue sky . . . (*Turns back to the room.*) Divine.

Petya   Lyubov Andreyevna! To pay my respects and I'll go immediately. (*He bows.*) I was asked to wait until tomorrow but I was impatient.

Lyubov *smiles, puzzled; she doesn't recognise him.*

Varya   Peter Trofimov, mamochka.

Petya   Petya, your Grisha's former tutor. Have I changed so much?

Lyubov *starts to weep.*

Gayev   Luba, Luba, now-now, you mustn't.

She embraces **Petya,** *weeping.*

Varya (*tearful*)   I told him to wait until tomorrow.

Lyubov   My son, my little boy in that river.

Varya   God's will, mamochkamine: there's nothing we can do.

Petya   There, there. (*He's awkward, stiff in dealing with an embrace.*)

Lyubov   My little boy, drowned. Why do these things happen? What for, my friend? (*Drying her tears.*) Anya's sleeping in there and I'm shouting and making a scene . . . So, well, Petya! But your hair's thinning, you're wearing spectacles, why have you become so plain, why-have-you-grown-so-old?

Petya   Mildewed, I heard an old lady say of me on the train.

Lyubov   And you yourself were just a boy then, a little thing of a student. Surely you're not still a student?

Petya   I probably always will be.

Lyubov   Well, get some rest now. (*She kisses her brother, then* **Varya**.) You've got old too, Leonid.

Pishchik   Off to bed, are we? (*Rising.*) Aaarrrgh, gout! I'm staying the night, my dear, and in the morning, respected lady, I'd dearly like two hundred and forty roubles.

Gayev   He keeps on.

Pishchik   A trifling sum.

Lyubov   My dear Boris – (*Gesturing she doesn't have it.*)

Pishchik   But the bank must have it! You will, you will! – and I'll pay you back, my dear, no fear.

Lyubov   Oh I give in! (*Laughs.*) Give it to him, Leonid.

Gayev   Will you take it now or wait till you get it?!

Lyubov (*going out, laughing*)   What else can I do? He needs it . . .

Petya, **Pishchik**, **Firs** *and* **Dunyasha** *follow.* **Gayev**, **Varya** *and* **Yasha** *remain.* (**Yasha**, *exceeding his station, seems to find* **Gayev** *funny.*)

Gayev (*clucking over his sister's extravagance*)   Tck-tck, not the way, not the way. (*To* **Yasha**, *annoyed.*) Move aside, my man, out of my way. Why is he in – ['*here*']? ['*You*'] Smell of – hens.

Yasha (*smirking*)   And you, Leonid, are still the same.

Gayev (*to* **Varya**)   Wha-oo did he say?

Varya   Your mother has come from the village, she's been sitting in the servants' hall since yesterday!

Yasha   Can I help that?

Varya   How dare you! – You should be ashamed of yourself! She came to see you!

Yasha   She could've come tomorrow! (*Going out.*)

Gayev   . . . No, tck-tck, my sister hasn't changed her ways.

Varya   She'd give everything away if we let her. (*And she gestures hopelessly at their situation.*)

Gayev   . . . If. If lots of remedies – not one, but lots – are available for a disease, it means, basically, the disease is incurable. I rack my brains for a remedy and I come up with lots of them: which means, I haven't got one . . . If – it'd be good if someone died, left us a legacy. Marry our Anya to a rich man. One of us to go to Yaroslavl, try our hand there with the old aunt. She's very rich, mmmm.

Varya   If only God would help us. (*Crying.*) I pray to –

Gayev   Stop – don't start-tck-blubbering! But our old Yaroslavl auntie, 'the countess', doesn't like us, doesn't approve. For a start, my sister married beneath her, a lawyer, not 'a lord', my dear. Mmmm.

Anya, *in nightdress, appears in the doorway.*

And it has to be admitted – I love my sister dearly, but it has to be admitted, no matter what the stretching of it, my sister has been a bit easy on virtue. What? And still is: mm, loose. Somehow – hmm? – it's in her every movement!

Varya (*whispers*)   Anya's at the door.

Gayev   Wha-oo-something in my eye! I can't see. It happened too the other day when . . .

Anya *comes to them.*

Varya   Why aren't you asleep? Can you not sleep?

Anya   I can't sleep.

Gayev   My little one, my child. (*Kisses her forehead, her hands, emotionally.*) You are not my niece, you're my angel, you mean everything to me, believe me, do you believe me?

Anya   I do, I do, and everyone loves you, uncle, and *respects* you, but you must stop talking, you –

Gayev   Yes, I –

Anya   Must keep quiet more –

Gayev   I must, yes!

Anya   You were talking about mama just now –

Gayev   Tck! – I was –

Anya   Your *sister*. Why did you say that?

Gayev   Because – dreadful, stupid – I'm a fool! God rescue me, I talk and talk! I talked to the bookcase earlier!

Varya   Just keep quiet, that's all there's to it.

Anya   You'll feel the better for it.

Gayev   Done! I am silent. (*And he takes their hands in earnest of his purpose.*) There's just one thing – No, this is business! I was in the district court in town on Thursday, usual gathering, chit-chat, and then it came up: it seems there's some funny way of borrowing money against promissory notes. Now that could be a way of paying the interest on the mortgage to the bank, couldn't it?

Varya (*becoming tearful again*)   I keep praying to the saints –

Gayev   Couldn't it? A start? On Tuesday I'll go back to town and – (*To* **Varya**.) Don't start whingeing! – and talk to them some more.(*To* **Anya**.) Two: Your mama will talk to Lopakhin. Is Lopakhin going to refuse *her*? And, as soon as you are rested – Three – you will go to Yaroslavl to see your grand-aunt. Three-pronged attack, cat's in the bag! (*Warming to himself.*) I swear by my honour, by anything you like, this estate will not be sold. Call me worthless, call me worthless if I let it come to auction. Upon my life! (*He has popped a sweet into his mouth.*)

Anya   Clever uncle! (*Embracing him.*)

Firs (*coming in*)   Leonid Andreich, have you no fear of God, are you ever going to bed?!

Gayev   I'm coming now – You go on, Firs, I'll undress myself. Well, my children, it's bye-bye beddy byes. More tomorrow. You go and get your sleep now. (*Kisses them.*) You know, the eighties is a most erroneously maligned decade. Now, I am a man of the eighties, I have beliefs, and I can tell you I have endured much for my convictions. It is no small wonder that the peasant loves me. You have to know the peasant if you –

Anya   Uncle?!

Varya   At it again.

Firs (*crossly*)   Leonid Andreich!

Gayev   Coming, coming. (*To them.*) Off to bed with you, now. Red: two cushions, into the middle. Pot the cueball: defensive shot . . . (*He's gone.*)

Anya   I'm calm now, thanks to Uncle Leo . . . Go to Yaroslavl: I don't like my great-aunt . . . But I'm calm now. (*She sits.*)

Varya   We must go to bed. (*She sits. To herself, silently.*) Oh. While you were away, I had a little bit of bother. As you know, only the old servants live in the old quarters. Yefimyushka, Polya, Yevstigney – of course! – and Karp. Well, they began letting various – oh, rogue-types – in to stay the night. I didn't say a thing. At first, that is. Then, what do I hear? The rumour is about that I've given instructions they're to be fed nothing but dried peas. *My* stinginess, you see, *my* meanness. You know? All Yevstigney's doing, of course. 'All right,' I thought, 'if that's how it is,' I thought, 'wait on'. I call Yevstigney. He arrives. 'What is this I hear,' I said, 'you very, *very* old and extremely *stu*pid person?' . . . Anechka? (**Anya** *is asleep.*) Yes, beddy-byes. Come on, up, little pet. Come on. Come on.

She has helped up **Anya**. *They move. A shepherd plays his pipe in the distance.* **Petya** *comes in to cross the room. He stops on seeing them.*

Varya Shh! Don't-you-dare.

Anya (*half asleep*) I keep hearing little bells.

Varya She's sleeping . . . Come on, my darling.

Anya Dear uncle.

Varya Come on, my own.

Anya Dear mama and uncle.

Varya My pet, my love, my darling little sister, my . . .

They've gone into **Anya**'s *bedroom.*

Petya My sunlight . . . my springtime.

Act Two

Open country. An old shrine, lopsided, long-abandoned. Some large stones which were once tombstones, and an old bench. A track that leads to the estate. To one side, a tree ('tall dark poplars: beyond them the cherry orchard starts'.) In the distance a row of telegraph poles. The sun will soon set.

Charlotta, **Yasha** *and* **Dunyasha** *are on the bench.*
Yepikhodov, *somewhere, strums a guitar.* **Charlotta** *wears an old peaked cap. She has taken a rifle off her shoulder to adjust its sling.*

Charlotta (*as if thinking aloud*) Who I am, where I am from, *why* I am . . . I do not know . . . I do not have real identity papers . . . I travelled from fair to fair with my mother and father when I was a child, doing shows. We were very good. It made sense. I did the *salto mortale*. Various tricks. They died and a German lady took me in and gave me a different education . . . I grew up. I became a governess . . . But who I am, why I am? . . . How old I am? . . . I think of myself as young . . . Or timeless? I think, maybe my parents were not married. I do not know. (*She takes out a ridge cucumber and eats it.*) I know nothing . . . I should so much like to talk to someone . . . But there is no one . . .

Yepikhodov (*strumming and singing*) 'What do I care, oh what do I care for city, town or plain?/ What do I care for friend, foe, or kin?/ What do I care?'

Charlotta (*to herself; though it is a comment on his singing*) Ay-yi-yi!

Yepikhodov . . . 'Tis pleasant to play the mandolin.

Dunyasha Is that a mandolin? (*She powders her nose.*)

Yepikhodov To a man in love, it's a mandolin. (*Plays, sings.*) 'Ah, requite my love, hear my plea –'

Yasha 'Melt thy cold heart, beloved, beloved –'

Yepikhodov 'Else what is life to me –'

Yasha and **Yepikhodov**   'What is life to me – beloved – beloved? Ah what is life to me?!'

Charlotta   Ee-aw, ee-aw, ee-aw! (*A good imitation of a donkey.*) Jackasses.

Yasha *yawns elegantly and takes out a cigar.*

Dunyasha   The luck of some people to have lived abroad, God!

Yasha   *Peut-être.*

Yepikhodov   But absolutely. Abroad, everything's been fully constituted – for ages . . . Hasn't it?

Yasha   I should have thought that went without saying. (*He lights his cigar.*)

Yepikhodov   Absolutely.

Yasha   Quite.

Yepikhodov   . . . I'm an intellectual . . . I read a remarkable amount of serious stuff . . . in endeavour to find the slant of what it is exactly that I want: whether I should live or, strictly speaking, shoot myself. (*They continue unimpressed.*) In fact, I always carry this, just in case, you see. (*He has produced a revolver.*)

Charlotta (*shoulders her rifle*)   Yes, you are a terrifying man, your cerebrations too. Women ought to dream about you. (*She stands. To herself.*) Cerebellum people. . . I am alone everywhere. (*She goes off, unhurriedly.*) It is a mystery.

Yepikhodov (*impotently; his frustration is growing*)   Actually, other considerations apart, *inter alia*, I must evince about myself that life is treating me unmercifully. If I am mistaken, why then when I awoke this morning was there a spider the size of this – (*his hand holding the gun*) – sitting on my chest looking up at me? Or! To take another case in point because I really must express myself: I'm thirsty, I lift my glass and there is something unwise swimming in it . . . May I, Avdotya Fyodorovna, trouble you for a word?

Dunyasha   Fire away.

Yepikhodov   In private. If it isn't too costly to ask.

Dunyasha   Well . . . yeh. Only, would you fetch my little cape first, my talma. It's in the kitchen by the dresser. It's getting a trifle *damp* here, Yasha, isn't it?

Yepikhodov (*bowing*)   Madame, '*mamzelle*', *tout suite*! Now I know what to do with this. (*The gun. Takes his guitar and leaves – tripping over something.*)

Dunyasha   God forbid he don't shoot himself – over me!

Yasha   He's too ignorant.

Dunyasha   . . . Yasha I've become anxious about . . . everything. I cannot sleep. Worries, you see. Heigh-ho! It's because, partly, I've worked in the big house since – (*Gestures 'I was so high'.*) It's as if common life never existed. I've lost the habits of simple folk. I'm afraid . . . of everything. (*She holds out her hands, hopeful that he will admire them.*) So white . . . And if you deceive me, Yasha, God only knows what'll happen to my nerves.

Yasha (*a peck on the cheek*)   You're a cuke! (*Then.*) Of course, if a virgin is a virgin she should remember it.

Dunyasha   Eh?

Yasha   Morality. I've given it some thought. It's pleasant to smoke in the open air.

Dunyasha   You're so educated, you've such taste.

Yasha *has to agree with her.*

Dunyasha   I've fallen for you.

Yasha   Yes, but –

Dunyasha   Madly.

Yasha (*his perfect logic again*)   Of course. But if a girl loses control it means that she's – grown up. The difference between a good cigar and a bad. (*He listens.*) Here they come.

She hugs him, impulsively.

Go home! That way! If they see us together they'll think we've been meeting. (*He's brushing the air of cigar smoke.*)

Dunyasha (*annoyed with him; coughing*)   And the top of my head is lifting from that rotten cigar! (*She goes.*)

Yasha *disappears too – just out of sight.* **Lyubov**, **Gayev** *and* **Lopakhin** *arrive.*

Lopakhin   Decide. Time isn't dragging its heels on your convenience. The question is simple –

Lyubov   Who's been smoking cheap cigars?

Gayev   It *is* convenient having the railway.

Lopakhin   Do you agree to lease the land for building or don't you?

Gayev   In and out of town, had lunch, home again in . . . (*Checking the time it took on his watch.*) Hm, impressive. (*Then:*) Who's for a game?

Lyubov   There'll be time later ['*for billiards*'].

Lopakhin   Give me your answer.

Gayev   Wha-oo? (*Yawning.*)

Lyubov (*laughs at her purse*)   Look: yesterday, this was a fat little thing, today, skin and bone. And our poor Varya scrimping, trying to economise, and, I hear, giving our old dears in the kitchen nothing but dried peas. (*Tossing her purse in the air.*) And I'm throwing it away. (*She fails to catch the purse coming down: coins scatter.*) Bother!

Yasha (*appearing out of nowhere*)   Allow me, madam.

Lyubov   Thank you, Yasha. Why did I go to town with you for that stupid lunch? That ghastly restaurant of yours, and its ghastly music. Tablecloths smelling of soap. And why drink so much, Leo, eat so much and talk so much? – And to no purpose. You would talk the legs off whatever-that-animal-is. Making speeches about the seventies and the eighties and the Decadent Movement – and to the poor waiters!

Lopakhin   Correct.

Gayev   All right, all right, I'm! ['*incorrigible*'] (*To* **Yasha**, *annoyed*.) What's this? – Why are you always smirking around and under our feet wherever I look?

Yasha (*chuckling*)   You're funny.

Gayev   Lyubov, it's him or me!

Lyubov   That will do, Yasha, now run along.

Yasha   Madam. (*He goes, chuckling*.)

Lopakhin   D'you know who they're saying is interested in the estate? Deriganov. Now he *is* becoming rich. (*To himself*.) Oh-ho-ho, Deriganov. ['*Now there's a grabber for you*'] They say he says he's coming to the auction in person.

Lyubov (*dismissive*)   'They say?' Who say? Where do you get all your information, Yermolay?

Lopakhin   Oh, I hear things. (*And to himself*.) Oh-ho-ho, Deriganov.

Gayev   Our Yaroslavl aunt is going to send us some money.

Lopakhin   How much?

Gayev   How much and when is not yet clear.

Lopakhin   Two hundred thousand? A hundred thousand?

Lyubov   Oh. ['*hardly that*'] Ten or fifteen. And we shall be thankful for it.

Lopakhin   Excuse me – forgive me, madam, sir – I've never met anything like you! You're told in the plainest language the ground is going from under your feet and you simply won't understand.

Lyubov   Tell us what to do, Yermolay.

Lopakhin   I'm going to! ['*scream*'] I tell you every day, I talk about nothing else! Lease out the land for summer cottages. The auction is nearly on top of us. Make a decision *now* and you're saved.

Lyubov   But, cottages, 'bungalows'. (*The vulgarity of the idea.*)

Gayev (*emphatic agreement with her*)   Mm!

Lopakhin   I *am* going to scream. You've worn me out. (*Turns as though to go; turns back.*) And you're an old woman!

Gayev   Wha-oo?

Lopakhin   You! (*Turns again, as if to leave.*)

Lyubov   No, stay with us, our dear friend, please. Maybe we can think of something.

Lopakhin *rolls his eyes/whatever.*

Lyubov   Don't go, Yermolay. It is happier when you're around . . . (*To herself; worried.*) I *do* have a feeling something is happening. Something. As though the roof were to come in on top of us.

Gayev (*to himself; a billiard shot*)   *Croisée*: Middle pocket.

Lyubov   We have sinned so much.

Lopakhin   You're a great sinner. What're your sins?

Lyubov   Squandering my inheritance.

Gayev   I ate up mine in sweets. (*Popping a sweet in his mouth.*)

Lyubov (*sighs*)   Oh, my sins . . . Running away, throwing money away, marrying foolishly against advice. A man who could throw it away even faster. He drank like a fish, he died of champagne . . . What then? . . . Another profligate. I fall for a gallant, began an affair. And then came the first chastisement, the blow straight to the head. My little boy drowned in that river . . . I closed my eyes, went abroad, never to return, see that river, never to return . . . Ran . . . But I was pursued. Ruthless, brutal pursuit . . . My gallant pursued me. I became his unofficial wife. I bought that villa in Monaco when he became ill there. Nursed him. For three years. I had to do 'everything' for him. And I did it . . . Everything . . . Then that house had to be sold. Debts. To Paris, where he robbed me, before leaving me, that is, for another woman. And, I tried to poison myself . . . So stupid. So shameful . . . And . . . suddenly, I needed my homeland, my own people. My beautiful little girl . . . (*She wipes away a tear.*) Lord have mercy, Christ have mercy, forgive me my sins. Don't punish me more . . . (*She has a telegram in her hands.*) This one too today from Paris. He asks my forgiveness, begs me to go back. (*She tears it up. Listens.*) . . . Is that music?

Gayev   That's our famous Jewish band, d'you not remember? Four fiddles, flute and double bass.

Lyubov   It still exists? Wouldn't it be nice to have them over one evening? We-ought-to-have-a-party.

Lopakhin   I don't hear anything. (*He dances. He sings / recites quietly.*) 'And to make their mark, the Germans turn the Russians into francs'. (*Laughs.*) I saw a great ['*funny*'] play the other day.

Lyubov   I'm sure! Watching plays when you'd be better off taking a look at yourselves more often, and the endless nonsense you all talk.

Lopakhin   Well, I suppose. It's a fool's way of life somehow. I think of my father and I think I'm not much different, and he was an idiot. I haven't trained in anything – You've seen my handwriting? Like something the pig walked over.

Lyubov   You should get married, Yermolay.

Lopakhin   I suppose.

Lyubov   Varya's a good girl.

Lopakhin   No question about it.

Lyubov   And she's from simple people too. And like yourself, also, a worker. And what is more, she loves you, which is the main thing.

Lopakhin   I've nothing against it.

Gayev   Six thousand a year: I've been offered a job in the bank. Did I tell you?

Lyubov   You did. I'd stay as you are.

Firs *comes in with an overcoat.*

Firs   Here it is, now put it on.

Gayev   I didn't ask for my –

Firs   The air is damp. (*Helps* **Gayev** *into the coat.*)

Gayev   I'm fed up with you!

Firs   And you went off to town without telling me.

Lyubov   How very old you've grown, Firs.

Firs   What can I get you, madam?

Lopakhin   'How very old you've grown, Firs'!

Firs   I've been alive a long time. They were arranging to marry me off once, you know. Yes. That was before your father had even come into the world. (*He turns away, laughing.*) Oh yes. (*Turns back.*) And I was already head valet when the freedom happened, the Emancipation. I wasn't having any of that: I stayed with the master. And I remember the rejoicing, the rejoicing, and what they were so pleased about they didn't know themselves. (*He laughs.*)

Lopakhin   And in the good old days, people were flogged soundly and properly?

Firs   I'll say they were! The peasants had their masters and masters had their peasants. Now you don't know where to lay your hand on a blessed thing.

Gayev   Shush, Firs. Here come the children. Town again tomorrow for me: business. I'm to meet a general.

Lopakhin   A waste of time.

Lyubov   Yes, be serious, Leonid – (*Calls.*) Yoo-oo! Children! Over here!

Anya (*off*)   Mama!

Anya, **Petya** *and* **Varya** *are arriving.*

Lyubov   Come over here!

Gayev   Here come ours!

Lopakhin   And our eternal student.

Lyubov   My darling girls!

Lopakhin   And always with the ladies.

Lyubov   Sit beside me. That's right.

Lopakhin   How old are you now, Peter?

Petya   Mind your own business?

Lopakhin   Fifty?

Petya   You're very funny.

Lopakhin   Oh? Surely, never pique from our intellect-u-al.

Petya   I've nothing to say to you, Mr Lopakhin.

Lopakhin   Y'have. What d'you think of me?

Petya   You're a rich man, soon you'll be richer.

Lopakhin   Y'can do better.

Petya   I can. Metabolistically, just as in the food chain, the predator is necessary to devour everything in its path, you too are necessary.

All laugh, together with:

Varya   Oh don't say that. Tell us about the planets, Peter.

Lyubov   No, what were we talking about yesterday?

Petya   What was I saying yesterday?

Gayev   Man's pride.

Petya   Ah yes! Now as I understand you, as you see it, there is some mystical reason why man, the human being, should be proud, but if we *really* reason it, I mean simply, dispassionately – leaving out your mystical – what has he to be proud of? Physiologically, is the human being well-equipped? The vast majority of human beings are coarse, unintelligent and unhappy: we should be proud of that? We must stop admiring ourselves, we must just work.

Gayev   It's all the same –

Petya   We must *work*!

Gayev   But you'll die anyway.

Petya   Will I? Will I? 'To die': what does that mean? What if the human being has a hundred senses and only the five that we know die with him?

Lyubov (*fervently*)   Yes.

Petya   And the other ninety-five remain alive.

Lopakhin   Hmm?

Lyubov   He *is* clever.

Lopakhin   But? (*But*) Who is the one being 'mystical' now?'

Petya   Everything that is unintelligible to you, and unattainable, will one day be understandable and within reach. Humanity is moving forward, perfecting its powers. That's why we have to work, apply our energy to helping those who are seeking the *truth*. Trouble is with Russia at the moment, very few of us are working. The intelligentsia – or the majority of them – and I know them – are doing *nothing*, they merely talk, talk-talk. And with long faces. They *call* themselves the intelligentsia and they address their servants as 'you', they look on the workers as if they were still their slaves. Are they possessed of culture, knowledge of the sciences, political initiative? The long, serious, philosophising faces are what's important. And while they sit around talking, people are starving, sleeping in the streets, sleeping thirty-forty to a room, with fleas, in filth and damp, and all leading to foul language, greater ignorance, obscenities, eruptions of mindless, barbaric violence, immorality. Where are the crèches, health care, reading rooms, amenities? They don't exist, you only hear about them or read about them. All this fine talk serves merely to avert our eyes from reality. Work! I have a fear of serious faces, I do not like them, I am wary of speechifiers. Better let's say nothing.

Lopakhin   You know, I get up before five every morning, I'm handling money, my own and other people's, and I see what the human being about me is like. And, you know, you only have to start doing something to realise how few honourable people there are. And, you know, sometimes, when I can't sleep, I think, Sweet Jesus, you gave us all this: forests, fields, vast horizons. We ought to be giants.

Lyubov   In fairytales, Yermolay, but outside of that – Brrr! ['*frightening*'] Cumbersome creatures, giants.

Yepikhodov *strolls across (upstage) playing his guitar.*

Anya (*in a world of her own*)   There goes Yepikhodov.

Lyubov   (*absently*)   There goes Yepikhodov.

Gayev   There: the sun has set.

The setting sun stills them.

Gayev (*to himself*)   Good people one and all . . . (*And declaiming quietly.*) Oh wondrous Nature sempiternal, radiant at rise and fall, beautiful and indifferent Mother, thou givest and takest, embracing life and death.

Varya   Uncle, at it again.

Anya   Dearest uncle. (*She laughs softly to herself.*)

Gayev   I'm silent.

Silence. Only **Firs**, *mumbling, is heard. They are deep in themselves. Suddenly, a distant sound, a string snapping, vibrating, dying away. (A metallic twang.)*

Lyubov   . . . What was that?

Lopakhin (*shakes his head; listens for more*)   . . . Somewhere far off . . . A cable snapping in one of the mines?

Gayev   Bird, perhaps . . . A heron?

Petya   . . . An eagle owl?

Lyubov   Not nice somehow.

Firs   It was the same, you know, before all that bother: the owl went on screeching, the samovar humming.

Gayev   What bother?

Firs   Freedom, the Emancipation.

Lyubov   All right, *mes enfants*, let us go, shall we, it's getting dark. (*To* **Anya**.) Why, what is it? You have tears in your eyes.

Anya (*sincerely*)   No, nothing.

Lyubov   Little one?

Anya   Absolutely, mama.

Petya   There's someone coming.

A **Vagrant** *is approaching. (Old clothes, a battered peaked cap.) He's drunk.*

Vagrant (*off and entering, singing-reciting*)   'They chained her body to the cruel stone;/The beast begot of sea and slime had marked her for his own;/The callous world beheld the wrong and left her all alone'. (*He grins drunkenly.*) Can I come through here? To the station!

Gayev   You may. Keep along that path.

Vagrant   Thankin' you – Excuse me! – much obliged! (*In praise of the weather.*) The weather! 'Brother of mine, oh suffering brother, come to the Volga whose gr-o-o-o-ans . . .' (*He goes into a bout of coughing-laughter.*) 'Like falling rock, on fierce Siroc – No savage or marauder –'

Lopakhin   There's your path –

Vagrant (*talking over* **Lopakhin**)   'Son of a slave! – First of the brave! – Hurrah for Abdel Kadar!' Thankin' you! (*He sees* **Varya**.) Ah! *Mademoiselle*! What kind of wine d'*you* have for me?

Varya *recoils, frightened.*

Lopakhin   That'll do now – even where you come from!

Vagrant   Charity or a copper, then, for a broken soldier?

Lopakhin   That's your path!

Lyubov (*flustered, looking in her handbag*)   No, here's something, take this – Oh, I've no small – Doesn't matter, take it.

Vagrant   Thankin' you! Long life to your ladyship! (*Leaving.*) 'That glorious noon! – God send it soon – Hurrah for human freedom . . .'

They start to laugh. **Varya**, *too, out of the fright she has had. Then:*

Varya   No! I'm going to leave here, I *must*. Why did you give him all that money?

Lyubov   Because I'm young and because I'm silly! When we get home I'll give you every last thing I have and Yermolay Alekseich will give me another loan.

Lopakhin *bows.*

Varya   He frightened me. (*Referring to the* **Vagrant**.)

Lyubov   And – Varya, dear – congratulations: we have promised you in marriage to 'someone'.

Varya   That's not a joking matter, Mamochka. (*She's tearful again.*)

Lopakhin   Euphoria, get thee to a nunnery!

Gayev   Billiards. (*Meaning: 'Time to go'. He checks the steadiness of his hands.*)

Lopakhin   Euphoria, in thy orisons – in thy prayers let all my sins be remembered.

Lyubov (*chiding* **Lopakhin**)   Come-come! (*And laughs. Going.*) Come, ladies and gentlemen, it's almost suppertime, come! Everybody!

Varya (*following*)   I'm still shaking.

Lopakhin (*following*)   And – Everybody! – let me remind you that on the twenty-second day of August in this year of Our Lord, Cherryorchard will be sold! Think about that! . . . Think! . . .

Anya *and* **Petya** *remain.*

Anya (*laughs*)   Varya!

Petya   She keeps following us.

Anya   Thank you, Mr Vagabond, for frightening her off and making her forget us.

Petya   She's afraid we'll fall in love. That narrow head cannot understand that we are above such petty illusions. Forward! – Unstoppably! – That's where we're headed – No lagging behind, friends! – Truth is out there!

Anya (*claps her hands, silently, joyful at his words*)   . . . It was like heaven here today.

Petya (*mimics the* **Vagrant**)   'The weather!'

Anya   . . . Why, though, don't I love the cherry orchard as I used to? I used to think there was nowhere on earth better.

Petya   All of Russia is our orchard. The world is great and beautiful . . . Just think, Anya, your grandfather, your great-grandfather owned living souls. Those souls are looking down from every tree in that orchard. From every leaf . . . Owning living souls: that has changed you all. Not just your ancestors: your mother, you, your uncle. The debt you're living is off the living souls you won't let in your front door . . . We haven't come very far. We have no *conscious* attitude towards the past. Theories, melancholy and vodka. And to live in the present the past has to be consciously acknowledged, and atoned for by suffering and work.

Anya   The house we live in hasn't been ours for a long time.

Petya   If you have keys, fling them into the well. Let go.

Anya   Oh I shall.

Petya   Believe me.

Anya   I give my word of honour.

Petya   I'm not thirty yet, I *am* still a student, but I've seen a lot. When winter comes it'll be my fate again to be hungry, ill, penniless as a beggar. But ill, starved, careworn, every moment I'm filled too with visions of happiness.

Anya   The moon is rising.

Petya (*watching the moon*)   . . . There it is. It's getting closer . . . Slowly coming . . . (*The moon in and out of a cloud.*) Happiness . . . And if we don't see it fully realised, what does it matter? Others will.

Varya (*off, calling*)   Anya! Anya!

Petya (*annoyed*)   Varya!

Anya   Again! (*And laughs softly.*)

Varya (*off*)   Anya, where are you?

Petya   Merciless!

Anya   Let's go down to the river.

Petya (*a whisper*)   Forward!

They go.

Varya (*off*)   Anya! . . . Anya! . . .

Act Three

A reception room separated from a ballroom by an arch. A lighted chandelier. The Jewish band mentioned in Act Two can be heard playing. It is evening. In the ballroom a grand-rond is being danced.

Pishchik (*off, in the ballroom*)   Promenade! . . . Promenade à une paire!

The dancers come through into the reception room. The first couple: **Pishchik** *and* **Charlotta**; *the second:* **Petya** *and* **Lyubov**; *then* **Anya** *and* **Post Office Clerk**, **Varya** *and* **Stationmaster**, *and so on.* **Dunyasha** *is in the last pair.*

Pishchik   Promenade! . . . Grand-rond, balancez! . . . Les cavaliers à genoux et remerciez vos dames!

They go out again.

Firs *has come in, in tails, to cross the room with seltzer water on a tray.* **Pishchik**, *puffing, out of breath, and* **Petya** *return.*

Pishchik   I'm pretty robust, oh yes, constitution of a horse, oh yes, but – blood pressure? So! Out of puff. So! (*Boasting.*) I've had two strokes – Two! So! Can't dance as I could one time, what! Still, if you run with the pack y'must wag yer tail, even if you can't raise a bark, what? What! (*Sits.*) That's better.

Petya   Shall I fetch us another drink?

Pishchik   (No/Yes.) My dear father, too, was a great joker, the heavens be his bed. Used to say our family was descended from the horse, the same one was sat in the Roman Senate by Caligula. Mischief is, mischief is there's no money. Spent all my life looking for it.

Petya   And if you'd spent that energy on something else you'd have turned the world upside down.

Pishchik   What's that?!

Petya   You are built like a horse.

Pishchik   Aren't I? (*He's pleased. And winks:*) Y'can sell a horse.

A lull in the music during the above. Sounds of a game of billiards in the next room. **Varya** *appears in the archway.*

Petya (*teasing*)   Ah, Mrs Lopakhin!

She mutters something.

Pishchik   Wonderful musicians the Jews!

Varya   And what are they to be paid with?

Petya   Cheer up, Mrs Lopakhin!

Varya   And look at you! Frayed, shabby, moss-grown, dog-eared! (*Going out.*) Out-at-the-elbows!

Petya (*calls after her*)   I'm *proud* to be out at my elbows!

Pishchik   Nietzsche, now there's a man for you! Famous philosopher? Of the greatest intellect. Says it's all right – nothing wrong with it – to forge your own banknotes.

Petya   Have you read Nietzsche?

Pishchik   No. Daughter, my dear Dashenka. But the way things are I'd give it a go, give it a shot, I would. Day after tomorrow, *again*, I've to come up with three hundred and ten. I've managed to get hold of . . . (*He is groping in his pockets; he becomes panicked.*) Where is it? My money's gone! I managed to get hold of a hundred and thirty – It's fallen out – I've lost my money – I've . . . (*He finds it.*) Phew! My word! I say! Here in the lining. Close call.

Lyubov *and* **Charlotta** *come in.* **Lyubov** *is humming a dance tune to herself. She's restless throughout.* **Charlotta** *has a deck of cards. Others follow and come in by degrees to watch.*

Lyubov   Still no Leonid, still no sign. What can be delaying him in town, why is it taking so long?

Petya   The auction most likely didn't come off.

Lyubov Dunyasha, offer the musicians some tea. Have we chosen the right evening to have our ball?! Never mind. (*And she's singing again to herself.*)

Charlotta Here is a deck of cards!

Pishchik What's that!

Charlotta My darlink, dotey, peachy, Herr Pishchik, think of a card.

Lyubov Yes, Charlotta!

Charlotta Have you thought of one?

Pishchik I have.

Charlotta Now, shuffle the deck and give it back to me. Very good, you are an expert. *Eins, zwei, drei!* And the card is . . . (*Pretends puzzlement.*) Herr Pishchik, will you look in your side pocket?

Pishchik (*produces the card; astonished*) Eight of spades: it's absolutely true!

Lyubov Bravo, Charlotta! (*And others applaud.*)

Charlotta (*with the deck of cards on the palm of her hand; to* **Petya**) Name the top card?

Petya The-the-the-the –

Charlotta Quickly!

Petya The Queen of spades!

Charlotta And it is! (*To* **Pishchik**.) Now, what is the top card?

Pishchik Ace of hearts!

Charlotta The lady's done it again! (*She claps her two hands on the pack and the pack disappears. Now a languid pose.*) Oh, the heat, the heat, this night!

Voice (*seductive, as from under the floorboards, answers*) Vat wery varm veather, madame?

Charlotta   Hot. So nice, so warm, quite my ideal, the heat inspires me.

Voice   And I am wery font of you too, madame.

Applause, laughter, etc., together with.

Stationmaster   Bravo, Madame Ventriloquist!

Pishchik   'And I am wery' – Did you ever!

Petya (*giggling without knowing why, slaps* **Pishchik** *on the back*) Giddy-up, horse!

Pishchik   I'm madly in love with her!

Charlotta   L-o-o-o-ve? Are you ca-pa-ble? *Guter Mensch, aber schlechter Musikant!* ('*A good person, but a bad musician'. Sexual overtones. Now she claps her hands.*) *Mesdames et Messieurs, attention s'il-vous-plait! – Achtung!* One last trick. (*She has taken a rug off a chair.*) Here is a very good rug, I want to sell it! (*Shakes it, holds it open.*) What am I bid for it?

Pishchik (*rapt, fascinated: to himself*)   What am I?

Charlotta   This is a special rug, will no one buy it? . . . *Eins, zwei, drei!* (*Quickly lifting the curtain-rug.*)

And **Anya** *is standing there. She curtsies and runs to her mother to kiss her.* (*In a moment she will run off to the ballroom again.*) *Applause.*

Pishchik   Well, I never!

Charlotta   And again!

Lyubov   Yes, more!

Charlotta   *Eins, zwei, drei!*

The same trick and **Varya** *stands revealed. She bows.*

Charlotta   The end! (*She throws the rug over* **Pishchik**, *curtsies and skips off.*)

Pishchik   What a! What a rascal! (*Following/chasing* **Charlotta**.) *Eins, zwei, drei . . .*

Lyubov   Still no Leonid, still no Leonid, I don't understand it, what can be delaying him? The auction surely would have happened hours ago, either the estate's been sold or it hasn't.

Varya   Uncle has bought it, I just know it. (*Hands in prayer to heaven.*)

Petya (*mocking*)   Oh – God! – She just knows it.

Lyubov   Why are we being kept in the dark?

Varya   The power-of-attorney from auntie to buy it in her name and transfer the mortgage.

Lyubov   With the fifteen thousand she sent us? That isn't even enough to – (*She clicks her fingers.*) And to buy 'the property' in *her* name. How our doting Yaroslavl auntie loves us!

Petya (*to* **Varya**)   God replies?

Lyubov   Today my fate is being decided, my *fate*.

Petya   Madam Lopakhin?

Varya   You've been dismissed from university twice! Students are meant to be clever, not smart!

Lyubov   Why are you so angry, Varya?! He's only teasing you about Lopakhin – What of it?! Be serious! If you want to marry Lopakhin, marry him, if you don't, don't! No one is forcing you, my dear! (*Then.*) I just don't understand this delay. It means something, I tell you.

Varya   I am serious, Mamochka –

Lyubov   Then marry him!

Varya (*tearful*)   I can't propose to him myself.

Lyubov   I don't understand people – shilly-shallying!

Varya   He's too busy getting richer! Well, d'you know what: if I had some money, ever so little, I'd leave here now, this minute, and go far away – yes, to a *nunnery*.

Petya   And it would be *bliss*!

Varya (*would like to hit him with her fist, but she switches to pitying, plaintive retaliation*)   How old you look, Peter. How plain, ugly and thin. (*New tone.*) But *I* must do my work: I work and I love it. Now what have I to do?

Yasha *comes in, highly amused, to cross the room.*

Yasha   Yepikhodov has managed to break a billiard cue! (*And he continues off, laughing.*)

Varya   Yepikhodov, our *clerk*, is playing billiards – Who allowed him? Or! – (*Indicating the departed* **Yasha**. *She leaves busily to deal with the matter.*) I don't understand some people . . .

Lyubov   Don't tease her, Petya, the girl has griefs enough already.

Petya   Then let her mind her own business. She hasn't let me or Anya alone all summer. She's afraid of an – *affaire*: 'There is something going on between them, I tell you.' Have I shown any semblance of 'something going on'? Vulgar sentimentality. Anya and I are above love.

Lyubov   Then I must be beneath it. (*She's off again, worried.*) Where-is-Leonid? Calamities are happening and I do not even know what I should be thinking. Am I lost, are we *all* lost? Talk to me, Peter, or I shall – *scream* – or do something foolish. Talk to me – speak – about anything!

Petya   Be calm. Does it make a difference whether it's been sold today or not? It was finished, done for, long ago. And all paths back are overgrown. Stop denying it. For once in your life, Lyubov Andreyevna, look truth in the face.

Lyubov   Truth? You see where it is and where it isn't and I have lost my sight? It's easy to have the answers when you haven't yet had time to suffer through the questions. You –

Petya   *I've* suffered! *I've* –

Lyubov   My dear, my dear! You look ahead, boldly, with your young eyes, because you don't know that life is going to frighten you: you don't expect it: it's still hidden, waiting. You *are* deeper, bolder, honester than us – you *are*. But don't be proud. Be – generous? If only that much? (*'A little': space between thumb and forefinger. She smiles, a grin born of fear.*) After all, this is my house, I was born here. My father, my grandfather. I love my cherry orchard and, right now I cannot begin to conceive of life without it. (*And a laugh.*) And if it really has to be sold, well then, sell me along with it.

She kisses him on the forehead, embraces him. (As in Act One, he is stiff/awkward in response to an embrace?)

. . . Yes. And my son drowned here. (*Wipes away a tear, smiles.*) Have pity, my dear young good philosopher.

Petya   Lyubov Andreyevna Ranyevskaya, be assured of my unvarnished and sincere sympathy.

Lyubov   Ah, but not like that. Differently, you should say it differently. (*She has taken out her handkerchief at some point and, with it, a telegram.*) Don't judge me. My heart is heavy today. And it's been so noisy here. And I don't want silence . . . I love you like one of my own, Peter, I'd gladly allow Anya to marry you. Gladly. But you must finish something, whatever it is you are studying now, you must get your degree. Because, this – Fate – of yours that you talk about, that you welcome, is just blowing you about from pillar to post. Isn't it true? You do nothing. But isn't it? Hmm? Petya? And you really must-do-something with that beard of yours to make it grow. (*And she laughs.*) Oh you're such a funny little fellow. (*The telegram slips off her lap.*)

Petya (*picks it up for her*)   I'm not going to be a dandy or a cheat.

Lyubov   I get one every day now. (*Telegram.*) The wild thing has fallen ill again. He's begging my help. Peter, you're becoming like Varya with that serious face . . . But what can I do?! He's ill, he's unhappy. Who is there to look after him, stop him doing stupid things or give him his medicine on time? He's alone now, this minute. Oh, why hide it, I love the so-an-so. It's a stone around my neck and it's taking me to the bottom but I-love-that-stone. And I cannot live without it. (*She takes his hand.*) You're thinking badly of me, but don't say anything to me now.

Petya   Lyubov Andreyevna, forgive me, but he robbed you of everything you had.

Lyubov   No he didn't.

Petya   He's a cheat, a miserable –

Lyubov   You mustn't say such things –

Petya   Good-for-nothing scoundrel –

Lyubov   You mustn't speak of him like that –

Petya   Out-and-out, a nonentity! And you're the only one refusing to see it!

Lyubov   Oh? (*Containing her temper.*) And you are – What age are you?

Petya   I'm – Maybe!

Lyubov   And you're like a schoolboy.

Petya   I'm – What if I am?!

Lyubov   You should fall in love! A man of your age! And maybe then you'd understand something. (*Angry.*) Yes! And you're *not* pure: you just like the idea of it. Like all the other nonsense you carry about in your head. Ridiculous little freak – prude – crank!

Petya (*shocked*)   What're you saying?

Lyubov   'I am above love'! You're *not* above love, you're just as our Firs would put it, a bungle-arse simpleton!

Petya   . . . I'm leaving.

Lyubov   Ridiculous little monster. (*But she's containing herself again.*)

Petya   I'm leaving this minute.

Lyubov   Not to have a lover at your age.

Petya   It's all over between us.

He leaves, purposefully. **Anya** *and* **Varya**, *who are coming in, have to step out of his path.*

Lyubov   Petya, come here, I was only joking!

A crash, off. **Anya** *and* **Varya** *gasp. Then* **Anya** *starts laughing.*

Lyubov   What has happened?

Anya   He's fallen down the stairs. (*She goes out, laughing, followed by* **Varya**.)

Lyubov (*follows them off*)   What a queer little fellow . . .

In the archway, the **Stationmaster** *is reciting a poem, 'The Sinful Woman', to a group. He isn't very far into it when a waltz strikes up and he breaks off.*

Stationmaster   'The Sinful Woman'. (*As required.*) 'Midst the bustling throng and laughter,/Where music strikes each gilded rafter,/Lush palm trees and exotic flowers/Form here and there cool private bowers,/And twixt the pillars rich brocade/Is gathered up with curious braid./The chambers, sumptuously adorned/With gold and silver . . .'

Everyone is dancing again.

Lyubov, **Anya** *and* **Varya** *are returning with* **Petya**.

Lyubov   Poor thing. You poor, poor, *poor* thing. Forgive me, you do have a pure soul, dance with me, let's dance together. Let us dance . . . (*They dance off to the ballroom.*)

Anya *and* **Varya** *dance off together, too.*

Yasha *appears from somewhere. He watches the dancers, humming, swaying affectedly.* **Firs** *comes in on his stick.*

Yasha   Well, Speedy?

Firs   I don't feel well. (*He gets rid of his stick, props it somewhere.*) In the past, you know, we used to have barons, admirals, generals attend our evenings. Now, the post office people are sent for, the stationmaster. And, you know, they don't come running.

Yasha   What're you drivelling on about now?

Firs   Yes. I've grown old somehow. The old master, their grandfather, he gave sealing wax for everything, dosed us all with it and, you know it, it cured every ill. I think that's why I'm still alive.

Yasha   Just about.

Firs   Yes, sealing wax.

Yasha (*amusing himself with* **Firs**)   High time, Speedy, for you to croak it – *Oui-oui?!*

Firs   Shit! You no-headed gawpsheet! (*Continues to himself.*) Shit! Jolter-headed dummkopf! Shit! Rimstitch rantipoles today, tomfools and simpleton bungle-arsed girls . . .

Yasha, *laughing, moves aside – or just out of sight.* **Lyubov** *is returning, dancing with* **Petya**, *from the ballroom.*

Lyubov   *Merci!* Now I must sit down. (*Sits.*) I'm tired.

Anya (*coming in*)   There was some old man in the kitchen saying Cherryorchard is sold.

Lyubov   What man? Who has it been sold to? (*She's up again.*)

Anya   I don't know if he said to whom – he's gone. Petya! ['*Dance with me*']

They dance off.

Lyubov (*agitated again*)   What man – what man?

Yasha   Some old fool babbling down there, not one of ours.

Firs And, madam, Leonid Andreich has not returned and he's only wearing his light coat.

Lyubov I'm losing my reason.

Firs He's going to catch cold, madam, I tell you!

Lyubov I'm going to drop dead – Go and find out, Yasha, who it's been sold to.

Yasha He's gone – long gone! (*He laughs.*)

Firs Tck, youngsters nowadays! (*Continues muttering.*)

Lyubov I'm going out of my mind in a mad-house! And, Firs, dear soul, if Cherryorchard is sold, where will *you* go?

Firs Wherever you tell me to, madam.

Lyubov Why d'you look like that? Are you ill? You should be resting, you should lie down.

Firs Ah! (*Smiles a little triumph.*) But if I do, who will look after things? There's only me now, you know. (*He goes on muttering to himself.*)

Yasha Madam? Madam Ranevskaya, may I? ['*have a word*'] (*He is being rather confidential and hushed.*) Lyubov Andreyevna, if you go back to Paris, take me with you. I can't stay here. I mean, I don't have to tell you, you see it for yourself, the whole country is uncivilised, they're all ignorant. And immorality? Everyone of them. Lyubov Andreyevna, please? The boredom, the food down there: disgusting. And him, (**Firs**.) mooching about – the *language* out of him? Very inappropriate. He's a head-case.

Pishchik (*approaching*) Beautiful lady, there you are!

Yasha (*whispers*) Take me with you. (*And withdraws a little.*)

Pishchik Most beautiful lady, may I have the pleasure? (*She takes his arm.*) And I'll relieve you of a hundred and forty little roubles. (*They dance off to the ballroom.*) Oh I will, I will . . .

Yasha (*sways to the music, singing confidently to himself*)   'Could you but know the turmoil in my soul, will you ever understand the . . .'

In the ballroom a figure in a grey top-hat and check trousers is cavorting about to cries of 'Bravo, Charlotta Ivanovna!'

Dunyasha, *detaching herself from the ballroom scene, comes in as though to powder her face, very much aware of* **Yasha**. **Yepikhodov**, *at a cautious distance, is stalking her.*

Dunyasha (*as though to* **Firs**)   I'm all of awhirl, how my poor heart beats! Miss Anya says, 'Dance, Dunyasha, dance, dance'. *Everyone* insists, heigh-ho! So few ladies, so many, many gentlemen. (**Yasha** *is ignoring her.*) And, Mr Firs, you'll never guess what the post office clerk just said to me.

Firs   What did he say to you?

Dunyasha   Fair took my breath away. I'm like a flower.

Yepikhodov *sidles in.*

You, he said, are like a flower. D'you like sensitive words?

Yasha (*leaving*)   Philistines! Illiterates!

Dunyasha (*to his disappearing back*)   I adore sensitive words! (*To herself.*) I *am* like a flower.

Yepikhodov   Avdotya Fyodorovna?

Dunyasha *What?*

Yepikhodov   A word.

Firs (*to* **Yepikhodov**)   She's going to get herself into trouble. (*He moves off or aside.*)

Yepikhodov   Your attitude towards me lacks definition. Respectfully, therefore, might I enquire if the reason you keep avoiding me is because I'm an insect?

She flutters her fan in annoyance.

(*He experiments with the informal use of her name – and startles himself with its formality.*) Dunyasha!

Dunyasha   Tell me, what-do-you-want of me, what is the matter with you?!

Yepikhodov   Precisely. Because the matter with me, since you ask and if I may express myself candidly, is that I thought I knew the extent of my unhappy and inelegant lot and could face same with a smile, but you have brought it to complete reduction. Further, Avdotya Fyodorovna! – (*He raises his hand to emphasise his next point and sends her fan flying.*)

He nods grimly, futilely, and lets her gather up the fan for herself.

Dunyasha   I ask you!

Yepikhodov   I –

Dunyasha   Simon Panteleyevich, *please*! I need this time to – *dream* in! Tell me later, but leave me alone now in peace.

Varya (*coming in, to* **Yepikhodov**)   Are *you* still here? (*To* **Dunyasha**.) Run along, Dunyasha, you're required. (*To* **Yepikhodov**.) First, you play billiards in the billiard room and manage to break a cue, now you walk round like a guest.

Yepikhodov (*hurt*)   In reply, permit me to remark, you have no right to persecute me, either.

Varya   I'm not persecuting you, *either*, I'm telling you, it's my job. We employ you as a clerk here – though God knows why.

Yepikhodov (*doubly hurt*)   The matter of how I effect my stewardship – and, indeed, whether I walk, wander, eat or try to play billiards are matters for more senior people of understanding to judge me on.

Varya   How dare you! *Understanding*? Are you saying that I don't have understanding? Get out of here! Get out this minute, this instant!

Yepikhodov (*frightened of her*)   I should request – I'm going! – but I request that you express yourself in a more delicate mode of human commerce.

Varya   This minute, out, Two-and-Twenty Troubles!

Yepikhodov (*going, returns*)   I'm going, Varvara Mikailovna, but take note, I shall refer the matter of your last to the proper authority. (*He goes.*)

Varya   Don't you ever set foot in here again! (*To herself.*) Understanding: how dare he!

Yepikhodov (*off*)   Mark my words, I shall be lodging a serious complaint!

Varya   Oh, he's coming back again, is he? (*She has found the stick left behind by* **Firs**.) I'll give you cause to lodge a serious complaint.

Lopakhin *comes in and she takes a swipe at him.*

Lopakhin   Thank you very much.

Varya   I beg your pardon.

Lopakhin   Not at all, a Russian welcome.

Varya   Did I catch you?

Lopakhin   It's just a gash. (*Clowns, winces.*)

Voices (*in the ballroom*)   'Lopakhin is back!' 'Yermolay Alekseich is here!'

Pishchik (*coming in*)   You're back – Here he is – The very same, in person! (*Embraces* **Lopakhin**.) Dearest heart! Whiff of the old brandy, what? – What! ['*We're*'] Not doing too badly here either.

Lyubov (*coming in*)   Is that Yermolay?

Lopakhin   Oof! (*A stagger, holding his head. He's drunk/he's not that drunk/he's uneasy about facing her.*)

Lyubov   What took you so long? Where is Leonid?

Lopakhin   Leonid is coming. Right behind me.

Lyubov   Well, what happened, did the auction take place? Let us hear – did it?

Lopakhin   Four o'clock. (*And he's afraid of betraying his excitement.*)

Lyubov (*silently or just a frown*)   Four?

Lopakhin   We missed the train and had to wait for the half-nine one. Oof, my head is spinning!

Gayev *comes in, downbeat. He has some packages.*

Lyubov   Leonid! Well? Tell us quickly!

Gayev (*a despairing gesture, and gives his packages to* **Firs**) Some anchovies and Kerch herrings.

Lyubov   Give us the news!

Gayev   I haven't eaten all day. I'm very tired. Help me change my clothes, Firs. (*He goes out through the ballroom,* **Firs** *following.*)

Pishchik   . . . What's that?!

Lyubov   Is Cherryorchard sold?

Lopakhin   It is.

Lyubov   Who bought it?

Lopakhin   I bought it.

In the silence that follows, **Lyubov** *supports herself between the back of an armchair and table, lest she should fall.* **Varya** *takes the keys off her belt and dumps them on the floor and she walks out.*

My head is in such a state. (*A mock stagger*) I can hardly speak . . . . We got to the auction, who was there before us? Deriganov. Deriganov, oh-oh-oh! Leonid has – (*he shrugs 'only'*) – fifteen thousand. Straightaway, Deriganov bids thirty over the mortgage. I see. (**Lopakhin** *said to himself.*) 'Forty': I take him on. He bids forty-five, I go fifty-five. He keeps adding fives, I go up in tens, until? I bid ninety, over

the mortgage, and that's it, it stops – that's it – it's mine –
that's it – the most beautiful estate in the world –
Cherrylands! I don't believe it! (*He starts laughing; exceeds
himself; beats a dance on the floor.*) Can you believe it? Tell me
I'm drunk! I *know* I'm drunk! But am I dreaming this? Don't
laugh! Don't laugh at me-e-e-e-e, be-cause! If my father
with his stick – ouch! – if my grandfather with *his* stick –
ouch-ouch! – could see that their Yermolay, could see that
their 'half-wit' has bought the whole place where they were
ignorant slaves. Is it a dream, am I fan-tis-ising? (*Sing-songs.*)
'Tis a figment of your mind in a shroud of misteree.'

The musicians, off, are tuning up.

Yes, music, let's have some music, and see the trees come
'tumbelling' down to the tune of Yermolay Lopakhin's axe!
And he'll build cottages – all over! – and our children or our
grandchildren will see a new life here. Heigh-yeigh,
musicians, play!

The band is playing. **Lyubov** *has sat in a chair to weep.*
(**Lopakhin**'*s wild gesture on his very last nearly has him fall on top
of her?*)

. . . Why wouldn't you listen to me? . . . My *kind* friend . . .
Someone had to buy it . . . It's changing. ['*the world is*'] You
can't stop the clock . . . Lyubov Andreyevna . . . I'm not
happy either . . . If only the changing wasn't so dragged out
in this unhappy life of ours. (*He touches her hand, perhaps.*) If
only everything could be put right all at once.

Pishchik (*takes his arm; quietly*)   She's crying. She'd rather
be alone. Dear heart, let's go out here. (*He leads* **Lopakhin**
towards the ballroom.)

Lopakhin   What's the matter with that band? (*He bumps
into a small table, almost knocking over its contents.*) It's all right, I
can pay for it, I can buy anything! You out here, play up! –
Decent music! (*Going into the ballroom.*) Here comes the new
squire! Let everything be as I say! Heigh-yeigh, musicians
play! . . .

Lyubov *now sits alone, weeping.* **Anya** *stands in the archway.*

Anya   Don't cry. (*She comes to her mother.*) Why are you crying? Cherryorchard is gone, that's true, but your life too is out there in the future. My beautiful mother, I'm so grateful to you. I'm so grateful for you. Come with me, pure good soul: we shall plant a new orchard, a better one, you'll see, you will, and like the sun in the evening it'll all make sense. And you'll smile. Come with me, my dear.

Act Four

The same as Act One, but now the emptiness: the room has been stripped. The furniture that remains is stacked in a corner, and there is a pile of luggage.

Varya's and **Anya**'s *voices can be heard in* **Anya**'s *room.*

Lopakhin *stands by, waiting;* **Yasha**, *too, with a tray of glasses of champagne.*

In the background ['*in the front hall*'] **Yepikhodov** *is roping up a box, unsuccessfully. (In a while he will enlist the aid of a hammer and a nail, to his regret.)*

Gayev (*off*)   Goodbye! Goodbye! My good people, goodbye! Thank you, my brothers, my little brothers! Yes, goodbye! . . .

Yasha   It's touching: the simple folk saying their goodbyes. Salt of the earth, Mr Lopakhin, but – ah! – lack of education.

Lyubov *and* **Gayev** *are coming in from outside, to pass through the room. She looks pale, she doesn't want to speak.*

Gayev   That's not the way, Lyubov –

Lopakhin   Please? (*Inviting them to have a drink.*)

Gayev   You gave them your purse.

She gestures 'I couldn't help it', and continues off.

Lopakhin   Won't you?

Gayev   You shouldn't do that, Lyubov. (*He's off, too.*) That's not the way . . .

Lopakhin (*calling after them*)   Have a glass together before we all go?! (*Calls again.*) Champagne! A parting glass, my friends?! They don't want any. (*Calls.*) What?! . . . All right, I won't have any either, then. (*To* **Yasha**.) You have a glass.

Yasha   To those that are leaving, to those we leave behind! (*Drinks.*) Take my word for it: this isn't the real article.

Lopakhin   That bottle cost me eight roubles. It's bloody cold in here.

Yasha   They didn't light the stoves today: No point!

Lopakhin   October, and it's still sunny out there. Good building weather. (*Looks at his watch and calls.*) Forty-six minutes until the train leaves! That means, ladies and gentlemen, we must be out of here to get to the station in twenty! (*To* **Yasha**.) Why are you smirking?

Yasha   Because I'm glad.

During the above, carriages drawing up outside, and **Petya** *is coming in dressed in his overcoat, to search about the place.*

Petya   The carriages have been brought round. But where are my galoshes? Where-oh-where?

Lopakhin (*calls*)   A little haste, please! If you would! I'll be on the train with them for a few stops, then I get off to get to Kharkov. I'm spending the winter there. Mm, Kharkov. (*It's not his favourite place.*) But better than the nothing I've been doing, hanging around here with you lot.

Petya (*calls*)   Anya, I still can't find my galoshes! (*To himself.*) They've vanished.

Lopakhin   I'm worn out doing nothing. My hands are fed up with me. (*Waving his hands.*) They'd prefer to be someone else's.

Petya   Well, shut of us, they'll be your own again and you can set them to making more money.

Lopakhin   Have a drink.

Petya   No.

Lopakhin   Fine. You're off to Moscow.

Petya   I'm accompanying them to town. Then the Moscow train for me. (*Continues his search for the galoshes.*)

Lopakhin   The professors at the university suspend everything, I suppose, when you're not there?

Petya   Stale, Monsieur Lopakhin, can you come up with something new?

Lopakhin   How many years – how many, Peter – have you been a student? No, I'm interested.

Petya   You know, we'll probably never see each other again, so may I give you a parting piece of advice?

Lopakhin   Do.

Petya   Stop waving your hands about. (**Lopakhin** *mouths a silent 'what?', waving his hands, then he laughs at himself.*) And building all these cottages, your calculations and projections about how long it will take the tenant to become the owner, small-holder, self-producer on his hectare, well, that's just, that's just –

Lopakhin   Yes?

Petya   *More* hand-waving.

Lopakhin   (*laughs and hugs him warmly*)   My young old friend!

Petya   And you are a sensitive man, you've a sensitive soul! I like you. You could've been an artist.

Lopakhin   (*flattered/touched, but dismissive of himself*)   Ah! (*Then.*) Thank you. (*Then, a silent:*) Oh! Take some money from me – I mean, if you would?

Petya   What for?

Lopakhin   The journey, you'll need it –

Petya   Where are my galoshes?

Varya   Here are your galoshes.

Petya   Thanks! (*Pleased.*)

Varya   Take your muck! (*She has appeared briefly to throw galoshes into the room and is gone again.*)

Petya   Why is she always angry?

Lopakhin   But you don't have any money?

Petya   I do. Here. (*In his pocket.*) I just got paid for a translation.

Lopakhin   And I just got paid for –

Petya   These are not my galoshes!

Lopakhin   Peter – Peter, last spring I sowed three thousand acres of poppies. That was some picture, three thousand acres of poppies in flower. And I just made forty thousand clear on them, so, won't you let me give you –

Petya   Put away your purse.

Lopakhin   A *loan*, then, no strings attached, why turn up your nose at it? Merciful hour, I'm only a simple man! My father –

Petya   Was a peasant, your grandfather was a – so what? Mine was a chemist – so what? In debate, can conclusions be drawn from the basis of what your father was? Can they?

Lopakhin (*opening his purse/wallet*)   Ah, here –

Petya   Offer me two hundred thousand! Put it down there in front of me, now, this minute, and will I take it? (*He most certainly won't.*) Offer me anything you like – *everything* you have! All that you prize so highly has no power over me, not the slightest influence – no more than fluff in the air. Why? Why?

Lopakhin   Why?

Petya   Because *I* am a free man.

Lopakhin   I see.

Petya   I can do without all that. Why? Because I am *truly* free. And I'm strong.

Lopakhin   You are.

Petya   And proud.

Lopakhin   Yes. (*He puts away his wallet; contains a sigh.*)

Petya   Humanity, Yermolay, *is* moving forward towards the highest truth and I am in the first ranks.

Lopakhin   And you'll get there.

Petya   Yes, I shall. Or if I shan't, I'll show others how to. Now, galoshes.

And he's scratching his head again over his missing galoshes. Outside, off, the sound of an axe striking a tree, which they don't register.

Lopakhin   Well, whatever, farewell, far-thee-well, my friend. You and I are always squaring up to each other and the sun out there is just shining down on us. Life will go on its own sweet way no matter what. I don't know, it's only when I'm working that anything makes sense. How many people are there living who believe that there's no sense in anything? A great many, I think. But that's neither here nor there. I hear Leonid is taking up that job in the bank in town. He won't last it, he's too lazy.

Anya (*in the doorway*)   Mama asks that you don't start cutting down the trees before she leaves.

Petya (*registers the sound of the axe; then to* **Lopakhin**)   Really! (*And he goes out.*)

Lopakhin (*is embarrassed. Going out.*) Tck, stupid!

Anya   Has Firs been taken to hospital?

Yasha   I told them to this morning so what d'you think?

Anya (*to* **Yepikhodov**)   Simon Panteleyevich, when you've done there, would you please find out if Firs has been taken to hospital?

Yasha   I said I told Yegor to this morning.

Varya (*off*)   Has Firs been taken to hospital?

Yasha   How many times does it have to be spoken?

Anya   He has!

Varya (*off or in the doorway*)   Why then – why! – wasn't this letter taken with him for the doctor?

Anya (*going out*)   We'll send it after him.

Dunyasha *passes through on some ostensible business;* **Yepikhodov** *looks after her.*

Yepikhodov   In the matter of the ill and aged Mr Firs, I can only express my envy at his going off to meet his maker. (*He sets to hammering and hits his thumb or some accident befalls him.*)

Yasha   Two-and-Twenty! (*Laughs derisively.*)

Varya (*off, angrily*)   And where is that Yasha! His mother has come to say goodbye!

Yasha   Give-me-patience. (*He gets another glass of champagne for himself.*)

During the above, **Yepikhodov** *has been hopping about on one foot, silently – afraid of* **Varya**'*s voice – holding his thumb under his arm. Now, he thinks to sit down quietly and finds he has sat on a hatbox, squashing it. He limps off.*

Dunyasha *has returned. Now that she's alone with* **Yasha**:

Dunyasha (*silently or a whisper: an experiment in drama*)   My love!

Yasha *knocks back the champagne.*

Dunyasha   Yasha, look at me. Look at what you've brought me to. (*She starts to cry, or an experiment with tears.*)

Look at me once before you leave. You're abandoning me. (*She throws herself around him.*) Why?

Yasha   *Alors! – Mon Dieu! – D'accord! – Comment allez vous!* That's why! *Un instant.* (*He gets more champagne.*) I cannot live here, it doesn't suit me. Cannot you see that? I was made for Paris – *Vive la France!* (*And his logic.*) So what're you crying for? (*He drinks.*)

Dunyasha   Sensitivity, I suppose.

Yasha (*confidentially*)   Don't mind that. Just – yeh know? – if something comes up, play your cards right – *Comprendez?* – get someone to behave decently, and you'll be fine.

Dunyasha (*looking at herself in her compact-mirror*)   Well, will you write to me? Because I did, did, love you and I'd love to get a letter from Paris.

Yasha   Of course I will – *Certainement.* They're coming. Scoot!

Lyubov, **Gayev**, **Anya** *and* **Charlotta** *come in in silence and stand.*

Gayev   . . . We ought to be going.

Lyubov   These walls have seen so much . . . We'll do the traditional thing: sit for a few minutes. (*She moves about, slowly.*)

Gayev   Anyone get the – (*He sniffs the air.*) Smell of herrings. (*A quiet dig at* **Yasha**. *He sits.*)

Lyubov   Dear old grandfather house, winter will pass, spring will come, and you won't be here either. They'll have laid you to rest. (*To* **Anya**.) You look radiant, your eyes are sparkling, are you happy?

Anya   New life, mama!

Gayev   And it's quite true. Everything's fine now. Until it was sold we were worrying and fretting – up in a wretched heap. Now that it's all been decided, once for all, we're calm. We're even quite cheerful, hmm? (*And.*) I've landed on my feet: banker now, financier now. Yellow! Cannon off the red, middle pocket! And you, Lulu, say what you like, but you're looking better, no getting away from it.

Lyubov   It is true. My nerves are better. (**Dunyasha** *is now helping her on with her coat and hat.*) I'm sleeping well again. Take my things out, Yasha, it's time. (*To* **Anya**.) My little girl, and we'll see each other soon. I'll live – while I can – in Paris on that money from your great-grandauntie. Long live our Yaroslavl cousin!

Gayev   God bless her.

Anya   And you'll come back soon, mama, soon, won't you?

Lyubov   I shall, my darling, I shall.

Anya   And I'll get my exams –

Lyubov   Yes!

Anya   Oh, I'll get my exams!

Lyubov   Yes!

Anya   And I'll get – a job! I'll have a salary! And I'll be able to help you. And we'll do all sorts of things together, read all sorts of books – read in the winter evenings!

Charlotta *is singing to herself.* **Lopakhin** *is returning.* **Gayev** *indicates* **Charlotta**: *more evidence of their happiness.*

Gayev   Charlotta too: Happy.

Baby's Voice   Waaw! Waaw! (**Charlotta**'s *ventriloqiosm.*)

Charlotta (*picks up a bundle from the luggage, holds it as if it were a baby*)   'Hush, little baby, slush, don't cry, / Poor little munchkin, all is well, little boy' – And you will find a position for me in town.

Lopakhin   That'll be arranged, Charlotta, don't worry.

Charlotta   Because I do not exist without a position.

Baby's Voice   Waaw! Waaw!

Gayev (*to himself*)   And Varya's leaving.

Charlotta   Town of course is nowhere, there is no one there. Nothing, no one. It's a mystery. (*Dumps the bundle, unceremoniously.*) Goodbye, little maggot, I'm going away.

Gayev (*to himself*)   *Every*one's leaving. Suddenly, we're not needed. (*Like a momentary realisation.*)

Lopakhin   What have we here? – Who is this arriving?

Pishchik *is coming in, out of breath.*

Lopakhin   Wonders of nature will never cease!

Pishchik   Dearest friends – Out of ['*breath*'] – Let me get my ['*breath back*'] –

Gayev   Wha-oo?!

Pishchik   Can only stay a – stay a minute. Give me some – give me some –

Gayev   Money. I'll forgo this honour, thank you! (*He leaves.*)

Pishchik   Beautiful lady –

Lyubov   Boris?

Pishchik   Some water. I haven't visited you in so long. (*To* **Lopakhin**.) Glad you're here – Dearest heart – so pleased to see you – This for you. (*He gives money to* **Lopakhin**.) Four hundred. I owe you another eight-forty: To come.

Lopakhin   'Tis a figment of my mind in a shroud of! Where'd you get this?!

Pishchik   Hold on – I'm hot – Phew! Most extraordinary thing. Englishmen. They found a sort of white clay on my land. And four hundred for you, most beautiful lady. (*Money to* **Lyubov**. *He drinks water.*) The rest later.

Lopakhin   Who are the Englishmen?

Pishchik   Extraordinary! White clay! They came to see me. I've leased them the land it's on for twenty-four years. I'll tell you again – I have to gallop, call on the others. I owe money to everyone. God bless you! I'll – (*He drinks again.*) I'll call again on Thursday.

Lyubov   We're leaving for town, Boris, and tomorrow I'm going abroad.

Pishchik   What's that?! (*Only now noticing the stripped room and the luggage.*) Oh. I see. Yes. Well, that's all right. Never mind, what! People of the highest intelligence the English. (*Tears are running down his face.*) So, be happy. God bless you, everything has to end, what? (*He kisses* **Lyubov**'s *hands.*) And if the rumour ever reaches you that this old horse has met his end, you might remember me. Say, 'There was such a person once, Pishchik, God rest him.' Wonderful weather, what! Yes. (*Leaving. He turns back.*) Oh, Dashenka sends her regards. (*He goes.*)

Short pause. **Lopakhin** *takes out his keys.*

Lyubov   We have another few minutes. I'm leaving with two worries. There's Firs, who is ill.

Anya   Yasha had him sent to hospital.

Lyubov   And there's Varya. She's used to getting up early and working. Now her eyes are *always* red from crying, and she's losing weight. The creature is like a fish out of water. Anya. (*She whispers something to* **Anya**, *who whispers/nods to* **Charlotta** *and they both leave, leaving* **Lyubov** *alone with* **Lopakhin**.) . . . *You love her!* . . . It's been going on now for a long time, Yermolay . . . And you know very well what I had in mind for the two of you. It's the natural conclusion. You love her! And a blind person could see that she dotes on you. And why the two of you now go round avoiding each other is a mystery to me, it's *strange*. I don't understand it, Yermolay. Do you?

Lopakhin   I don't.

Lyubov   You see! D'you see my point?

Lopakhin   It's strange all right, I suppose.

Lyubov   Well?

Lopakhin   Well . . . if there was still time.

Lyubov   What does it take but a minute?

Lopakhin   I suppose . . . Let's do it then, straightaway. ['*Get it over with*']

Lyubov   I'll call her. Varya! (*To* **Yasha**, *who is coming in.*) *Sortez! Hors d'ici!* ('*Go out!*' *Calls to* **Anya**'*s room.*) Varya, leave everything and come here at once for a moment! Come! (*Going out; to herself.*) Wonderful!

Lopakhin, *alone, needs a prop for the occasion: the champagne. But someone has drunk it all.*

Varya *comes in. She inspects the luggage in silence for a long time.*

Varya   That's odd.

Lopakhin   What is?

Varya   . . . I can't find it anywhere.

Lopakhin   . . . What're you looking for?

Varya   Oh! (*Gesturing vaguely* '*something*'.) I packed it myself and can't remember where.

Lopakhin   . . . Where are *you* off to, Varvara Mikailovna?

Varya   Me? To the Ragulins . . . To look after things for them . . . A sort of housekeeper, I suppose.

Lopakhin   The Ragulins, in Yashnevno? . . . That's a fair bit away.

Varya   . . . Yes.

Lopakhin   . . . So life in this house is over.

Varya (*inspecting/counting the luggage again*)   Maybe I packed it in the big trunk. Or . . . Yes, life in this house is over. And it won't come back.

Lopakhin   I'm off to Kharkov. The same train as them, for a few stops. I've so much work on. Yepikhodov is going to clerk for me.

Varya   You've taken him on?

Lopakhin   I have.

Varya   I see.

Lopakhin   . . . It's calm out there. Sunny. Last year, if you remember, it was snowing at this time . . . Cold, though. Three degrees.

Varya   Three degrees?

Lopakhin   Three degrees below.

Varya   I haven't looked at the thermometer.

Pause.

Voice (*from outside*)   Yermolay Alekseich! Can you come out a minute?

Lopakhin   Coming! (*He goes out quickly.*)

Varya *weeps.*

Lyubov (*comes in, the question 'Well?' on her face. She can do no more*)   . . . We must go.

Varya (*dries her eyes*)   Yes, it's time.

Lyubov (*calls*)   Anya, put your things on!

Varya   I can get to the Ragulins today if I don't miss my train.

Anya, **Gayev** and **Charlotta** *come in, dressed for leaving.* **Coachmen** *come for the luggage.* **Yepikhodov**, *too, dressed to leave, getting in the way.*

Anya We're setting out!

Gayev My friends, my dear friends, of whom I am so fond: how to remain silent, how to refrain from giving farewell voice to the feelings that now well-up within —

Anya (*laughing*) Uncle!

Varya Dear uncle, we know.

Gayev: *finger to his lips, then mimes a billiard shot.*

Petya *and* **Lopakhin** *come in.*

Petya Time to go!

Anya Time to go!

Lyubov Just one minute more. (*Sits – rather abruptly.*)

Lopakhin Yepikhodov, my coat!

Lyubov It's as though I've never seen these walls before. Now I devour them.

Gayev Trinity Sunday, I was six years old, sitting on that windowsill, watching father go off to church.

Lyubov Has all the luggage been taken out?

Lopakhin By the look of things, yes. (*Takes his coat from* **Yepikhodov**.) See that everything's in order.

Yepikhodov Affix your confidence to me, Yermolay Alekseich. (*In a husky voice.*)

Lopakhin What's the matter with you? ['*with your voice*']

Yepikhodov Swallowed — swallowed something. (*He leaves.*)

Yasha (*to himself*) *Il ne connait pas le monde!*

Lyubov And not a soul will remain. ['*here when we're gone*']

Lopakhin Until spring. (*Now he clowns, ducking, as though to protect himself.*)

Varya *has been tugging at an umbrella to extricate it from a bundle and it has come free in a swipe.*

Varya (*to* **Lopakhin**)   What? (*She realises she is holding the umbrella aloft. Then, innocently.*) I wouldn't ever. Here are your galoshes, Peter, they were under the luggage.

Petya (*slipping on the galoshes*)   Now muster up, everyone!

Gayev (*to himself*)   Muster up –

Varya (*the galoshes*)   How very worn they are.

Petya   Our carriages await –

Gayev   Very worn – Carriages –

Lopakhin   Is everyone here?

Petya   The train will be in!

Gayev (*continues*)   Train – *Croisée*, into the middle – To the station, everybody – Double back, white to corner: end of break. (*He's smiling, gamely, in a private panic, afraid of crying.*)

Lyubov   Yes! We're leaving!

Lopakhin   (*He locks a side door.*) Some stuff stored in there so better lock it up. All ready?

Anya   Goodbye, old house, goodbye, old world! (*She leaves, laughing.*)

Petya   Hail, new life! (*He goes, cheerfully.*)

Varya *follows, looking up and around at the ceiling.* **Charlotta** *and her dog,* **Yasha** *stepping aside, elegantly, to let them precede him.*

Lopakhin   All right then, till spring, out we go, far-thee-well!

Lyubov *and* **Gayev** *stand there on their own. And suddenly, as though they'd been waiting for the moment, they throw their arms around each other and weep quietly, afraid of being heard.*

Gayev   Sister, sister. . .

Lyubov   My gentle cherry orchard.

Gayev   Sister, sister . . .

Lyubov   Happiness, goodbye.

Anya (*off, laughing*)   Mama! Mama!

Lyubov   Our dear mother walking this room.

Gayev   Sister . . .

Anya (*off*)   Mama, come on!

Petya (*off*)   Ah-ooo!

Lyubov   One last look.

Petya (*off*)   Ah-ooo!

Anya (*off*)   Mama!

Lyubov   We're coming!

They leave and the stage is empty. The sound of doors being locked and then the carriages pulling away. It grows quiet. The thud of the axe from the orchard. Footsteps. And **Firs** *comes in. He is dressed, as always, in his jacket and white waistcoat, but he is wearing slippers. He is ill.*

Firs   . . . They've gone? . . . (*He tries a door, finds it locked.*) Locked. Shit . . . And I expect he left in that light coat. Tck, I should have seen to that! Sit for a bit? (*He sits, muttering something.*) . . . Yes, young people . . . And, you know, life slips by. It goes by, somehow. As though you never really live it . . . (*He smiles, blows a puff of air: ephemeral life.*) Here, gone. Forgotten . . . I'll lie down for a bit. (*He mutters something we can't make out.*) . . . Yes, and you've nothing left in you, you know . . . Have you? No . . . Shit . . . Good-for-nothing.

A distant sound, as though out of the sky, the sound of a breaking string (a metallic twang) vibrating and dying away again. Then all that is heard is the sound of the axe on the trees far off in the orchard.

The Drunkard

For Jane

Acknowledgements

The Drunkard, after the melodrama by W.H. Smith and A Gentleman, is indebted to *Fifteen Years of a Drunkard's Life* by Douglas Jerrold; and for lines, freely used, from *'Let The Toast Pass'* by R.B. Sheridan in Scene Two Act Two. Songs: the lullaby, 'Child and Mother' is by H.A.J. Campbell and Eugene Field; 'O Kisses They are Plenty' (anonymous); 'Down Among the Dead Men' is by Dyer; 'Soft Music is Stealing' is by F. Pax.

Additional music

Additional, original music for the premiere of *The Drunkard* was composed and performed live by Ellen Cranitch and Helene Montague. It included some set pieces – the wedding scene, the tavern scenes and the final 'hymn'. Extensive underscoring was also used almost continuously – this was devised in response to the rhythm of language, and the actions and interactions of the characters.

The Drunkard was first produced at the Town Hall Theatre, Galway, on 18 July 2003, by b*spoke theatre company in association with Galway Arts Festival, with the following cast:

Sir Arden Rencelaw	Nick Dunning
Edward Kilcullen	Rory Keenan
Phelim McGinty	Stephen Brennan
Mother/Agnes Earley/	
Floozie 1	Pauline McLynn
Arabella/Floozie 2	Sarah-Jane Drummey
William Earley/Loafer 3	Jack Lynch
Widdy Spindle/Tavern Keeper/	Dylan Tighe
Loafer 1/Bartender/	
Policeman 2	
Farmer/Loafer 2/Policeman 1	Rory Nolan
Alanna/Village Girl/Floozie 3	Sarah Brennan
Village Girl	Gemma Reeves

Director Lynne Parker
Set and Costume Design Monica Frawley
Lighting Design Rupert Murray
Music arranged, composed, and performed by Ellen Cranitch
    and Helene Montague
Stage Manager Aisling Mooney
Assistant Stage Manager Gemma Reeves
Producers Jane Brennan and Alison McKenna

Characters

Sir Arden Rencelaw
Edward Kilcullen
Phelim McGinty, *a lawyer*
Arabella
Mother
Agnes Earley
Tavern-Keeper
William Earley
Alanna, *a child*
Widdy Spindle
Bartender
Man
Villagers, Loafers, Floozies, Policemen

The play benefits from a musical accompaniment.

Prologue

The prologue is delivered by **Sir Arden Rencelaw**, *dramatist and philanthropist. He is innocently himself.*

Rencelaw   When steadfast man, with riches to enjoy, well-born and nobly to ambition's cause intent, begins to slide into perdition's way, what topples him? What insidious attraction tempts the tender heart from that straight and goodly narrow to the rude bent and vulgar broad? Why, when in safe harbour, his wont to drift the foul-hard foetid waters from the soft moorings of a lovely wife?

Apply to Intellect's highest school, man's overflowing treasury of light, Philosophy, and draw a blank. And the Holy Alternative in His infinite wisdom guards His motives still. Our heavenward appeal is not for answer but to implore first aid.

Yet, I have some, and not a little, knowledge of this turpitude, for I was once – though never wedded – one such.

Taxing to credit when you see before you a personage of my conduct. But 'tis shining reformation o'er my erstwhile fault that you perceive; a figure staunch again in the ways of righteousness, reconstituted in fortune and, though I am not one to boast, in just and rightful claim to fame. Indeed, in recognition of a life spent penning works for the edification of my fellow man, titled. Don'tcha know.

But that is perfunctory by the way, for the protagonist of the drama to be here enacted is not its humble author: the role I take is more modest one, God's instrument on earth.

Lights briefly up on a bundle of rags that is **Edward**, *lying in a heap on the ground.*

There he is, the hero, master of the earth and all its creatures. There he lies, man, who binds the elements to his will, at death's door, gorged to the throat with wine.

Is't too late for him to mend? Can the luminous, once noble light, now guttering to its shivering last, have rekindle? Is't too late? Is't too late for YOU? Fellow, fallible man, I stand before you, renovation's living proof! All can be saved.

Light briefly up on **McGinty** *– his back towards us, perhaps.*

Most all. For there are some, into whose hearts, black and adamantine, no ray of sweetness is allowed to penetrate, who will continue blind to example's lamp and resolutely deaf to the reproving shafts of conscience. Why? In this request we are afforded no difficulty. For no reason other than that someone *pitied* them.

Take observation then and attend the tale of human weakness about to be revealed, of selfless and unfaltering love to rend and yet uplift the gentle heart; a tale of remorseless hatred, cruel injustice and salvation.

Poor woman.

The last, as he leaves, of **Mother**, *who is entering Scene One. Music.*

Act One

Scene One

An idyllic, rural cottage. A chair . . . **Mother**, *an apple-cheeked, old lady, has entered, leaning on a stick. She starts, totters, cries, as if seeing a ghost.*

Arabella, *who will come hurrying in in a moment, alarmed, with a basket of flowers, is young, beautiful, spirited and very kind.*

Mother   Oooooo!

Arabella   Mother! Mother!

Mother (*to her*)   Bartholemew!

Arabella   Mother?

Mother   Your dear father – (*She points to a spot, whispers.*) Bartholemew.

Arabella   Shriek! (*Then.*) There is nothing there. Morning light through the lattice contrives in variegated hues to dissemble, amusingly.

Mother   No, my dear. It was on that spot your dear father breathed his last.

Arabella   Oh, Mother. Let me help you to the chair.

Mother   That chair is indeed dear to me.

Arabella   There. (*Seating her.*)

Mother   For it was in this chair he sat the day before he passed away. Oh, how he loved this calm retreat! And 'twas often in his last illness, he . . .

Arabella   He rejoiced in you, Mother.

Mother   He rejoiced in me, Arabella. The comfort he drew from the knowledge that it should be myself would close his eyes at last to these rural shades; ah yes, and soon follow him, to be laid in yon little nook out there beside him.

Arabella   Dearest, dearest, *dearest*, Mother, it is true that this cottage, and its contents, are most dear to us, but we are not its proprietors, and word is now abroad that our worthy landlord, Patrick Joseph Kilcullen, is failing fast.

Mother   Aa no! Old Paddy Joe?

Arabella   I fear so. And should he cease the world we would be in the hands of his son, Young Edward Kilcullen, who has come down from college, word on whom is scant other than that he has been paying nocturnal calls on the village tavern of late.

Mother   My beloved child! Who will protect you when I am gone?

Arabella   Oh dear, I did not mean to alarm you.

Mother   Hark!

A knock at the door.

That must be someone. Come in!

Enter **McGinty**.

McGinty   Good Mrs Clancy – Remember me? – One of the McGinty family below? – Now Lawyer McGinty. I once ran barefoot in this village and knew your husband Bartley well, indeed I did and he knew me – Good morning!

Mother   Good morning, Sir!

Arabella   Sir! (*Curtseys.*)

McGinty   Mmmm, young lady!

Mother   Arabella, child, a chair.

McGinty   Won't sit. A sad calamity has befallen the village.

Mother   Not? Aa no!

McGinty   Paddy Joe. I have lost a client, may he rest in peace.

Mother   The lenient creature! Many a poor person, I feel, will have reason to mourn his passing.

McGinty   Indeed they will, how true! A good old skin, a grand old stick and we'll leave it at that. He placed great confidence in me towards the end and I am now sole trustee and executor of all he owned, except this cottage.

Mother   Which favour he bequeathed to us in his final testament!

McGinty   Aaa, no now. (*'Not so fast.'*) Which favour was transferred by *deed*, to his son, sometime in the past.

Arabella   To Young Edward Kilcullen?

McGinty   To the young buck Ned.

Arabella   Sir, you are skilled in pleading causes and I perceive in you a worthy advocate who has –

McGinty   A heart for business and a head to feel for the unfortunate – yes! So why prolong a matter that perhaps another dreads: do ye have the money to purchase this property?

Mother   This calm retreat!

McGinty (*to himself*)   They don't have it.

Arabella   The young gentleman wishes to sell it?

McGinty   What else can he do?! It's all that he possesses. Cut off with a shilling in his father's will – I saw to it myself!

Mother   It's the streets for us then!

McGinty (*to himself*)   The streets!

Mother   Is my child to be exposed to the thousand temptations of life?!

McGinty   Bear up! Your daughter's young and roundly beautiful: avid public interest must await such usefulness.

Arabella (*to herself*)   What if the rumour of this young man's character be in mistake or a tarnish put about by idle tongues?

McGinty (*to himself*)   What's the young fruit thinking?

Arabella (*to herself*)   And I, with safety, could approach him with petition?

McGinty   No!

Arabella   Sir?

McGinty   Let me plead your case.

Arabella   But some instinct tells me deep inside –

McGinty   The young man's gay! Grows fond of the world, fond of – Not edifying for the ears of sweet innocence.

Arabella   But –

McGinty   He's giddy! Be advised, my dear: do not approach him, nor let him see you – unless I find advantage in it. I shall go to him at once and, man to man, make trial on your behalf.

Mother   Oh Sir! –

Arabella   Kind Sir! –

Mother   Dear Sir! –

McGinty   Tut, tut! Think nothing of it, that's the sort of man I am. In the meantime, lest my best entreaties fail of course, be looking for a place before he moves in the matter. Now I must be off. May heaven look down on you with blessings, if it can. (*Exit.*)

Mother   A comfort to have such a friend in the hour of trouble?

Arabella   Yes, Mother. He appears a very feeling man. (*To herself.*) But what if *he* be in mistake about Young Kilcullen's character? Arabella Clancy, it's vainalorious of you to be setting conjecture against the opinion of a learned man! But my instinct, now awakened, grows obstinate to see him. Tck, Arabella Clancy! That is female curiosity aroused, for you have heard too the young man's not too badly landscaped. Yes, but what if I, *in concert* then with our lawyer friend, made proposal of our own? Dare I? Arabella, will you stop! I won't! Mother, how much have we put aside to purchase fuel for the winter?

Mother   It's all here in the box.

Arabella   And if that were offered to him?

Mother   Thirty shillings –

Arabella   It would partially do for our rent arrears.

Mother   And when the young man finds we are disposed to fairly deal with him? Yes, go to him!

Arabella   Yes, I shall go to him! –

Mother   And he'll relent! –

Arabella   He'll relent! (*She is putting on her village bonnet, etc. To herself.*) And yet, I tremble with a sad foreboding.

Mother   Why, child, you turn pale!

Arabella   Dearest Mother, it is nothing. A severe task is imposed on us, but it must be done.

Mother   And he'll relent! And if he be one whit like his father, he'll have the manners of a gentleman and, however wild his conduct when at large among the loafers, he'll not insult an unprotected woman.

Arabella   You give me courage.

Mother   Hand me down my book

Arabella *gets the Bible, kisses it for strength and gives it to her mother.*

Mother   Go forth, my child; go as the dove from the ark of old and return with the olive branch of peace.

Arabella   Should I fail?

Mother   Return to find consolation here in the bosom of your fond old widowed mother. But you shall not fail.

Scene Two

Drop scene. A landscape.

McGinty *and* **Arabella** *separately, en route to see* **Edward Kilcullen**, *alternate, coming forward and retiring.*

McGinty   Well, that little scene of sympathy and concern with Bartholemew Clancy's widow and daughter went well. Now for this young milksop puppy Kilcullen.

Arabella   In a few moments I shall come face to face with this young man whose tarnished reputation now alarmingly enlarges in my brain. Oh courage, Arabella!

McGinty   I now control all the Kilcullen family ever owned except the cottage, which final clause, when I possess it, will clinch a life's ambition.

Arabella   I'm nearly there – Dare I go on? I must go on, suppliant to a dangerous reprobate for shelter beneath the roof where I was born.

McGinty   Why? Firstly, for the *kindness* I for years endured from Patrick-Joseph-Paddy-Joe Kilcullen and, secondly – secondly, it doesn't suit me to think about it now.

Arabella   Do my mother's cheery urgings, my own innocent expectations deceive in leading me to hope of a notorious dissipated collegian?

McGinty   Ha! There he is.

Arabella   Shriek! A gentleman approaches.

McGinty   Wish-washed and starry-eyed.

Arabella   His fear-inspiring countenance informs me it is he.

McGinty   I cooked the father, now to prepare easier fare, the son. (*Exit.*)

Arabella   I am tongue-tied. I must pause a moment for valour to recover. (*She retires.*)

Enter **Edward**, *another innocent; young, handsome, earnest, somewhat dreamy and romantic.*

Edward   For the very sacred life of me I know not what to think. The situation bears no comprehension. All these acres should be mine. What offence to merit disinheritance? That I enjoy a – tipple – now and then? Hardly. Or that my father thought I lacked 'drive', that my bashfulness was 'unmanly'? I must say I am a trifle upset. (*To heaven.*) And what now up there, Papa, has Mama got to say to you in heaven, what does *she* think of you? 'Out and out with you, Paddy Joe!' she is saying, I'll wager. 'Out and out with you to treat your son – your *only* son – our only child like that!' (*He produces a hip-flask.*) She at least left me a little something in cash. But that will hardly keep whatever-the-animal-is from the stable door when the fox has run off with all the chickens, will it? Hah! Out and out with you, Paddy Joe! (*And he has a sip from the flask.*)

McGinty (*without*)   Holloo! Young Master Kilcullen, Sir! (*Entering.*)

Arabella (*from afar*)   Lawyer McGinty goes earnestly to plead our case.

McGinty   I bring good news!

Edward   You have found another will!

McGinty   What strange idea! There cannot be other than the one that cut you off: I conducted all your late dear father's business.

Edward   It don't make sense! Adoringly he looked me at the last. – He drew me close. My very image was reflected in his eye – as I stand here I saw it there – an apple! Before heaven's very threshold he turned back and said, 'Forget the poetry, put your knuckles to the grindstone, and ever keep a special eye on those that heaven chose to bless less well than you, the tenantry.' Where is explanation? What tenantry?! for me to keep a special eye on.

McGinty   Your father was a saint sure. Who, but I, has reason never to forget the superiority of his existence? But like many a saint before him, he rambled at the last.

Edward   But father was so *wise* – 'Paddy Joe'! The man could not even – *blink* – without there being something in his eye. What could he have in mind that is so encoded in his dying scripture? (*He is throwing his hands up.*) I am bereft!

McGinty   But, Young Sir, you have the cottage, previously inherited by deed, which is the matter I have come about. I have opportunity of selling it.

Edward   Lost! (*He's not listening; sighs and has a sip.*)

McGinty   For – a hundred pounds?

Edward (*absently*)   Did I not hear that it is occupied?

McGinty   By an impecunious old widow and her child.

Edward   Who have lived there long.

McGinty   In arrears for rent.

Edward   And that the widow is in poor health.

McGinty   She has a claim upon the poorhouse.

Edward   Hmm? (*He continues dreamily.*)

McGinty   I have the eviction papers here, ready to be signed.

Edward (*then, suddenly*)   I have tenants! Maybe I have little else but I have tenants to keep a special eye on! Do I at last begin to decipher some of father's philosophy?

McGinty   Young man –

Edward   Hold! Though I am now myself in somewhat straitened circumstances, that condition shall not make me less gentlemanly. Deprive peasant simplicity of a caring landlord! Of a home dear to them as a, perhaps a – popsy! Send them forth from the flowers they have cultivated, the vines they have trained in courses –

McGinty   No vines – (*'Hot air.'*)

Edward   From an abode endeared to them by tenderest recollections and domestic remembrances of things past.

McGinty   Oh, all that and more! The fences they've neglected, garden gate off its hinges, limbs of birch and fruit trees broken down for firewood – a window decorated with a battered hat!

Edward   Cease, McGinty! All this was explained to me by Billy Earley in the tavern last evening. The trees were broken down by idle schoolboys, and with regard to the battered hat in the window, whose hat was that, Sir? I ask you! It was a *man's* hat, Sir, the hat of Bartholemew Clancy, Sir! Can as much be said of yours, McGinty?

McGinty   I see you are pleased to be pleasant this morning and I bid you good day! (*He walks away, stops. To himself.*) This does not turn out.

Arabella (*from afar*)   He has argued well our case but his sombre face tells not of victory.

McGinty   I'll play my next advantage.

Arabella   He tries for us again – Courage to the lawyer!

McGinty   Beg pardon, Master Kilcullen, I now comprehend what underlies your plan the better. Let them stay on in the cottage for a term. The daughter, growing girl, eh? Tender, rosy, firm?

Edward*'s lack of comprehension.*

McGinty   Aa, you have not seen her!

Edward   Never.

McGinty   Aaaaa!

Edward   Explain yourself.

McGinty   Continue them in residence till you're – satisfied? Traps for wild fowl? Mother, daughter grateful – free access to the cottage at all hours – love, passion?

Edward   Do you know the girl has no father?

McGinty   That's it!

Edward   Are you aware that she is brotherless?

McGinty   A garden without a fence! All you have to do is step inside.

Edward   That is – McGinty! – shocking! To enter like a wolf an innocent fold and lie down with a lamb! Tear from a mother's arms the last hope of her old age! If I had a horsewhip I would seize you by the throat and dash you prostrate to the earth!

McGinty (*aside*)   He's drunk!

Edward (*loudly*)   Unmolested, the widow and her child shall remain in the cottage – for ever!

Arabella   Heavens! (*And she approaches.*)

McGinty   Hell!

Edward   This is the widow's – *child*?

McGinty   And she is a dear girl. But I am deeply upset that a member of the family I have esteemed my lifelong years should so misconstrue my words.

Arabella (*to* **McGinty**)   Oh thank you, Sir! And blessings – blessings! – shower on you, Sir! (*She kneels at* **Edward***'s feet.*)

Edward   She – she weeps?

McGinty   As I do. (*As he exits.*) I'll be revenged on them both for this.

Edward   By – by my soul!

Arabella (*weeping; to herself*)   This is unexpected kindness, Arabella.

Edward   The lovely girl excites my sympathy, strangely. No! R-r-rise, M-m-miss.

Arabella   Clancy. I have an errand, Sir, for you.

Edward   What's this?

Arabella   'Tis portion of the rent money we owe. Oh, but be assured of the remainder as soon as willing hands can earn it.

He stays her with a gesture.

But you declared that Mother and I should remain in the cottage!

Edward   And I s-s-spoke it plain.

Arabella   What reason then to hold from you your due? – Take it!

Edward   N-n-nay!

Arabella   I entreat! Especially now you are in need of it. (*Hand to her mouth: was her last presumptuous?*)

Edward (*is not offended; he is mustering himself against his shyness. Loudly.*)   Perish the rent money, Miss Clancy!

Arabella   What do I do with it?

Edward   Keep it!

Arabella   Ay?!

Edward   As portion of your dowry.

Arabella   Sir?

Edward   Shall I undisguise my feelings? Shall I?

Arabella   'Twould be impertinent of me to order you in aught.

Edward   In plenitude are there comely maidens with beauty to astonish in this section of the country. But I have now discovered something more: a purity of mental excellence, noble sentiment and filial piety. These qualities my mother had, these were the charms that bound captive my father's heart and made man of him. I too would be such success as he. (*He throws the flask away behind his back.*) I speak plainly for I speak honestly, and when I ask that you keep the contents of that box as portion of your dowry, need I say into whose hands I should like to have it fall at last?

Arabella   (*to herself*)   Shriek! But to affect not to understand you further, Sir, would be idle return for your kindness and condescension.

Edward   M-m-miss Clancy

Arabella   Arabella.

Edward   I sometimes stroll in the vicinity of your cottage.

Arabella   Should I, M-m-mr Kilcullen –

Edward   Edward –

Arabella   See you go by without stopping, why then, why then –

Edward   Why then, why then, Miss Clancy?

Arabella   Why then – Oh Mr Kilcullen, I should suppose that you'd forgotten where I lived!

Edward   Yes, my father's wisdom worked in ways mysterious. A cottage, gifted to me by this deed on the day that I was born: that it should become a casket for a priceless jewel! Miss Clancy, in earnest of my trust, would you consent to have your name lie with mine on this document?

Arabella   Edward!

Edward   Arabella!

Music.

They exit.

In the transition, **McGinty** *returns and looks off in the direction they have taken.*

McGinty   Thus ends my efforts? (*He sees the discarded hip-flask and he picks it up.*) Thus ends my efforts, for now.

He exits.

Scene Three

A platform on the village green for a celebration. Villagers in festive spirit enter for the party. **William Earley, Girls** (*including an oddly dressed* **Widdy Spindle**), **Farmer** *and* **McGinty** *too, affecting goodwill. They are led in by* **Rencelaw,** *who is in peasant dress his 'disguise' a pied piper with a tin whistle. The men have tankards of drink.*

All   Ha, ha, ha, ha, ha, ha, ha!

Rencelaw   The village keeps holiday for the newlyweds!

All   Ha, ha, ha, ha, ha, ha, ha!

Rencelaw (*calling off*)   Stay you a while there, the rest of you! You shall all have chance to show your mettle!

McGinty   Ha, ha, ha! – Great happiness attends us all!

All   Ha, ha, ha, ha, ha!

Rencelaw   Yes, warm the village green with honest, wholesome merriment for the arrival of the happy couple! Select partners!

William   Widdy Spindle, let's see what's left in them relic pins!

Spindle   William Earley, how uncouthful!

They dance. All dancing.

Rencelaw   Vary partners!

All dancing, change partners.

Rencelaw   Single dancers!

Others   Widdy Spindle, take the floor! Widdy Spindle! (*Etc.*)

Spindle   (*coyly*)   Nay! 'Tis too much for my temerity!

And she leaps into the dance, the others cheering on her solo performance.

Farmer   Now be William's turn!

Others   William! Billy! (*Etc.*)

William (*dancing solo*)
When I was a young and roving boy,
Where fancy led me I did wander;
Sweet Caroline was my pride and joy,
But I missed the goose and hit the gander!

Clapping, cheering – 'Next!' 'Who's next?' – and **Rencelaw** *takes the floor.*

Rencelaw   Well executed, honest William, but – Everybody! – Observe how I do it!

When I was a young and roving boy,
Where fancy led that road I'd take;
Sweet Angeline was my pride and joy,
But I missed the goose and hit the drake!

Laughter, applause etc.

Spindle   Who is he? Who is that handsome, vigorous (young) man?

Rencelaw (*aside*)   When visiting the provinces, I sometimes conceal myself lest my fame put them in awe.

Farmer   That be Sir Arden Rencelaw in his disguise.

William   Likes to be up and down the country –

Farmer   A-couragin' what be right, a-curin' what be wrong.

Girls   A ring-play, a ring-play!

Rencelaw   Form a circle!

William   Fall in here! –

Girls   A ring-play, a ring-play!

McGinty   Sweet golden age of youth!

Spindle   Who'll go in the middle?

McGinty   Aa, that I were young again!

William   Lawyer McGinty!

McGinty *protesting.*

All   Honest Lawyer McGinty!

He is pushed into the centre.

William   There's a right, rich catch for you, ladies!

And they circle him.

Girls
    I am a rich widow, I live all alone;
    I have but one son and he is my own.
    Go, son – go, son – go choose you one –
    Go choose a good one or else choose none!

All   Choose! Choose! . . . (*Laughter.*)

Improvise. **McGinty** *succumbs to a shy, giggling side of his nature.*
Girls *are pushed at him or he grabs at the* **Girls** . . . **Spindle**
finds herself with **McGinty**.

Men   Kiss her, McGinty!

Spindle   Mortifications!

Girls   Kiss him, Widdy Spindle!

Spindle   Petrafactions!

Farcical kiss. Cheers. And **McGinty** *and* **Spindle** *dance, while:*

All (*circling them*)
    Now you are married, you must obey
    What you have heard your parents say!

Now you are married, you must prove true
As you see others do, so do you!

William Mary and Joseph!

He's impatient at this 'clumsy' dance; he sweeps **Spindle** *from* **McGinty** *and they dance together, vigorously.*

Mercy on me! What have you done?
You married the father instead of the son!
His legs are crooked and ill put on,
They're all laughing, Widdy Spindle, at your young man!

Laughter, cheering. Then a gradual hush and they pull back as **Agnes** *comes in, singing to herself, smiling, laughing crazily, and strewing some withered flowers.*

Agnes *(without)*
Brake and fern and cypress dell
Where slippery adder crawls . . .

McGinty The maniac, Agnes Earley. Her voice haunts me like the spectre of that young shuffler she was to marry.

Agnes
Brake and fern and cypress dell
Where slippery adder crawls,
Where grassy waters well
By the old moss-covered walls . . .

To various people, in turn.

Will you come to my wedding today and see the coffin go in?
Will you come to my wedding today and . . . (*Etc.*)

Spindle (*to* **Rencelaw**) She were to be married, Sir, but night afore wedding her young man up and died –

Girl Outside the tavern.

Spindle Fell 'n' died in a drunken fit.

Farmer Aye!

McGinty Her eyes! Maniacs have strange insight. She knows too much for my happiness.

Agnes (*to* **McGinty**)   Will you come to my wedding today –

McGinty   Go home, Agnes, you creature!

Agnes   And see the coffin go in?

McGinty   Who let her out?! Why is she here?!

Agnes   And we shall dance!

She dances gaily.

> Upon the heather, when the weather
> Is as mild as May,
> We'll all prance as we dance
> And we'll all be happy and . . .

(*It's dying on her.*) And we'll all be happy and . . . (*She cries.*)
Water! Water! He only wanted water! Water . . . But they
kept feeding red . . . *red-red-red* water . . . into poor young
Kevin's glass.

Rencelaw   Ah, *red* water!

Agnes   Quick! – Give him water – Oh hear him cry for
water! Quick, quick! He turns cold. Quick! His lips, the lips
I love . . . turn blue . . .

McGinty   Why can't the almshouse keep these maniacs
chained up?! It's a disgrace! She should not be at large! Look
at her!

Agnes (*laughs / sing-songs*)   The lawyer is a creepy man, now
owns the brick house yonder!

McGinty   She ruins our honest celebrations, she distresses
the entire neighbourhood! – The poor wretch! Agnes, you
witch, clear off from here!

Agnes   And the will – Ha, ha, ha!

McGinty   Wha's that?! –

Agnes   The will – Ha, ha, ha!

McGinty   So, you want a nice warm whipping?

206   The Drunkard

He fetches a cane.

Agnes   The will – Ha, ha, ha!

McGinty   Then you shall have one!

*His cane is raised to strike **Agnes**. **Rencelaw**, with deft flick of his own cane, knocks the cane out of **McGinty**'s hand; and **William**, too, has rushed in to throw **McGinty** aside.*

Rencelaw   Fie!

William   Ho! Strike my helpless, little half-crazed sister Agnes, would you?!

McGinty   Assault and battery! All here are witnesses!

William   Ho! Ho! Mr Honey! – I won't wait for Bezzelybub down there –

McGinty   I'll have you, William Earley, between stone walls! –

William   To treat you to a brimstone bath! –

Rencelaw   Silence! . . . I have some, and not a little, knowledge of physic and I suspect this young lady's malady to be temporary . . . Miss Agnes?

Agnes   Sir? Will you come to my wedding today and . . . (*She is in tears.*)

Rencelaw   I should be greatly honoured.

Agnes   Then walk up, young man, there's a lady here, with . . .

Rencelaw   With jewels in her hair.

He has approached her and is holding out his hand to her.

She considers his hand, hesitates, withdraws into herself, and retreats from them:

Agnes   'Brake and fern and cypress dell where slippery adder crawls . . . '

And she is gone. **Rencelaw**, *interested, follows her a little way. The dancing has started again. This turns into a guard of honour for the arrival of the bride and groom,* **Arabella** *and* **Edward**, *accompanied by* **Mother**. *Church bells, rose petals, cheering.*

> Hooray! Hooray!
> Hail, hail, the happy pair!
> Long life!
> Peace! Health and joy!
> Progeny!
> Happiness!
> Hooray! Hooray!

The **Girls** *surround* **Arabella** *to kiss her and admire her ring. And* **Arabella** *throws her bouquet of flowers up among them. While the* **Men**, *with their tankards, surround* **Edward** *to shake his hand and toast him.* **Edward** *is a happy groom; shy, too, and nervous.*

McGinty   Toast to the groom!

Farmer   Aye —

William   Toast to the groom!

McGinty   Your health, Master Edward!

William   Long life, Ned, and —

First Farmer   Aye!

William   May the Kilcullen name be perpetuated!

McGinty (*as they are about to drink*)   Why, he has no cup!

And he sends **Tom**, *the* **Farmer**, *off to get one.*

Edward   Nay, Tom, thank you – (*Too late.*)

McGinty   Nay? And offend us by not returning the traditional toast?

Edward   My thanks, good friends all, but I have given up the practice and left the brawl of the tavern for a new beginning: from today I am an altered man.

And gestures 'No' to the **Farmer**, *who has returned with a tankard of drink for him.*

McGinty Excellent! An altared man – he's been to the altar – A wit, a wit! – He's jesting! (*Laughter.*)

Edward (*laughing, nervously*) Nay –

William Ah, here's to the bashful groom then!

McGinty (*holding up the toast*) Bashful?! Bashful?! His dear father once told me his bashfulness was such that he went to bed without a candle. (*Laughter.*) What is to happen at bedtime tonight? (*Laughter.*)

Edward (*takes the tankard*) Well, *one* draught then. And – dearest and best of good fellows – so as not to be discourteous to your salute, this to *your* good health!

They drink. **McGinty** *draws* **Edward** *aside, produces the hip-flask and slips it to* **Edward**. **Edward** *is unsure.*

McGinty As a precaution for later, lest your courage fail and take from the pleasure that lies ahead.

Mother My children! This is a day of great joy. May blessings rest on you always.

She joins the hands of **Arabella** *and* **Edward**.

Mother And blessings be upon us all!

Applause.

Edward From tomorrow all happiness shall be ours.

Arabella Tomorrow? Why from tomorrow?

Edward It will be the first full day of our union. (*He slips the flask into his pocket.*)

Arabella My husband.

Edward My wife.

Music. They kiss. And they waltz off.

Scene Four

Arabella *sits alone by a cradle.*

Rencelaw   Tempus fugit. No longer does she address herself as Arabella Clancy, no longer the charming little cries of innocent astonishment that marked her girlhood. She is now wife and mother . . . See her. She sleeps? Ah, no! She waits, hopes. She listens, ears pricking up like terriers for the rattle of the latch, the bride of only yesteryear shorn of glorious bloom. Or for the thunder of drunken fists upon the door that will alarm the ancient mother, now failing fast; that will awaken the newborn babe from sleep. She sings.

Arabella
    Oh, daughter-my-love, if you'll give me your hand
    And go where I ask you to wander,
    I will lead us away to a beautiful land
    The Dreamland that's waiting out yonder;
    We'll walk in the sweet posey garden out there,
    Where moonlight and starlight are streaming,
    And the flowers and the birds are filling the air
    With perfume and music of dreaming.

Rencelaw   Night after night she wastes the light of two candles. A hundred times has she crept to the casement, bending low her ear his step to catch. Many a despairing look has she cast at the black sky. Then moving back again, she pauses . . . 'Mother?'

Arabella   Mother? Are you all right?

Rencelaw   And returning to her child, she sits once more . . . See her. She weeps? Ah, no! Stoically, she restrains her anguish . . . 'Edward?'

Arabella   Edward?

Rencelaw   Edward.

Edward (*a light comes up on him*)   I shall give it up. I promise.

Rencelaw   'She is a good wife.'

Edward   And I worship her. And I shall reform.

Arabella   Kiss me?

Edward   I kiss you.

Rencelaw   'Edward?'

Arabella   Edward?

Edward   I shall have one glass more.

Light down on **Edward**, *then down on* **Rencelaw**.

Arabella
So, daughter-my-love, let me take your dear hand
And away through the starlight we'll wander,
Away through the mists to the beautiful land
The Dreamland that's waiting out yonder.

Scene Five

Exterior of the village tavern. A tree. Night.

Rencelaw   Half-a-dozen years elapse.

Noise and shouting in the tavern: **Edward**, *without his jacket, is being thrown out of the tavern – and is resisting it – by* **Tavern-Keeper** (**Tubbs**). *He goes back in again to be thrown out again.* **McGinty** *comes scurrying from the tavern – out of harm's way – to watch, pleased, from a distance.*

Farmer, *too, is here, paralytic; his monosyllabic contributions – 'Aye!' – are both belches and half-conscious responses to the drama going on about him.* **William**, *who has not been in the tavern, will arrive shortly.* **Rencelaw** *stands on the opposite side to* **McGinty**.

A sextet that grows: six voices in competition, in counterpart, overlapping and simultaneous.

Tavern-Keeper   Come along now –

Edward   I shall not leave –

Tavern-Keeper (*continuous/overlapping*)   Come along, I say –

Edward (*continuous/overlapping*)   How dare you, Sir –

Tavern-Keeper   Out of here –

Edward   I shall not leave –

Tavern-Keeper   Get out!

Tavern-Keeper *reurns to the tavern.* **Edward** *barges into the tavern again.*

Rencelaw   The business of his day is to get drunk!

McGinty   Life works admirably!

Tavern-Keeper (*throwing* **Edward** *out again*)   Come along now! –

Edward   I shall not leave! –

Tavern-Keeper   Come along I say! –

Edward   How dare you, Sir! –

Tavern-Keeper   Out of here! – Get out!

Edward   I shall not leave! – I shan't!

Farmer   Aye!

Rencelaw   The infatuation every day increases!

McGinty   Admirably! Admirably!

Tavern-Keeper   You'll have nothing more in this house tonight! –

Edward   Do you know whom you address?!

Tavern-Keeper   Clear off! (*Returns to tavern.*)

Farmer   Aye!

Rencelaw   He expels reason, drowns the memory, defaces beauty!

McGinty   Ha, ha, ha, ha!

William   Holloo! Holloo! What sport goes forward here?
(*Arriving.*)

Edward *is trying to get back in to tavern.*

Tavern-Keeper   Out, out-out!

Edward   Release! – Unhand! –

Tavern-Keeper   Out, out-out! –

Edward   Release! – Unhand!

Tavern-Keeper   Out, out-out, out-out!

Farmer   Aye!

Rencelaw   He thieves his pocket, devils his soul, diminishes his strength!

McGinty   Ha, ha, ha, ha! Ha, ha, ha, ha!

William   Mary and Joseph, this be no sport!

Tavern-Keeper   Nothing more for you in this Christian house –

Edward   I am a Kilcullen! –

Tavern-Keeper   Nor any other night!

Edward   Dare you refuse service to a Kilcullen?!

Farmer   Aye!

Edward   In this townland of Glencullen?!

Tavern-Keeper   Nor – any – other – night!

William   Steady on, Edward, friend! Steady on, Landlord Tubbs!

Farmer   Aye!

Rencelaw   He bewitches his senses, corrupts his blood, drinks to others' good health and robs himself of his own!

McGinty   And he won't stop now – Ha, ha, ha!

Tavern-Keeper   Take 'His Lordship' out of this, William Earley!

Edward   If it were not for your greying hairs I'd thrash you within an inch of up-and-down the village! –

William   Where's his coat then, Landlord Tubbs?

Tavern-Keeper   There's his coat then! (*Throws it on the ground.*) Now, pack off! (*Exit.*)

In the comparative quiet, **Edward** *is fuming, his anger and impotence making him pace/strut.*

Edward   This is an outrage, this is a scandal.

Farmer   Aye!

William   Come, Ned, let me advise you to go home.

Edward (*calling*)   Tubbs! You in there! Don't want your flat, polluted, rot-gut liquor!

Tavern-Keeper (*off*)   Ho, ho, ho, ho, ho!

Farmer   Aye!

William   Come, Ned –

Edward   Pack off! (*A shout at* **Farmer**.)

William   Put on your coat –

Edward (*at tavern*)   Ho, ho, ho, ho, ho!

Farmer (*exit*)   Aye!

Edward (*to himself*)   But I know where liquor can be found.

William   Ned, friend, Ned! Your wife and child await.

Edward   And mother-in-law?

William   She's near the end, and suffering.

Edward   She is preparing for hell!

William (*helping* **Edward** *into his coat*)   You go more astray by the day than my little half-crazed sister Agnes.

Edward (*'sincerity'*)   William, Billy, shipmate, brother! I need a moment alone to collect myself. You go on and, should you be passing, tell them that I shall be there, the briefest of anons, twinkling of a lamb's tail.

He watches **William** *go. Then he looks about:*

Edward   No one sees. Yes, I know where liquor can be found.

He goes to the tree and, from a hollow, produces a bottle.

McGinty   The arch cunning!

Rencelaw   Is this to be the issue of that young man's life?

Edward (*drinks. And:*)   Aaaaa! It relieves.

McGinty   He has tasted well and will not stop now short of madness or oblivion.

Edward (*drinks again, and*)   Aaaaa!

And he sits under the tree to drink the rest.

Rencelaw   Must he ever yield to the fell tempter and, bending like a bulrush to the blast, bow his manhood lower than the brute?

Edward   Aaaaa!

McGinty   I now know his nature well. I bide my time. (*Retires.*)

Edward (*to heaven: laughing to himself*)   Papa – You up there – Dad! – whatchoo think of me now?

Rencelaw   And he could earn his bread.

Edward   If I wanted to.

Rencelaw   He has hands to work with, feet to walk, eyes to see.

Edward (*of his hands*)   Merest of shakes.

Rencelaw   A brain to think.

Edward   Slight head – (*Headache.*)

Rencelaw   Yet these best gifts of heaven he abuses, and puts out the light of reason.

Edward (*to the bottle*)   Shapely friend, why do people so rail against you? (*And drinks.*)

Off, in the night, eerily, faintly, plaintively:

Agnes (*off*)   'Brake and fern and cypress dell, where slippery adder crawls . . . '

Rencelaw   But another mission that brooks no wait calls upon my conscience and attention. (*He exits, purposefully.*)

Edward   Poor Agnes, too, abroad the night again. (*To the empty bottle.*) And you, my friend, have nothing more to say to me. Can I now go home? Face them? (*Rises.*) Mama, send down a little cash for Teddykins. (*Sighs.*) If I had one more. From where?

McGinty   Master Edward, dear friend!

Edward   Tempter, begone!

McGinty   What means this?

Edward   Were you not with me in the tavern when that vile fray began?

McGinty   Fray? What fray?

Edward   And did you not desert me?

McGinty   But I was summoned out on urgent business!

Edward (*angrily*)   Oh yes, oh yes, McGinty, you know only too well how to sit on the fence of the faraway hills buttering your bread on both sides without batting a single blind eye when a friend is in trouble!

McGinty   But I left you jovial there! Remember, we two, 'Ha, ha, ha!'? . . . As I am a Christian!

Edward   Ha, ha, ha, ha!

And he throws his arms round **McGinty**.

Tempter, begone! (*Then sighs.*) Oh my friend, I am so ashamed and want for money.

McGinty   Want for? Pooh-pooh! Do you see yon smoke, Sir, rising up among the trees?

Edward   Where?

McGinty   There.

Edward   Rising from – cottage?

McGinty   Your cottage.

Edward   My cottage.

McGinty   And do you know how much it's worth, Sir?

Edward   How much, Sir?

McGinty   A full one hundred and fifty pounds, Sir.

Edward   A full . . . (*And mouths the rest of it.*)

McGinty (*to himself*)   I have him.

Edward (*to himself*)   Is he be pulling a trick down the sleeve of his mind? (*He points at* **McGinty**, *breaking away from him, laughing.*) Aaaaaa . . . !

McGinty   The idiot's going to confuse it. Young Sir?

Edward   Do you know, do you know who had that cottage built, McGinty?

McGinty   Your father had that cottage built – *Kilcullen*.

Edward   My father had that cottage built, McGinty.

McGinty   And you came into it by the deed that's in your pocket on the day that you were born.

Edward   Is – that – so?! Well, can you tell me, then, by whom it was first occupied?! On the day that I was born.

McGinty   By a Mr Clancy.

Edward   By a Mr Clancy, McGinty.

McGinty   Bartholemew Clancy – *Kilcullen*.

Edward   Who?

McGinty (*to himself*)   This is stumbling search for cunning.
Your point of argument, Sir.

Edward   Who lives there now?

McGinty   You do.

Edward   I do! I do!

McGinty   And your point!

Edward   Where do you live?

McGinty   Brick house yonder.

Edward   Brick house yonder, and see! – (*points*) – no smoke
curlings. But see – there! – smoke rising up among yon trees?

McGinty (*exasperated*)   And 'tis well established that you live
there!

Edward   And no one else?

McGinty   Your family!

Edward   Beg pardon?

McGinty   Family!

Edward   . . . Exactly! And you counsel me to sell it? Take
a – a *nest* from a mourning bird and her – her *chick*! Make of
them wandering – *scratchers* – of the world! And for what?
I ask you! To put a little – *pelf* – into these leprous hands of
mine – one hundred and fifty pounds, pah! – and to then
squander it on – *rum*?!

McGinty (*to himself, 'I see'*)   I shall have to up the offer. But
I must have that cottage.

Edward   And I must now go home.

McGinty   But not thus! You should first wash, refresh yourself.

Edward   Ought I?

McGinty   Yes!

Edward   Should I?

McGinty   Come with me.

Edward   Is it indeed for the best?

McGinty   Yes!

Edward   And not too late?

McGinty   No! And I have – *rum*?

Edward   Brandy.

McGinty   A *feast* of it.

Edward   Well . . . But you are dry, McGinty, dull and steady. No man sits down with Teddy that don't drink glass for glass with him.

McGinty   Why, I can drink like an emperor.

Edward   Can you?

McGinty (*exiting*)   This way! Come!

Edward   We shall see who is last to finish first under the table.

He exits, following **McGinty**. *And* **Agnes** *now enters, cautiously, to watch him go. Now she looks about, as* **Edward** *did earlier.*

Agnes   No one sees.

And she goes to the tree to draw from the hollow an imaginary bottle – or the empty one. She drinks from it, and:

Aaaaaa! (*And again, and:*) Aaaaaa!

The moon is in and out of the clouds and shadows appear to move.
Agnes, *a substantial fairy, dances in and out of the pools of light and talks to 'people'.*

When we are married, will you come and visit? We shall live but a little way away. In the valley, my dear. (*To another pool of light. She appears to be pouring tea.*) This is special. For when I lived in the big house there was a blend that Mrs Kilcullen liked: not to my stomach. No, taste this. Dock tea. What did I tell you? From your own back yard, made from the seeds of the dock.

She thinks she hears something, and she is poised to run if needs be. She forgets it.

> We shall live down the valley
> In a house all painted red –

Again, she thinks she hears something. And forgets it.

> And every day the birds will come
> To pick the crumbs of bread.

Indeed, she has heard something, because two crouched **Figures**, *using the shadows for cover, are entering stealthily . . . One* **Figure** *now is whispering:*

Figure   Hist! Do not make a sound . . . Be ready to spring if she tries to escape . . . Hist! Cut her off!

The last because **Agnes** *is now darting this way and that, to escape. The* **Figures** *are* **Rencelaw** *and* **William**. *We establish who they are at whatever point. They have cut off* **Agnes**'s *escape. She is frightened, but a kind of delighted terror, too, is growing in her. She begins to tremble, half-laughing, half-crying, half-defiant; indeed provocatively.*

Agnes   Kisses they are plenty as the blossoms on a tree!

Rencelaw (*whispering*)   Miss Agnes . . . Miss Agnes . . . I am a friend to the unfortunate . . . Hist! Cut her off!

Agnes (*has darted again; stopped*)   Kisses they are plenty as the blossoms on a tree!

Rencelaw   We may yet need the net, William . . . Miss Agnes, it is I, Sir Arden Rencelaw.

Agnes (*darts again, stops, and*)   Oh, kisses they are plenty!

William (*tearfully*)   Oh, Sir, be you sure that you know what you're doing with my sister?

They are closing in on **Agnes**; *all three, dipping, swaying, lunging, as in a kind of dance.*

Rencelaw (*singing quietly*)   'Oh kisses they are plenty' – I am taking her back to the big city, honest William, and putting her into care – 'Oh kisses they are plenty as the – ' to have her malady treated. Don'tcha know. And you shall accompany us – Hist! Cut her off!

Agnes (*darted again, stopped again*)   'Kisses they are plenty as the blossoms on the tree!'

Rencelaw   And I suspect she is the key to much that is awry in these parts. Sing, William!

Rencelaw *and* **William** *sing the following as they close in on* **Agnes**.

> Oh kisses they are plenty
> As the blossoms on a tree.
> And they be one and twenty
> And are sweet to you and me;
> And some are for the forehead,
> And some are for the lips,
> And some are for the rosy cheeks,
> And some for fingertips;
> And some are for the dimples,
> But the sweetest one is this –

Agnes
> When the bonny, bonny sweetheart
> Gives his lady bride a kiss.

During the above, **Rencelaw**, *magically – as only he can – has produced a stream of long, coloured ribbons, which – with* **William**'s *assistance – is cast over/draped upon* **Agnes**, *calming the trembling* *creature. She is tearful, but smiles at them, and she walks off with them, her pages, like a bride.*

Music.

In the transition, **Edward** *and* **McGinty** *appear.* **Edward** *first, backing away from* **McGinty**, *pointing at him with the rolled-up document (deeds to the cottage), laughing.*

Edward   Aaaaaaaa . . . !

Both are drunk. **McGinty**, *indeed, who is following, is drunk to the point of being on his hands and knees, his hand reaching out to the document.*

McGinty   Let me touch it . . . Let me hold it . . . Let me feel it . . .

Edward   But look you!

He unrolls the document, shows it to **McGinty**.

McGinty   I'll give you, I'll give you . . . What did I last offer you?

Edward   But look! Two names on it, two signatures: my name and my wife's name.

McGinty   Nife's wame? Nife's wame?

Edward   You are, Maginty, killarneyed! Blind drunk! (*And exits.*) 'I've been drinking, I've been drinking where were wine and brandy good . . . '

McGinty   Nife's wame? . . . Wife's name! (*Thinks about it. And holds up his finger: he has the solution.*) I'll have that cottage. I'll have everything the Kilcullens ever owned. Why? It suits me – *pleases* – to brood upon it now.

Old Patrick-Joseph-Paddy-Joe, ever a man for counting his possessions and his beads, tracked me one day, feather by feather, to a chicken I had plucked from his yard. I was a boy of ten, and barefoot. He gave me personal pardon, soundly, with his whip, which I accepted and expected – which gratified me! For had he chosen to yield me to the authorities – minor though the offence – it would have meant imprisonment for someone of my station. But when he then informed me that he *pitied* me? In that moment I discovered myself. That he despised me thereafter is of no issue. From that moment I hated with an intensity – ha, ha, ha! – that has existed beyond the grave, descending unimpaired to his expensively educated 'clever' son. By cunning – of which I have in plenty! Is it not superior to hypocrisy? –I wormed back into favour – each wriggle nurturing within the spite I harboured – until I became necessary to him, indispensable – he all the while despising me – Ha, ha, ha, ha! What triumph then when in his dying hours his papers were delivered to my hands, what sweet revenge – *and* opportunity! I prepared a new will and, to sign it, I engaged a master forger, my brother, who then emigrated; but lest he should return to blackmail me, I dared not destroy the real will but cached it in a secret place.

I'll have that cottage. And I take this pledge: never again shall a drop of alcoholic liquor pass Phelim McGinty's lips until his mission is accomplished.

Scene Six

Interior, cottage. An oil lamp burns. A want of comfort now. **Alanna** *will enter in a moment. She is a child.*

Arabella   Heaven, weigh not this poor creature down with woes beyond her strength to bear. Much I fear my suffering mother never can survive this night, and Edward comes not. And when he does arrive, how will he be? Oh misery! This agony of suspense. Heaven, aid this wife who is now six years a mother.

Enter **Alanna**.

Alanna   Dearest Mother, do not cry.

Arabella   Forgive me, dear Alanna, but I sometimes cannot help it.

Alanna   I feel so sorry when you cry.

Arabella   There now: I am composed again.

Alanna   But when you cry it makes me want to cry too.

Arabella   My angel child! It is unjust of your mother to indulge her feelings. Have you eaten up your supper?

Alanna (*nods, then*)   I cry too each night when Father comes home late.

Arabella   When he arrives, smile, kiss him and then be very, very quiet.

Alanna (*nods, then*)   But when I kiss him, Mother, his face is hot as fire or cold as ice.

Arabella (*'Hush'*) – Is that a step?

Alanna   And why is he so pale, Mother?

Arabella (*to herself; her voice is trembling*)   I do not know.

Alanna   Mother, is he very ill?

Arabella, *to conceal her emotion, turns her back, shakes her head.*

Alanna   What makes him so very ill, Mother?

Arabella   He is perhaps unhappy with me.

She is weeping, goes to the 'window' to conceal it.

Alanna   Dear Grandmama too. Will she die tonight, Mother? Mother, will she die tonight?

Arabella   Father of Mercies – Be quiet, Alanna! Hush, my sweet innocence. I go to look in on her again. (*As she exits.*) Oh, religion!

Alanna   Poor Mother: the colour drains from her face and her lips quiver. Oh religion, sweet solace, support this family in these horrible, horrible trials.

A knock at the door.

Enter!

William *comes in. He is dressed for travelling and has his belongings in a roll.*

William   Alanna, darling! You're huge! You are! A foot taller and a power comelier every time I see you – huge!

Alanna   Mr Earley!

William   Be your father not at home yet?

She shakes her head.

And your mam?

Alanna *puts a finger to her lips and points.*

William   A-sittin' with the grandma. How is the poor creature?

Alanna   The nurse was here and shook her head, Father Harty held her hand and prayed in Latin.

William   Latin: The game is up then. She's kitted to take off.

Arabella *comes in.*

Arabella   William!

William   Ma'am!

Arabella   Have you seen Edward?

William   Why, I saw him earlier outside the – in the village and he bade me to precede him – and that no one was to fret, mind! – and I'm sure he'll soon be here sure.

Arabella   Ever a good and loyal friend, William. Alanna, sit with your grandma.

Alanna   Yes, Mother. (*Exit.*)

Arabella   Was he . . . ? How to frame my question. Is he sober?

William   Oh! He . . .

Arabella   William?

William   Then I mustn't tell a lie, Ma'am. He'd been taking – *some* – intoxicating liquor: I'd have to say that: I would. But, then, maybe not that much maybe: and maybe all'll maybe'll be well.

Arabella   Oh, heavens, if something could restore him to his former self. But you are all dressed up!

William (*proud of himself*)   And somewhere to go!

Arabella   Oh?

Alanna *comes in for the Bible and stays to register the reference to* **Rencelaw** *before going out again.*

William   I'm off to the big city in the post chaise tonight with my little half-crazed sister Agnes. See what might be done about her malady. Sir Arden Rencelaw himself –

Arabella   Oh! –

William   Yes! – has took an interest and is gone before us on his steed.

Arabella   The world famous philanthropist!

William   Friend to the unfortunate!

Arabella   That great, good man!

William   Sure, he played the penny whistle at your wedding sure!

Arabella   I have done a likeness of him which hangs over our bed.

William   Whist!

Edward (*without*)   'Wine cures the gout and whiskey makes you sing . . . '

Arabella   'Tis Edward!

Edward (*without*)   'Stout makes you fat, but – ' Ow! Ow!

Arabella   He has fallen!

William   'Tis Edward right enough.

Edward   'But good brandy makes you king!' (*Entering.*)

Arabella   Edward!

Edward   Who else should it be?

William   Ho, Ned!

Edward   Oh! You have company. Why, each time that I come home, is there a man here?

Arabella   He has come to –

Edward   So, it's stableboys now!

Arabella   Edward! –

Edward   What is your purpose in having a servant here at this hour?

Arabella   Servant? – He is our friend

Edward   Out of my house! –

Arabella   Edward! – Our last loyal friend!

Edward   Your friend, not my friend, I have no friends!

Arabella   He has come to say goodbye.

Edward   Goodbye, farewell, good riddance!

Arabella (*whispers*)   Go, William.

William   He's not himself, Ma'am. When he sleeps it off –

Edward   Still here! And *whispering* together? Leave, before I knock you down, Sir!

William   I'm going, Ned – I just called to –

Edward   Out of my house

William   Farewell, friend –

Edward   Out of my house

William   Fare you well. (*Exit.*)

Edward   Farewell! (*Muttering.*) Farewell.

Arabella   Sit, my dear.

Edward   Do you have to tell me?

Arabella   Hush! Where were you?

Edward   Questions?!

Arabella   It's twenty-four hours since you crossed that threshold.

Edward   Why remind me? 'I've been drinking, I've been drinking where were wine and brandy good – '

Arabella   I'll fetch your supper – (*Moving to go out.*)

Edward   'And I'm thinking and I'm thinking how to get out of the wood!'

Arabella   Oh hush, dearest, hush, oh hush –

Edward   Am I a child that I should remain silent in my own house?!

Arabella   Edward, Mother is –

Edward   This house that I could have sold tonight but for – Never mind! I sacrifice myself for everyone!

Arabella (*to herself*)   I must restrain myself. Our house, dear. Your daughter's house, yours and mine.

Alanna (*entering, coming to kiss him*)   Father! Dear Father –

Edward   Keep off! I'm hot enough as it is. (*Muttering.*) This is what I come home to – 'Where were you?' 'Hush, dearest.' Five, six years now I have borne these questions and complaints, endured food that you would not –

Arabella   *You* have borne, *you* have endured!

Edward   What's this?!

Arabella (*to herself*)   I *cannot* restrain myself.

Edward   What say you – *woman*?!

Arabella   Alanna, sit again with Grandmama.

Alanna (*whispers*)   His face is cut, Mother. (*And exit.*)

Arabella   You have borne, you have endured? And what have we borne and endured?

Edward   Insurrection!

Arabella   Without murmur! Maybe I, and *others*, were not nursed in the lap of luxury and so cannot mourn the comforts of ancestral halls, but have I not seen this once-warm home stripped and discomfited to a shell? Are we so unlike you – do *we* have no feelings – that we bear, endure, sacrifice, suffer nothing? Have we not had to watch you, day by day, sink to the footing of an outcast? Everywhere but here. Have we not been in receipt of your broken temper? Have I not seen your intelligence – everything about you! – coarsened and obscured by that infatuation of yours that my heart sickens to think upon, that my lips refuse to name?

Edward   Ho – ho! Well – *Madam* – granted that you have all this – martyrdom – you have still the satisfaction of your sex – to *talk* about it.

Arabella   It pleases you, too, to cheaply wound with glibness.

Edward   Well then, if I be sunk so low and grown so hideous, pray, do not longer violate the delicacy of your feelings, but . . . (*He indicates the door.*)

Arabella   Leave you. (*To herself.*)

Edward   And take with you your darling daughter.

Arabella (*to herself*)   How easy. No. Though you have brought us to this, though you have banished relations and every last friend from our home, though you draw the contempt of the world upon your head, though you are a mark for the good to grieve at, the vain to scoff, though abuse be levelled at you – and at us – you are still my daughter's father and my husband; though, in you, those designations – father and husband, both are now coupled with the opprobrious, scurrilous and shameful epithet of . . .

Edward   Complete your sentences. Of? . . . (*Shouts.*) I –
am – not – a – drunkard! It pleases you to punish with
imputation my sensitivity. I – am– not – a – drunkard! It
pleases you to impugn, with vices I do not possess, this
unlucky character. Why? Because – Madam! – behind your
persecution, the vice that you so carefully avoid to mention is
my lack of means, which deprives you of the life of sloth that
you would lead, which deprives you of the silks, feathers and
frippery that your vanity craves!

Arabella (*to herself*)   My vanity.

Edward   Hah! I have hit it.

Arabella   Do you believe, Sir, that only vanity has hunger,
that only empty pride of dress has appetite? Are these the
only wants and cravings? Know you how the food for your
supper was procured? How – was – it – procured? By what
magic came it here? How did I come by the money?

Edward (*dark, threatening; suspicion, jealousy*)   By what means?
How was it procured?

Arabella   For 'tis long since I received financial help from
you.

Edward   How? – Tell me! – Speak! How came you by the
money? Satisfy me or, by heaven and by hell's damnation,
you shall know all about it from me! (*His fist is raised.*)

Arabella (*holds out her hand*)   You do not even notice its
absence. Your ring. Your ring bought your supper. Your ring
provided you with the money you so artfully took from the
box before leaving here yesterday. The ring that was fixed
upon my finger by a gentle, loving, honourable, young man
called Edward, was wrested from its holy place to buy a little
food and to purchase intoxication for a degraded, selfish
drunkard. (*She is weeping.*)

*He backs away, aghast. She continues to weep. The following is very
gentle, in whispers, or little more than whispers.*

Edward   Bella.

Arabella   Dearest?

Edward   Arabella.

Arabella   Dearest?

Edward   All reveals your constancy, my disgrace.

Arabella   No. No.

Edward   No. No.

Arabella   Dearest, dearest, do not think that.

Edward   No. No.

Arabella   Forgive me for speaking thus.

Edward   No. No.

Arabella   Besides, all is past now.

Edward   No. No. I must leave.

Arabella   No, Edward, my adored.

Edward   No.

Alanna *is entering.*

Arabella   I'll do anything – I shall enlist aid from *somewhere.* There must be – *someone* – to whom we can apply for help!

Edward   I must leave for ever.

Arabella   No –

Alanna   Father –

Arabella   My husband!

Edward   Father, husband? (*He shakes his head, 'No.'*) Curse me as your destroyer.

Arabella   I shall follow wherever you go!

Edward   Forget this unfortunate man who never will forget you! (*He rushes out.*)

Alanna (*running out*)   Father!

Arabella (*follows*)   Edward!

Alanna   Faather!

Arabella   Edwaard!

Alanna   Faaather!

Arabella   Edwaaard!

Their voices continue, off, growing more distant and becoming distorted by the howling wind that has risen and that continues to the end of the scene.

The stage is empty. A breeze is catching the flame in the oil lamp, which, in turn, is casting shadows about the room; a nimbus appears to be forming round a shadow, creating – could it be? – the figure of an old man. And the ancient **Mother***, in shroud/nightdress, is now entering, her arms reaching out to the haloed, ghostly thing:*

Mother   Bartholomew! . . . I'm coming! . . . We are together again . . . Take me! . . .

The oil lamp flickers and gutters to its last. Music.

Act Two

Scene One

City street/alleyway. On the ground, there is what looks like a heap of rags and litter.

Rencelaw   Another year has come and gone. A new day has passed its noontide. Our hero awakens.

The rags and litter have stirred: **Edward**, *slowly sitting up. His condition has deteriorated. He looks terrible.*

Rencelaw   He sleeps now on the street. What his morning prayer? His thought? Feelings? Everything for him now starts and finishes in a bottle. City life speeds the downhill course.

Now two **Loafers**, *one each side of* **Edward**, *are waking up with headaches, coughs and what-have-you.*

Loafer 1   Oooooofff – ah-hah-haaa! Does I need a drink?

Loafer 2   Does *yous* need a drink? Oooooofff – ah-hah-haaa!

Edward   Is't tomorrow?

Loafer 1   Does he need a – Ah, ha, ha, ha, ha!

Leading to a bout of phlegmatic coughing and laughing from the three of them.

Rencelaw   Can habitual intoxication stand as epitome of every crime? Is't too harsh to make such claim? A Roman stoic – regarded as my near equal for imperturbable temper and balanced judgement – seeking to fix stigma on the man who had ruined his sister, called him not knave, destroyer, debauchee or villain, but wreaked every odium with one word, drunkard. And is it not at least debatable that all the vices that stain our nature may find ready germination in that state, and wait but little time to sprout forth in pestilential rankness?

But I leave perusal of the thought with you, for at this point in the narrative I am away in Switzerland, enlisting the opinion of Dr Carl Freung in the matter of Agnes Earley's malady, which, surprisingly, was proving recalcitrant to my solo efforts at renovation. (*To himself.*) A pretty girl. Don'tcha know. (*And exits.*)

A woman – **Floozie 1** *– oldish, down-and-out, is entering, followed by* **McGinty**. *She points at* **Edward**.

Floozie   Would that bowsie be your man, Sir?

Edward   I feel most shockingly.

Floozie   Him, round here, we do call Lord Teddy.

McGinty *gives her a coin and she retires.*

McGinty   There's the drunken vagrant.

Edward   I am quite on fire.

Loafer 1   Cheer up, Neddy, you'll soon be dead!

Loafer 2   Do we have the price of a drink?

Edward   'Tis a burning question.

They laugh and cough.

McGinty   With two bright friends. And by the looks of him, he has nothing left to offer by way of resistance to what I want.

Loafer 1 (*has produced a cosh*)   Time to go to work, we need money.

Loafer 2   There'll be more where the last came from.

Loafer 1   Yous stay put, Lord Teddy, mind our furnishings and effects. Joe and me'll take a turn down the docks, a liner from abroad gets in today.

The **Loafers** *exit.*

McGinty   Now for my design on him.

He crosses, affecting to be unaware of **Edward***'s presence.*

Edward   Sir! Sir!

McGinty   Someone calls?

Edward   Charity or a copper – hither, Sir! – for a broken-down soldier.

McGinty   Why, certainly, my poor, brave veteran. Here's something. Oh! Sir! Can it be you, Sir? Master Kilcullen, Sir, luminary, exceller, decoration of the Kilcullen family and empire?

Edward   Beg pardon?

McGinty   Never!

Edward   McGinty?

McGinty   Why, by all that's happy, it is my young master!

Edward   What's left of me.

McGinty   I don't see you much altered. A stitch, maybe two, about the elbows. But you can always count on my friendship for a little charity. Here we are. (*Offers money.*)

Edward   Well . . . (*He hesitates; a bit embarrassed.*)

McGinty   Yes, take it! After all, we are fellow villagers.

Edward   Well . . . Fellow villagers you say? (*Takes money.*)

McGinty   Yes! You once from the big house, I from the little.

Edward   Ha, ha, ha!

McGinty   Ha, ha, ha!

Edward   Dare I ask . . .

McGinty   He's going to ask about his wife and child. Young Sir, Sir?

Edward   Have you seen them?

McGinty   Sir? Oh! Your wife and child. (*Aside.*) I shall not tell him they are in this very town in search of him. They are exceeding well and happy, you'll be glad to hear! Your strange conduct, your – migrating – from them attracted the sympathy of the gentle folk about the area and your wife is given an abundance of washing and sewing. She is quite a favourite, and her pretty face helps.

Edward   She is happy then. (*His head is bowed.*)

McGinty   As the day is long. She is doing charmingly!

Edward   Well, I ought to be glad of it. And I am. And that she thinks no more of me.

McGinty   Oh, she thinks of you!

Edward (*eagerly*)   Does she – does she?

McGinty   Oh, yes! She says, what paradox! misfortune turning blessing. She says she never, ever would have realised the curious friendship of those dear hearts and gentle neighbours had you not left her.

Edward   Did she say that? (*His head is bowed again.*)

McGinty   And more! (*To himself.*) Further cripple him and make him more amenable to my scheme. Young Sir! She says she pities you.

Edward   *Pity?*

McGinty   What else?!

Edward   Well, that is, that is – Cursed taverns not yet open! Well, that is very kind of her, I'm sure.

McGinty   The world deals a tinch unfairly with you, Master Edward?

Edward   It treats me ill, McGinty.

McGinty   It misuses a little?

Edward   It abuses me!

McGinty   And what remedy for the casualty? There is but one. If the world ill treats, be revenged upon the world.

Edward   Revenged? But how?

McGinty   Have a drink.

Edward (*a beat, and*)   Ha, ha, ha!

McGinty   Ha, ha, ha! But, hold! Charity buys but poor revenge, retaliation requires higher fee than what is in your fist. I have it! Do you by chance still have about your person the deeds to that old cottage in the village?

Edward   Here. (*In his pocket.*)

McGinty   Fortunate! And I a purse in mine, containing a full two hundred pounds. All that is required is for the document to be signed.

Edward   But you are aware as I that the document requires two signatures.

McGinty   Easily resolved! You are an excellent penman. How your dear father boasted of your hand when comparing it to my scrawl.

Edward   The plaudits for calligraphy and Vere Foster Prize I won at school so pleased Papa.

McGinty   There you are then, show your skill! Sign your noble name with flourish and, in her fashion, the name of the wife who pities you, and you may laugh vengeance in the world's face.

Edward (*has the document in his hand*)   Ought I?

McGinty   Yes.

Edward   Should I?

McGinty   Yes! Come over here and do the signing.

Off, cheering has been growing in the streets. **Loafers**, *old* **Floozie**, *other* **Floozies** – *as available* – *and* **Bartender** *are entering, like the outlying members of a welcoming throng, laughing at and cheering someone, which distracts* **Edward**.

Edward   Has a war been truced?

McGinty   Yes – but let's –

Edward   Parade? St Patrick's Day?

McGinty   Yes-yes – But let's proceed with the transaction. An assemblage to welcome home that old duffer and affecter, Arden Rencelaw.

He gives his pen to **Edward**.

Edward   What! Do you mean Sir Arden Rencelaw?

McGinty   Yes, that old humbug – Come!

Rencelaw, *as if in an open carriage, is seen over the heads of those present, acknowledging the adoring populace.*

Edward   Do you mean the princely merchant, the noble philanthropist, who in disguise played tin-whistle at my wedding? Whose life-size picture hangs upon the bedroom wall at home, an astonishing likeness done in needlework stitches by my own wife's hand! Do you refer to Sir Arden Rencelaw, the poor man's friend, the orphan's benefactor, the great humanitarian reformer, on whose opinion the State awaits with bated breath, upon whose every sacred word the Church hangs, blessed?

McGinty (*to himself*)   Hot air.

Edward   Whose very presence – even at far proximity – can inspire greatness in others?

McGinty   Blether, blarney, twaddle, malarky. (*He's not impressed by* **Edward** *or* **Rencelaw**.)

Edward   Pardon?

McGinty   Talk!

Edward   Exactly! And talk does not put potatoes on the table of the foolish husband, does it, who stays in bed for half the morning cultivating his wife?! So, you see! (*Moves away, calls to the parade.*) Hooray for Sir Arden! (*Returns.*) Did you come here by any chance, McGinty, to bribe me with this so-called charity? Did you mean, Sir, that I should commit a forgery with this? (*Pen.*) For shame! Shocking! Out and out with you for a villain and a coward that you dare propose such baseness to my father's son!

McGinty (*to himself*)   A final fiddle-faddling puff of self-indulgent righteousness.

Edward   I would sooner perish on a dunghill.

McGinty   Would you?

Edward   Take back your poisoned quill!

He joins the others, cheering, laughing. 'Hooray, shipmates, hooray!'

McGinty   A last lickspittling token to virtue. The game is up. He returned the villain's 'poisoned quill', did he return the 'so-called charity' was given him? Yes, the ember may flicker but, anon, when he is moistened and burns for drenching, we shall see his true passion flare. My aspiration will fulfil itself before the night is out – with *bonus*. The wife – for is not she too a Kilcullen? – will be possessed.

Music. The lighting has changed during the above; it is now night-time and the cheering spectators from the street are raucous in the tavern, calling for drinks.

Scene Two

City tavern. **McGinty** *is here, too, watching, encouraging. The* **Bartender** *is a busy man.*

Bartender   Yes sir, yes sir, yes sir, yes sir!

Loafer 1   Whiskey there! –

Edward   Brandy here! –

Loafer 1   And for you, Joe? –

Loafer 2   A rum-rum-rum!

Bartender   Whiskey there, brandy here and a rum-rum-rum-rum-rum!

Loafer 1   Whiskey!

Edward   Brandy!

Loafer 2   Rum-rum-rum!

Bartender   Yes sir, yes sir, coming up!

Loafer 1   And for the ladies?!

Bartender   Three teas! With cakes or muffins, girls?

Floozies   And we'll pay you back with crumpet! (*Laughter.*)

Floozie 1 (*old whore*)   I'll have what killed Goliath!

Floozies 2 *and* **3**   A gin-sling! (*Laughter.*)

Bartender   Steady on, steady on, don't raise a row in a decent house!

Laughter, jeers, cheers. Toasts.

Edward   Here's to the maiden of bashful fifteen!

Loafer 1   Here's to the widow of fifty!

Bartender   Here! Give that to her highness, Pock Alley's Queen! (*A drink to be passed to* **Floozie 1**.)

Edward   To parchment-and-ink face, Sir Thrifty! (*Mocking* **McGinty**.)

McGinty   Here's to this lass with a bosom of snow!

He is moving/easing **Floozie 2** *towards* **Edward**.

Loafer 1   And to this one, brown as a berry!

Edward (*to* **Floozie 2**)   Here's to the wife with a face full of woe!

Floozie 1   Here's to myself that gets merry!

Edward, *above, has drawn* **Floozie 2** *to himself. Now he is backing away from her – he shakes his head as if to wake up. She looks, strangely, like* **Arabella**.

McGinty (*whispers to* **Floozie 2**)   Follow him, lass, follow him, lass – I'll warrant you'll prove an excuse for a glass.

Edward   'Nother round, another round!

Bartender   Yes sir, yes sir, yes sir, yes sir!

Loafer 1   Whiskey there! –

Edward   Brandy here!

Loafer 1   And for you, Joe?

Loafer 2   A rum-rum-rum!

Bartender   Whiskey there, brandy here and a rum-rum-rum-rum-rum!

Loafer 1   And for the ladies?!

Floozie 1   I'll have what killed Goliath!

Floozies 2 *and* **3**   A gin-sling!

Bartender   Steady on, steady on, don't raise a row!

Laughter, cheers, jeers.

Edward   Come, come, everybody! Is someone dead, this somebody's funeral, someone going to preach sermon?! Come, come!

Floozie 2   Then sing us a song!

Floozie 1   I'll sing a song!

Loafer 1   No, *he'll* sing a song! –

Edward   Neither of you shall sing a song! –

Floozie 1 (*singing, raucously*)   'Years ago out in the wilds of Australia – '

Edward   I'm master here! – Silence!

Bartender   No quarrelling, no quarrelling!

Edward   *He* shall sing a song – Joe!

Loafer 2
'Here's a health to the King and a lasting peace,
To faction an end, to wealth increase,
Come let us drink while we have breath'

All
'For there's no drinking after death –'

Loafer 2
'And he that will this health deny – '

All
'Down among the dead men
Down among the dead men – '

Loafer 2
'Down, down, down, down – '

All
'Down among the dead men let him lie.'

Edward, *revelling, sings the second verse. He is drawn to* **Floozie 2**; *his eyes are glazed, he circles her, he dances with her.*

Edward
In smiling Bacchus' joys I'll roll,
Deny no pleasure to my soul,
Let Bacchus' health round briskly move,
For Bacchus is a friend to love,
And he that will this health deny –

All
Down among the dead men let him lie –

They are amused at **Edward**'*s attention to* **Floozie 2**.

Edward   Your name, please.

Floozie 2   Can you not guess?

Edward   I should not like, Miss, actually, to hazard one, just now.

Floozie 2   Why it's . . . Prudence, of course. (*Laughter.*)

Floozie 3   Mine's Patience!

Floozie 1   And mine's Chastity!

Laughter, together with **Edward**'*s inordinate pleasure (and relief that* **Floozie 2** *isn't called* **Arabella**). *He keeps repeating the name.*

Edward   Prudence! Prudence!

Loafer 1   Lord Teddy's made a conquest!

Edward   Everybody, her name is Prudence!

Floozie 2   And yours, Sir?

Edward   Temperance!

All   Ha, ha, ha, ha, ha, ha, ha . . . !

Floozies
    May love and wine their rites maintain,
    And their united pleasures reign,
    While Bacchus' treasure crowns the board,
    We'll sing the joys that both afford,
    And they that won't with us comply –

Others
    Down among the dead men let them lie!

Edward   This calls for another round! Bartender, another
round!

Bartender (*a beat, and*)   You've perhaps the money in your
purse?

Edward   Perhaps I have – Ha, ha, ha!

Bartender   Then perhaps I can see it so that neither of us
is in doubt.

Floozies (*with others, as appropriate; quietly*)   'Down among the
dead men, down among the dead men . . . '

Edward *has searched his pockets: he has no money. He looks at*
Loafer 1 *who is also broke.*

Edward (*a plea*)   Sir, pour me a brandy . . . One more . . .
One . . . An ale, then . . .

Floozies (*and others*)   'Down, down, down, down – '

Edward   I must have a drink.

Floozies (*and others*)   'Down among the dead men let him lie.'

Bartender *is unforthcoming.*

Edward *(to himself)*   I must have a drink.

And **McGinty** *comes forward with his pen in one hand and a large roll of money in the other.* **Edward** *takes the document from his pocket and the pen from* **McGinty**.

Edward   Is this the end then? And that I am an object of pity to my once adoring wife. The friendship of others has made up my loss. I am a wretch with but one resource: liquor.

McGinty   Two signatures, yours and your wife's.

He is poised to sign the document; he pauses for the briefest moment to half-register a call from (the now near-dark) behind him:

Loafer 1   Prudence awaits you!

And he signs, gives the document to **McGinty**, *who, in turn, gives* **Edward** *the large roll of money.* **McGinty** *leaves. And* **Edward** *goes to the counter and puts the roll of money into the* **Bartender**'s *hand.*

Edward   You will, I know, Sir, be good enough to tell me when that is drunk.

Music.

Scene Three

A wretched garret. A single lamp burns dimly, by which **Arabella** *sits, sewing 'slop-work', an old shawl about her shoulders.* **Alanna** *is on a straw bed, pretending to be asleep.*

Arabella   Where is he on this very bitter night? In vain have I made every effort to gain tidings of his whereabouts. *(She is prey to her imagination.)* He is alone and he is ill! Even to enlist the help of Lawyer McGinty, whose offices I chanced upon today when abroad the streets in search of a few shavings. *(Prey to her imagination.)* He is fallen down and no one comes to his assistance! These shirts must be handed in by eight. My industry will be repaid by a miserable two shillings. (*Prey to her imagination again.*) He is the inmate of a prison! But at least, with that little money there shall be some kind of food upon the table for my child.

Alanna   I am so cold, but I shall not let dear mother know for she is careworn as it is, faint with hunger and fatigued from work. In the morning I shall be able to warm myself at Mrs O'Brien's fire downstairs. Little Dennis, her son, with whom I sometimes play, told me that I should. The mother of that little boy is blessed.

Arabella   My sweet lamb sleeps, and sleep offers some relief. (*Her imagination again.*) The earth is already closed over him!

*She steals to the bed and covers **Alanna** with her shawl.*

Arabella   Still, that ever I should see his child thus.

A clock chimes one. She returns to her work:

One o' clock, my work not yet near finished. Merciful heaven, restore to me my Edward and I shall pay any price, bear every burden, accept any hardship that . . . that can . . . that can be . . . heaped . . . upon me.

She is nodding to sleep. **Alanna** *watches, and to encourage her mother's sleep she begins to sing, softly:*

Alanna
Oh Mother-my-love, if you'll give me your hand
And go where I ask you to wander,
I'll lead us away to a beautiful land –
The Dreamland that's waiting out yonder.

Arabella *is asleep.* **Alanna** *has tiptoed from the bed, and returns the shawl to her mother's shoulders:*

Alanna   Ah, Mother, you tried to trick your little darling by giving me your shawl.

She takes up the work – shirts – and begins sewing them, one eye on her mother.

Arabella *stirs in her sleep.* **Alanna** *sings.*

Alanna
   I'll rock you to sleep on a silver-dew stream,
   And sing you asleep when you're weary,
   And no one shall know of our beautiful dream
   But you and your own little dearie.

Arabella (*in her sleep*)   Edward.

Alanna   We shall find him, Mother.

Arabella (*in her sleep*)   Edward.

Alanna   We shall find him. With the help of God, and the aid of my secret friend to whom I shall write yet again. (*And she sings:*)

   So Mother-my-love, let me take your dear hand
   And away through the starlight we'll wander,
   Away through the mists to the beautiful land
   The Dreamland that's waiting out yonder.

A knock at the door.

(*Whispers to herself.*) Father!

Arabella (*awakened*)   Who can that be?

Alanna   It is Father!

Arabella   Ah, that it were he! (*Calls.*) Yes?

And **McGinty** *enters.*

McGinty   The lovely Mrs Kilcullen! – Good evening, good evening!

Arabella   Sir! (*Curtseys.*) Good evening! But – *evening*?

McGinty   I saw your light as I was passing, remembered your address from our meeting today and friends are welcome at all hours and seasons?

Arabella 'Tis an untimely hour to visit, Sir, but if you have come with ought of Edward's whereabouts, even the slenderest of tidings, you would be welcome at any time.

McGinty Ah, the dear child! Here's a sixpence for you, take my hat and cane to the next room and wait there.

Alanna There is no other room.

McGinty Hmm! Not the most commodious for the interview I have in mind. May I suggest immediate alternative accommodation for the two of us?

Arabella Heaven help us, where could we go?

McGinty To a little – nest? You must know that I'm a man of means and can supply – the feathers?

Arabella Nest, feathers?

McGinty A reward for your compliance.

Arabella Ah! You refer to our cottage in the village. How we long for return to our home! But we made a vow to remain in this poor place until Edward is discovered.

McGinty So be it then!

Arabella What news, Sir, of him?

McGinty Young, young, *beautiful* lady, I find this infatuation of yours most strange!

Arabella Sir? Do you find love strange?

McGinty Indeed I do! And it would appear there is no cure for it but marriage. 'Tis very strange. And stranger still, since the love object in the case in point is a foolish, no-good, indolent profligate.

Arabella Sir, is it of my husband that you speak?

McGinty I mean no offence, but of – who else?!

Arabella Then he is alive!

McGinty And kicking!

Arabella   Thank heavens!

McGinty   Thank heavens, yes! And does charmingly in a circle of companions, whose company, clearly, he prefers to yours.

She takes a step backwards.

I mean not to distress, but a woman, practical as she is beautiful, should like to know the facts in order to take further 'dancing' steps. And to apprise you more of the company he keeps: with the male half, his revels are of one kind; tired of that, the sociability of the other half consoles.

Arabella *(another step backwards; and a whisper)*   Oh Sir, what do you say to me?

McGinty   I mean not to distress, my dear, but the things I speak of have always been, and will be, while the two sexes exist, let alone where there are drunkards on the one side and harlots on the other.

Arabella *(a whisper)*   Oh Sir, this cannot be, oh Sir, do not break my heart.

McGinty   My dear young lady, I fear it is so, and you know it is so, and a woman of your intelligence will begin immediately to salvage her one big mistake in life. Give me your hand.

She complies. She appears transfixed by him. He strokes her hand.

Arabella   What mistake?

McGinty   Choice of poor man.

Arabella   What? Nothing of what you say is true.

She comes to, snatches her hand away.

McGinty   Come, come, my dear, this part of the scene is unnecessary!

Arabella   You lie! You calumniate my husband – I know you do! – You lie like a rascal! – And now you slander me – and before a child! Gaze on her features where famine has already set its seal, look on this hapless woman who brought her into the world, then, if you have heart, speak further insult to us!

McGinty   The heart, hah! A little red dripping barrel of cruelty.

Arabella   I love my husband! I love him the more because he *is* poor, forsaken and reviled. It is why I follow him!

McGinty   He laughs at you in his drunken ribaldry!

Arabella (*tearfully*)   False! That is false – He would never laugh at me! False! False! The fault of my husband, the *only* fault, is his intemperance – Terrible, terrible, I acknowledge! But it is an illness! Call it a weakness, if you will, but it is one that has assailed the finest and most sensitive intellects of mankind: men who, though prostrated with the affliction, would, to the very last, scorn you and your kind – *your* sickness, your moral deformity and warped philosophy!

McGinty   I must say it is a good game you play.

Arabella   Game?!

McGinty   Yes. And you are proficient in the craft of tears.

He takes her hand again.

Arabella (*snatches her hand away*)   You are contemptible.

McGinty   Ha, ha, ha!

Arabella   Now you reveal the real purpose in your coming here. Get out!

McGinty   You know it better than I: a woman cannot have purity and intelligence, both.

Arabella   You scoundrel!

McGinty   Rapscallion!

Arabella   Ruffian!

McGinty   Scapegrace, slubberdegullion!

Arabella   Knave!

McGinty   Ha, ha, ha! You are young and you know it, beautiful – you know it – I desire you, you will yield to me and you know it –

Arabella   Unhand me! You are despicable and you *don't* know it! But *know* it, how much I despise you, *know* it that my husband, covered in mire, drunk at my feet –

McGinty   Perishing on a dunghill! –

Arabella   Unhand, unhand me! –

Alanna   Help! Help!

McGinty   You verge too close to insolence now. Remember your circumstances. – Remember it is late, you are helpless and unfriended –

Alanna (*this time, calling out of the window*)   Help! Help! Oh, won't someone come to our aid?

Voice (*without*)   Holloo!

Alanna   Help! Help! –

Voice   Holloo! Holloo!

Alanna   Mr Earley! Mr Earley! It is Mr Earley.

William (*rushes in*)   Mary and Joseph! It's Mrs Kilcullen's little darling, Alanna. And Mrs Kilcullen! And howdydo! What have we here? Oh bo, bo, bo, bo, bo: think of the devil and you meet his first cousin!

McGinty *tries to hide or slope away.*

William   Ho, Squire, you lizard! (*Throws* **McGinty** *about.*) Ho, Mr Honey! What's the lowest you'll take for your skin? Shall I turn auctioneer and knock you down to this bidder? Or this one? – Or here's a higher one!

McGinty   I'm a respectable man –

William   You, a man? Nature made a mistake!

McGinty   Strike me and I'll sue you!

William   Strike me, but if I don't set your paddles going all-fired-quick!

McGinty   I have two witnesses!

William   Out you get or see if I don't play The Wind that Shakes the Barley on your organ of rascality!

Throws him out, down the stairs.

McGinty (*without, tumbling*)   Ow-wow-wow-wow-wow!

William (*finds* **McGinty**'s *hat*)   Well, I declare: a silk hat for a man like that!

McGinty (*without*)   You'll find I have not done with you!

William   Nor I with you! (*Deftly aiming and pitching the hat out at* **McGinty**.)

McGinty (*without*)   Ow!

Arabella   William, ever friend!

William   It did ill behove me, Ma'am, to dust him further in your presence.

Arabella   But how came you upon us so opportunely?

William   Well now, that be a long tale. But mind you of Sir Arden Rencelaw?

Arabella   He is seldom from my mind.

Alanna   We keep his picture.

She takes the lamp to the wall, they follow, and we see **Sir Arden**'s *life-size 'picture' on it.*

Arabella   I would not be without it.

Alanna   We pray to it as we do to God.

Arabella   For anyone who knows Sir Arden Rencelaw wishes to know more of Sir Arden Rencelaw.

William   A truer word was never spoken, Ma'am. Well, on account he's been away in Switzerland with my little half-crazed sister Agnes – the same Agnes, you'll be glad to hear, is now – well, by Sir Arden's remarkable lights – is now but tuppence short of the shilling, but, dang me, if by my lights, there isn't more than tuppence worth of air still getting in up there. (*He means air getting into* **Agnes***'s head.*) Howandever, he did only on his return today get your letter.

Arabella   Letter, William? What letter, I wrote no letter?! (*What a puzzle.*)

Alanna   Please, Mother, I hope it does not vex you, but this picture has become my secret friend and inspired by the noble features delineated in it, I took it on myself to write entreaty to Sir Arden on our behalf.

Arabella   Oh, my child, it does not vex me. (*To* **William**.) And he sent you to us?

William   Aye, that be so.

Arabella   And you have found Edward!

William   Aye, well, that not be so.

Arabella   William?

William   Then I mustn't tell a lie, Ma'am. We haven't found him but, even if we do, by whatever accident Sir Arden's got to know of your Edward's present condition . . .

Arabella   Speak!

William   All efforts now to save his life may have come too late.

Arabella *faints.*

Scene Four

Agnes , *as one in adoration, is gazing at another life-size 'picture' of Sir Arden. (This 'picture' for instance, might be face-on as against the one in the last scene which could be in profile.)*

Agnes   His features. His features.

She carries a crucifix, which, now, she remembers, guiltily.

Oh, Christ's features too, oh our Blessed Saviour's too, of course, too, oh I wouldn't have it otherwise, oh Christ no, Christ knows! But . . . *(wistfully)* his features. Don'tcha know.

We are in the Sir Arden Rencelaw Foundation. **Agnes** *wears an institutional-type dress and she is now scrubbed clean. She appears quite dreamy – some might say lovelorn or, indeed, scatty. But she pulls herself together to get on with the business of the play.*

For three days now are we returned and for three days he has been abroad the city streets . . . *(She forgets her purpose.)* And I miss his daily instruction. *(She assumes* **Rencelaw***'s bearing and tone.)* 'With good economy, Miss Agnes, few need be poor.' Without economy, Sir Arden, none can be rich.

Rencelaw *(the 'picture' behind her speaks)*   Everything has a beginning, Miss Agnes, except?

Agnes   Except God.

Rencelaw   Don'tcha know.

She pulls herself together.

Agnes   For three days now are we returned from Switzerland and for three days he has been abroad the city streets, assiduously preaching temperance, and in desperate search of another soul to save: that of Young Edward Kilcullen. *(Beat.)* And I miss him. He says – with look I know not what to make of –

Rencelaw   You may address me, Miss Agnes, by my first name.

Agnes *(silently, whispered:)*   Arden. But I am much too shy.

Rencelaw   Address me by my first name –

Agnes   He says –

Rencelaw   Don'tcha know.

Agnes   Can't. And I am very much improved, he says, and how pleased his countenance that I respond to his tuition.

Rencelaw   Cabbage and carrots were unknown before?

Agnes   1545.

Rencelaw   It would take 27,000 spiders to produce?

Agnes   It would take 27,000 spiders to produce one pound of web. I weep with delight when he gives me a smile.

Rencelaw   But one last mist remains –

Agnes   He says, that I must –

Rencelaw (*declaims, frowning*)   Sunder and disperse! (*And he's gone – the 'picture' is gone!*)

Agnes (*now cowering in the corner*)   And I tremble with fear at his frown. (*She is lost. She grows agitated.*) Brake, fern, cypress dell where – no, cabbage, carrots, cypress dell where – no, one pound of spiders to make 27,000 webs – no, no, no! (*Repeat, as necessary. Her mind is reeling and a half-swoon perhaps. Then:*)

A strange fancy keeps forming in my brain: it flits across my mind like a half-forgotten dream: oh, what can it be? A remembrance vague of a moonlit night when I'd concealed myself to observe the strange goings-on of the sane section of mankind . . .

She swoons into a trance and, like one possessed, she begins to speak in a deep voice:

Wait. Wait . . . Night. The moping owl falls silent; night holds its breath, the shadows and the mist subside, hide under the trees, and across the sward, now bathed white in its lunar lover's tide – lo! – a man steals from the big house, *brick* house, *brick* house yonder. And neath his great black coat he conceals . . . What can it be? . . . Wait. A box, tin box, and buries it in the earth, tin box, in cypress dell, midst brake and fern, by the old moss-covered wall. And 'tis honest Lawyer McGinty! . . . I have sundered the last mist. He will be pleased. (*Silently, whispered:*) Arden! Arden! (*It will be a long time beofre she is able to say his name aloud. She does. though, run off excitedly:*) The will – ha, ha, ha!

Scene Five

A stable or outhouse. It is dark but nearing dawn. **Edward** *is on the floor, delirious. He is without coat, hat, shoes; the clothes he wears are torn and dirty. He is in 'the jigs'. At first, perhaps, he is quiet; staring eyes; slowly pulling up his knees and pulling back his bare feet, to protect them from something. His innocent horror. It is as if a tide is coming towards him. He thinks he has escaped, that this 'tide' is moving past him, but – 'Ah!' – something on his arm which he flicks off. But – 'Ah!' – another on his thigh. Another and another, in his hair, his mouth – 'Ah!' 'Thwuh!' . . . An infestation of creepy-crawlies have come for him. They are on his hands, around and in between his fingers. And he cannot yet bring himself to roar. They are making low-pitched sounds – like bees that have invaded his skull; they pant like dogs needing water . . . They are all over him. Now, a growing roar:*

Edward   OooooOOOO! MamaaaAAA! MamaaaAAA! Send them away, send them away, stop them, stop them . . . !

The tide recedes. (Made up of crawling **Floozies** *perhaps, and others as available – but* **Floozies** *in particular.)*

Edward   What hideous place is this, where am I? . . . Is it hell? Dream? Does dream occur after one is dead? . . . Is it night? Morn? Coming morn, coming night? . . . I wanted day but, if it come, what shall I do with light? How to hide my face away from . . . from me? . . . If it be night, how to bear again the unleashed terrors of Dark's enhancing powers? . . . Ah! dawn spreads a rosy hue over night time's troubled skies: the stars at last released from their ticking spasms, but, ah me! It is morn.

Now, again, he tries to make himself smaller, to hide, protect himself This time it is an invasion of snakes. He whimpers:

No . . . No . . . Off . . . Off me . . . Away . . . Get away . . . Take them away . . . Off! Off! (*He appears to be hurtling them away, but one snake is persistent.*) NoooOOO! Take it off me! Take it – MamaaaAAA – get it off me! . . . Mama, it tightens – How it coils – tightens! . . . Dash, dash, dash you to a pulp against the wall!

Snakes, **Figures,** *retiring.*

Edward   I breathe again.

Figures *returning. This time, upright, standing, or nearly so.*

Edward   Nooooo! I am awake – Mama, Papa, tell them that I am awake! Dreams – you are dreams – you are shockingly bad dreams! Will you return upon me when my eyes – see! – are gaping wide? (*Pleads.*) Please you, leave? Please?

Figures *draw back. Every fibre of him is shaking.*

Edward   I should not be so stricken were I in these hands to hold a glass . . . Nor so fearful, despairing, astonished, or ashamed . . . Ashamed? (*He shakes his head, 'No,' wearily.*)

A figure enters, a **Man.** (*He will, later, turn out to be real.*) **Edward** *watches him, at first suspiciously.*

Man   Who left the door open? Where is the horse? Where in blazes is my horse?

Edward   I say, you there!

Man   Who's there?!

Edward   Yes, you there, Landlord Tubbs from the village, pour us a drink!

Man   Who's there, I say!

Edward   It is I, Young Edward Kilcullen!

Man (*assuming a new voice*)   Ah, the scape-gallows, Kilcullen!

Figures   Ha, ha, ha, ha, ha, ha! (*Coming forward.*)

Edward   Scape-gallows – Ha, ha, ha! – Good old Tubbs, ever fond of a jest. You and I have long been friends – Don't draw back! pour us another and be quick about it!

Floozie 1   And the devil's to pay!

Figures   Ha, ha, ha, ha, ha!

Edward   But it is I, Edward Kilcullen, a respected worthy!

Floozie 2   You were that once, Teddy!

Floozie 1   And so was Lucifer!

Figures   Ha, ha, ha, ha, ha!

Edward   Fetch him here! – Tubbs, Tubbs, I am ill, faint, my brain I think's on fire – Give me a drink!

Man   Ho, ho, ho, ho, ho, ho, ho!

Edward   Think how I was when I first entered your shop! Make amends!

Floozie 2   Make amends for what, Lord Teddy?

Edward   Prudence, Prudence! assist me –

Floozie 1   You had your senses –

Floozie 2   Did he compel you in? –

Floozie 3   You walked in the man's door –

Man   Did I invite you in? –

Figures   Ha, ha, ha, ha, ha . . . !

Edward (*angrily, bitterly; overlapping them*)   Ha, ha, ha, ha, ha! Does hell send cards of invitation forth to its fires of torment? Curse you, Tubbs – Curse you all! If it had not been for you and your infernal shops I had been still a man! (*He lies back, whimpering.*)

Rencelaw (*light up on* **Rencelaw**)   The foul shops – dens! – where pockets are plundered, where death and disease are dealt in tumblers – with little thought from the noxious purveyors than to count the profits of the till; from whence goes forth the blast of ruin on our land, stealing and withering the beauty and intelligence of our youth. Youth! Our future! Our promise, pride, joy, our hope, turned into a generation of animals! The waves of that direful sickness extending, leaving none unaffected, wounding to futility the loving relatives, filling the mother's, sister's, brother's hearts with anguish, the widows' with grief, orphans cursed, blighting ambition and all that is glorious in man and casting him from his high estate!

Fade on **Rencelaw**.

Edward   And making of him such as I?

He chuckles, bitterly. **Man** *enters, as before.*

Man   Where, in nature, can my horse have gone?

Edward (*quietly*)   Here is your horse.

Man   Who's there? . . . Who's there, I say!

Edward   You common poisoner! It is I, Young Edward Kilcullen.

He springs on **Man** *and takes him by the throat.*

Man   Murder! Murder!

Edward   I have a claim on you now, a deadly claim –

Man   Release – release me –

Edward   So, a drink, one drink, a single glass –

Man   Let go your hold –

Edward   Or I shall have your last breath!

Man   Help! I am choking! Police! Arrrrrgh!

William (*without*)   Holloo! Holloo! (*Rushing in.*) What goes here?

He pulls **Edward** *off* **Man**. **Edward** *falls back.* **Man** *rushes off, calling:*

Man   Police! Police! . . .

William (*shocked*)   Edward? Mary and Joseph! Young master, friend, can this be you?

Edward   Shhhh! Hush, she sleeps.

William   Edward, don't you know who I am?

Edward   Shhh! Do not disturb her sweet slumber.

William (*frightened*)   Ned, dear soul, come to your senses.

Edward   Angels guard thee. And you, my darling child.

William   He's near gone from us. I must venture for assistance. (*He hurries out.*)

Edward   All is quiet, my beloved. I kiss these hands that were once mine. And yours, my child. And one last time let me kiss her lips while she sleeps, for awake she would spurn me did she know it . . . Yes, all's quiet now. (*He produces a phial.*) It's a sin to steal liquor. Is't sin to purloin lasting sleep with the universal antidote that – *quenches* – earthly cares?

He is about to drink the poison. **Rencelaw** *rushes in, followed by* **William**, *and with a deft flick of his cane sends the phial flying out of* **Edward**'s *hand.*

Edward   God!

Rencelaw   Nay! Take not your life, mend it!

Man (*without*)   This way, Officer! In here, Officer!

Man, **Policeman**, *followed by* **Floozies** *and* **Loafers** *are arriving.*

Man   There he is!

Policeman (*pushes* **Rencelaw** *aside*)   Step aside, Jimbo!

Man   Arrest him!

Rencelaw (*to himself*)   Jimbo?

All speaking together:

Policeman   Now who have we here? – (*And repeats.*)

Loafer 1   What's happening, what's happening? – (*And repeats.*)

Floozie 2   It's Lord Teddy, he's raving – (*And repeats.*)

Floozie 3   Let me see, let me see – (*And repeats.*)

Loafer 2   Sod's in the jigs – (*And repeats.*)

Floozie 1   He's dying, he's dying –

Rencelaw   Jimbo? Jimbo?

Edward (*shivering, and a continuous gabbling mantra*)   Give me a drink, give me a drink, give me a . . .

William   Do something, someone. Help him, help him –

Rencelaw   Silence! . . . Do you not know who I am?

William (*whispers to* **Policeman**)   Sir Arden Rencelaw.

And the whisper – 'Sir Arden Rencelaw' – goes round. All are impressed and they pull back to watch.

Rencelaw   I have come not to judge or condemn you.

Edward   Give me a drink, give me a drink . . .

Rencelaw   Consider ere it's too late.

Edward   'Tis too late to consider – give me a drink.

Rencelaw   You are a man and, if a man, a brother.

Edward   Give me a drink – I cannot be brother to anyone.

Rencelaw   Why?

Edward   I am lost, of no use, you put your friendship to waste here!

Rencelaw   Are you indeed lost?

Edward   Give me a drink –

Rencelaw   Are you indeed a fallen man?

Edward   Brandy – a glass, a drop, a sip, a taste –

Rencelaw   Edward?!

Edward   I am a drunkard.

Rencelaw   Then you have greater claim upon my compassion.

And he produces a glass of drink – as only he can – and places it on the floor.

There is the mouthful you crave. Take it. Take it. Or stand on your feet and once more become a blessing to yourself and to those dear ones you love.

Edward (*shakes his head; he is becoming tearful*)   That picture is too bright.

Rencelaw   You mistake, you misjudge the picture.

Edward (*whispers, silently*)   No.

Rencelaw   Well, you now have a choice.

Edward   There is no choice.

He's crying; hand and arm shaking, reaching out, weakly, as for someone to give him the glass.

Rencelaw   Then CRAWL!

Edward (*weeping; starts to crawl; stops*)   It's too late.

Rencelaw   Never! You see before you one who, for twenty years, was prey to that dreadful absurdity. Come, give me your hand. Reject not my plea. The journey back, as with the journey there, begins with one step. Come, my son, my brother, enrol your name among the free, become once more an ornament to society. Be a man again.

Edward *is very weak and frail but with a faltering effort he manages to stand. He takes* **Rencelaw**'s *hand and they leave together.*

William   He that lifts a fallen fellow creature be greater than the hero that conquers the world. (*Exits.*)

Floozie 1 (*to heaven*)   Please, your great Majesty up there, be nice to our Lord Teddy.

And she knocks back the glass of drink that has been left on the floor.

Scene Six

Drop scene. Day. **McGinty** *alternates with* **Rencelaw**, *coming forward and retiring. An air of urgency.*

McGinty   Good news: Young Edward Kilcullen is dying.

Rencelaw   His waste in health exceeds what I'd supposed: endeavour does not prosper.

McGinty   And good news more has just arrived: my brother the master forger has expired.

Rencelaw   The special fillip must be found to rally him.

Agnes (*entering*)   Sir! –

Rencelaw   Miss Agnes! (*Joining her, and they confer.*)

McGinty   Now my brother's dead at last, I must hasten to the village, retrieve the real will from its hiding place and destroy it –

Rencelaw   You saw the lawyer at the dead of night?

Agnes   Stealthily, Sir, put a document in a box and . . .

McGinty (*with deeds to the cottage*)   Then, with this, take possession of the cottage, thus concluding triumphantly my life's undertaking. (*He hurries off.*)

Rencelaw   The will – ha, ha, ha! This explains Young Kilcullen's disinheritance. We have not a moment to lose. (*Calls.*) William!

William (*entering immediately*)   Sir Arden!

Rencelaw   Instruct my footman run at once to Mrs Kilcullen's lodgings and tell her to prepare for a journey!

William (*hastening off*)   Sir Arden! –

Rencelaw   And William! –

William   Sir Arden! –

Rencelaw   Race you then to Collopy's Cross, bid the postillion to halt the post chaise and await my further orders!

William   Sir Arden! (*And he is gone.*)

Rencelaw   Miss Agnes!

Agnes   Sir! –

Rencelaw   Attend to your valise and see that my portmanteau's packed at once! –

Agnes   Sir! (*She runs.*)

Rencelaw   And Miss Agnes!

Agnes   Sir! (*Stops.*)

Rencelaw   Make haste!

Agnes   Sir! (*She runs.*)

Rencelaw   Agnes!

Agnes   Sir!

Rencelaw   I long to hear my first name issue from her lips!

Agnes   Sir?

Rencelaw   We shall together, my dear, lighten the journey into night with our favourite hymns. (*She races off.*) Her devotion actively stirs me. But now, with God's speed, to see if we can outgo the crooked lawyer to the village and set a trap there. And if my plan succeed, might I return with the special fillip to muster a dying man? (*Hurries out.*)

Scene Seven

Galloping horses: the coach is arriving, off. Night.

A landscape with moss-covered wall. **Farmer** (**Tom Moggan**), *paralytic (as in Act One, Scene Five), is going homeward with a lantern. He thinks he hears something, then, a belch.*

Farmer   Aye! (*And is going on.*)

But **William** *enters. He, too, has a lantern. He is bemused*

William   Tom. ('*Goodnight.*')

Farmer   Aye!

Now, **Rencelaw** *and* **Agnes**, *in travelling clothes. They are excited. And they have lanterns.*

Rencelaw   Cover those lanterns with your bodies! We have beaten him to it but he is on the upper road. Are you sure, Miss Agnes, this is the place?

Agnes   Brake, fern, cypress dell – moss-covered wall!

Rencelaw   The exact spot!

Agnes   Here! No, there! No! . . . I was hidden over here . . .

William (*bemused, scratching his head*)   Grand night, Tom!

Farmer   Aye!

Agnes   Here!

Rencelaw   Dig! – Make haste! – (*Going out urgently, to check on* **McGinty**'s *approach.*)

Agnes *is digging, on her hands and knees.*

Agnes   No! Here!

She has discovered that she is digging in the wrong spot and she tries another.

Rencelaw (*entering, briefly*)   Haste, hasten or we are done for! He approaches! (*Exit.*)

She hurries to dig in another spot.

Farmer   Something's afoot maybe?

William   Mary and Joseph, Tom! this be like Mother Reilly's addled eggs: can't make chickens or ducks of them.

Rencelaw (*entering*)   What luck, Miss Agnes? He's nearly upon us!

Agnes   Here! (*And she digs a third spot.*)

William   This don't tot, Sir Arden: why, she's more nuttier now than the hazel beyond!

Rencelaw   She's as sane as myself, honest William. (*And exits.*)

Agnes *finds the tin box, opens it, produces the real will from it, and full voice, calls*:

Agnes   Arden!

Rencelaw (*rushing in*)   Agnes! (*He looks at the will.*) It confirms possession of everything to Young Kilcullen. Replace the empty tin! He is here! Everyone draw back! And you, Sir, (*Farmer*) fetch a policeman here at once!

Farmer   Aye!

All move off. Music. And **McGinty** *enters, cautiously, with a lantern.*

McGinty   Safe. No one's about. Now to destroy the real will . . . What's this? The earth looks freshly turned. I like this not . . . Still, here's the box . . . Empty! The will! –

Agnes (*without*)   Ha, ha, ha!

McGinty   The mad wench Agnes Earley!

Agnes (*entering*)   Gone, gone, the bird is flown, the rightful heir shall have his own!

McGinty (*cane raised to beat her*)   You shall pay dearly for this!

But a **Policeman** *rushes in, followed by* **Rencelaw**, **William** *and* **Farmer**. **Policeman** *is pointing a pistol at* **McGinty**'s *head,* **William** *has seized his arm and* **Rencelaw** *holds up the will.*

Rencelaw   You are trapped, Sir!

William   All day to you, Squire!

Rencelaw (*deftly drawing the deeds from* **McGinty**'s *pocket*) And as for this – the deeds to the cottage – this 'forgery' is not worth the rosin dust off a fiddler's bow to you, Sir.

McGinty   Prove it's a forgery!

Rencelaw   I see here that this document is signed by Mr Edward Kilcullen and by – Hah! Call Mr Kilcullen's wife.

William   Mrs Kilcullen!

Arabella, *bewildered, and* **Alanna** *enter in travelling attire.*

Rencelaw   Madam, who are you?

Arabella   Sir?

Rencelaw   State your title and your name

Arabella   Why, Mrs Kilcullen.

Rencelaw   Mrs *what* Kilcullen?

Arabella   Mrs Arabella Kilcullen, Sir.

Rencelaw   Hah! And here is writ: Prudence!

Agnes   Hah!

William   Now for you, Mr Honey!

Farmer   Aye!

Rencelaw (*a stroke of his pen on the document before giving it to* **Arabella**)   To you and your heirs, freehold and in perpetuity, is given possession of that calm retreat.

William   Take him away before I have his skin for –

Rencelaw   Nay, William. – Hold, Officer! He is foul and shameful. Revenge and avarice have been his master passions and he is the perpetrator of deeds heinous: but let the superior power that has defeated him now look in compassion's box to see what might be found for this pitiable creature, who is, still, after all, a human being. Most unfortunate man –

McGinty   Spare me. (*Darkly, to himself.*)

Rencelaw   I shall see what can be done. Most unfortunate man, the deeds you have committed –

McGinty   Spare me.

Rencelaw   I shall see, Sir, what measure can be found for you!

McGinty   Spare me your speeches!

Rencelaw   What's this?

McGinty   Spare me your compassion's box!

Rencelaw   Unhappy wretch! –

McGinty   Happy wretch!

Rencelaw   Evil wretch! –

McGinty   Ha, ha, ha!

Rencelaw   Repentance is available to you!

McGinty   Who makes it available?

Rencelaw   The honest rule of the Establishment that I here represent: Church and State.

McGinty (*to himself*)   Church and State: Sir, give me the salt mines, Siberia, Van Diemen's Land. I promote life in a dungeon, in the company of foul-mouthed criminals, with the lash daily across my back, with verminous rats making dinner of my toes, than subscribe, submit or bow ever again to the scourge of your respectability.

Policeman *leads him away.*

Rencelaw   Poor, poor man. But I must follow at once and show this evidence (*the will*) to the magistrate, thence to see it safely lodged in Probate, and thence to Young Kilcullen to ascertain what effect on a dying man the knowledge that he is now a wealthy one.

William   What blessings, at all, at all, can repay you, Sir?

Rencelaw   My own approving conscience, honest William.

He goes to **Agnes**.

Agnes   Arden, you're exhausted.

Rencelaw (*has to agree that he is*)   Agnes. And with heavy heart I leave you.

Agnes   But you will return – sometime – with lighter one, and edge.

He leaves.

William   The heart of a feeling man, Tom Moggan, be like a tree that's wounded yet still gives forth its precious sap.

Farmer   Aye! Children and chickens must always be a-pickin'. (*Closing in, with his boot, one of the holes dug by* **Agnes**.)

Scene Eight

Interior of the cottage. A pretty picture. **Arabella** *and* **Alanna** *are completing a tapestry, a symmetry of motion between mother and daughter. They sing, unselfconsciously, as they work, a duet.*

Soft, soft music is stealing,
Sweet, sweet lingers the strain,
Loud, loud, now it is pealing,
Waking the echoes again . . .
Yes, yes, yes, yes ,
Waking the echoes again.

Join, join children of sadness,
Send, send sorrow away,

Now, now changing to gladness,
Warble a beautiful lay . . .
Yes, yes, yes, yes,
Warble a beautiful lay .

Without, a cheer from the **Villagers**.

Alanna   What can that be, Mother?

Arabella   I know not, my dear.

Edward (*without*)   Thank you, thank you, kind friends and neighbours!

Alanna   It sounds like . . .

Arabella   Edward!

Alanna   Father!

Edward   Where is my dear, my beloved wife? (*Entering, well-dressed.*)

Arabella   Edward! Is it you?

Edward   It is I! My blessed one!

Arabella   Oh my dear, dear, dear, dear husband! (*As they embrace.*)

Edward   And my child, my child!

Alanna   Father! Father!

Arabella   Bounteous heaven! (*To heaven.*)

Alanna   Accept our thanks! (*To heaven.*)

Arabella   Oh my beloved, are you returned to me?

Edward   And wiser. (*He is in tears.*)

Alanna   He is crying, Mother. Mother, you are crying too!

Edward   Yes, my child, we weep. But these are different tears to those we have known.

Arabella   Tears of joy. And our past troubles now are as nothing compared to this happiness.

A cheer from without.

Villagers   Hooray for Sir Arden Rencelaw!

Rencelaw *comes in, followed by* **Agnes, William** *and others.*

Arabella   Sir, what words can express our gratitude?

Rencelaw   Pay thanks where it is due. (*He means heaven.*) I am rewarded in your happiness.

Alanna *presents him with a little bunch of flowers.*

Rencelaw   Dear child.

Edward   I shall not wrong your selfless nature, Sir Arden, by fulsome show of praise, but humbly beg that heaven gives me the strength to continue in the path adorned by your example.

Rencelaw (*epilogue*)   What joy can equal the sensations of a thinking being returned from futility? With what happiness the erstwhile prisoned heart beats in the rediscovery of life's beauty. How it pulses with the spirit of the earth! And the soul listens to its own music – the diminuendo that held on – now swell in tune with the Infinite, the great mystery we all share.

Now full company. They pair as appropriate. And, led by **Edward***, they sing:*

> There came a change – the clouds rolled off,
> A light fell on my brain,
> And, like the passing of a dream,
> That cometh not again,
> The darkness of my spirit fled,
> I saw the gulf before,
> I shuddered at the waste behind,
> And am a man once more.

And – tableau.

The Last Days
of a Reluctant Tyrant

inspired by
The Golovlyov Family
by Mikhail Saltykov-Shchedrin

For Marie Mullen

The Last Days of a Reluctant Tyrant was first produced at the
Abbey Theatre, Dublin, on 3 June 2009. The cast was as
follows:

Arina	Marie Mullen
Peter	Declan Conlon
Paul	Frank McCusker
Steven	Darragh Kelly
Victor	Tom Hickey
Anna	Janice Byrne
Lena	Caoilfhionn Dunne
Vera	Eva Bartley
Ulita	Ruth McGill
Ivan	Barry Barnes
Anthony	Rory Nolan
Priest	Brendan Conroy
Kiry	Mick Lally
Doctor	Seán O'Neill
Man	Donagh Deeney
Maid 1	Aoife O'Donnell
Maid 2	Bríd Ní Chumhaill

Director Conall Morrison
Set Design Tom Piper
Lighting Design Ben Ormerod
Costume Design Joan O'Clery
Composer Conor Linehan
Sound Design Ben Delaney
Fight Director Paul Burke

My thanks to: Justin Harmon and Carmen Casey; Elizabeth
Keogh; Patrick Miles, translator and consultant; Aideen
Howard, Literary Director of the Abbey Theatre, and Jessica
Traynor, in the same department,

Tom Murphy

Characters

Arina
Steven, *her son*
Peter, *her son*
Paul, *her son*
Victor, *her husband*
Anna, *her granddaughter*
Lena, *her granddaughter*
Vera, *a servant*
Ulita, *a servant*
Ivan, *a steward*
Anthony, *a farm labourer*
Kiry, *a servant*
Priest
Doctor

Setting

Once upon a time in a provincial rural area.

Act One

Scene One

A cavernous place, a big room. Evidence of industry. The top end of a line of people, waiting. (Or they can be off in the next room.) **Arina** *comes in. She is an able, no-nonsense figure of authority, and she knows it. She is very much the matriarch. She nods her head and a* **Man**, *cap in hand, is ushered to her by a servant,* **Maid**. *The* **Man** *starts whispering to* **Arina**.

Two men, her sons, **Paul** *and* **Peter**, *are also present. They stand by and back, like observers come to attend a masterclass. The enthusiastic-looking one is* **Peter**.

Arina *(to* **Man**, *who has finished whispering)*   No business – cabbage patch to ten thousand acres – can be run on incompetence. It can't be done.

A gesture from the **Man**, *a plea.*

Arina   There are no second chances. You knew that.

Another plea – he's abject – and he looks at **Maid**.

Arina   Your wife's work is satisfactory, you're sacked.

Man *leaves,* **Maid** *seeing him off.*

Arina *stays next in line of those waiting to see her, and calls others to come forward: two schoolgirls,* **Anna** *and* **Lena**, *her granddaughters, in their going-back-to-convent clothes, come to say goodbye. She takes them aside. (The contrast in their personalities:* **Anna**'s *is open,* **Lena**'s *closed.)*

Arina   Be good, be obedient, be wise, do what you're told so that you'll be of use later. There's money being spent on you: don't waste it. *(She allows them to kiss her.)* Off!

They are leaving. **Anna** *runs back to press the back of* **Arina**'s *hand to her cheek, then she rejoins* **Lena** *and they leave together.*

Next in line come forward: **Ulita** *and* **Vera**. **Ulita**, *in some kind of servant maid's costume, is, say, in her twenties.* **Vera** *is very young, perhaps of an age with* **Anna** *and* **Lena**. *She is round-shouldered and has a broad back. A coat and headgear of some kind and, perhaps, her possessions in a roll. She is shy to the point of being speechless.*

Arina   How are things up the mountain then, that village of ours? (**Vera** *nods.*) Your father is well, your mother? (**Vera** *nods.*)

Ulita (*cueing* **Vera** *to the proper address*)   'Ma'am'.

Arina (*to* **Ulita**)   That's all right. Do your work well and your parents will do well and we'll all get on. Ulita will show you what you have to do and where you sleep. Turn around. (**Vera** *obeys.*) What a back! You're welcome.

They leave. **Ivan** *is next. He's* **Arina**'s *steward. He gives her a ledger and some receipts of sales.*

Arina   Ivan!

Ivan   Ma'am! Rent receipts. Corn market, hay market, cattle market.

Arina   Anything out of the ordinary?

Ivan   No.

Arina (*as she looks at the receipts*)   Young Townsend that's come to live on his late father's estate: how's that working out for him?

Ivan (*eager to please her*)   Parties every night, not just the weekends, ladies out from the town. He won't last the year if you want my opinion. If you want my opinion, he –

Arina   That'll do. Anything else?

Ivan   No. (*But he's shifting on his feet.*)

Arina   Tenants complaining?

Ivan   No – the usual – nothing.

Arina   What have you to tell me? . . . Don't I see it on your face?!

Ivan   Steven.

Arina   He's back.

Ivan   (Yes) Ma'am. He's in town.

Arina   And he's staying where?

Ivan   Here and there.

Arina   So he's roofless again. (*To* **Paul** *and* **Peter**.) Your brother!

Peter   Tsssssss!

Arina   I don't want him near that door. He ought to be shot. I'd do it myself: God or the law wouldn't have me answer for it. (*She dismisses* **Ivan**.)

Ivan   Awfully sorry. (*He moves to leave, but is shifting on his feet again.*)

Arina   You have more for me?

Ivan   He isn't well.

Arina   He isn't well.

Ivan   He doesn't look well.

Arina   He doesn't look well.

Ivan   He coughs a lot. Holding his sides.

Arina   Don't be too concerned about him!

Ivan   Ma'am. (*And he leaves.*)

Peter *and* **Paul** *come forward, to say goodbye.* **Peter** *to kiss her;* **Paul***, by comparison, seems indifferent; and though* **Arina** *is no indulgent mother or grandmother, it is possible to wonder if she doesn't like a show of admiration and affection for her from others.*

Peter   Mama.

Arina   A lot of men cough for thirty years and grow fat on
it.

Peter   Mama.

Arina   Holding their sides. I'll send for you if he shows up.

Paul (*more or less to himself, with a shrug*)   Why? Why should
she need us?

Arina (*to herself*)   Why am I only happy on my own? In
town, see that the orphans get safely from the railway station
to the convent.

Victor, *her husband, has come in. He's a bit of a dandy; he holds aloft
a cheroot behind his head. He is followed by a manservant* (*later,* **Kiry**).

Arina (*as she walks out*)   And I'm neither wife nor widow!

Victor   You're a bachelor! (*Calling it after her – though he's a bit
afraid of her.*)

Peter   Papa.

Victor *has a big voice though he is frail, unhealthy. He starts to declaim
a Barkov-type poem of his own composition; his delivery is both
ridiculous and heroic.*

Peter *and* **Paul** *leave him to it. And, outside,* **Arina** *pauses for a
moment or two to eavesdrop.*

Victor
    Now the wedding ritual's done,
    Cherrymaid, it's time for fun!

    O glorious member mine,
    Patient in abstinence,
    Come, now arisen, unto your reward!
    Timidity discard as boldly you undo
    The box and claim its treasure;
    Do justice t'it, and to yourself
    No shaming bring but rigidly plunge in.
    Ram to the balls and in the depths,
    Within those moistened walls,

Run deliriously distracted!
Then t'it, t'it and t'it again!

O glorious member of mine,
By goddesses be praised
And by cherrymaids remembered!

Scene Two

The open road.

*Two men. One, with a pack, in battered army tunic or coat. He's about
forty; unkempt; gaunt, maybe; ravaged; a garrulous man; garrulity,
though, on this occasion has something to do with fear of what lies ahead
(his mother and home). This is* **Steven**. *He's accompanied
by* **Anthony**, *a farm labourer, who also has a pack or bag.*

Steven   Yes, brother, it's the devil of a world and I've had
the devil of a life of it, so it's time I had a rest. Unlike you,
comrade, I served my country: now it's other people's turn to
help me. What's in your bag, brother?

Anthony   Are you hungry?

Steven   A T-bone steak would be the very thing right now.

Anthony   I'm sorry, sir, there's only this.

Steven   Sausage? Sausage will do nicely.

They've stopped to eat.

Anthony   And you'll have a sup of this to drink.

Steven   Cold tea? No. (*He produces a bottle of his own.*) But you
will have a sup of this, my friend.

Anthony   I never once touched it in my life, sir.

Steven   That's wrong, brother. Filling yourself up with tea:
that's why you have the belly. And it tightens the cough.
Whereas, whereas vodka – (*He drinks and it is followed by a bout
of coughing, and:*) Y'see?! Y'see?!

Anthony   I don't know. I suppose.

Steven (*of the sausage*)   It's a bit salty. But I can tell you we ate worse than this on the march. D'you know what my father once told me? (*He goes off on a tangent, declaiming a few lines of a Barkov poem.*)

> A traveller overta'en by night,
> Spent it at an old crone's quarter,
> Inside he found it warm all right,
> The crone she had a lovely daughter!

(*And he laughs.*) I always got on with my old man. But d'you know what he once told me? He told me he knew of an Englishman that betted he would eat a dead cat.

Anthony   Eat a?!

Steven   Dead cat. And he did.

Anthony   He didn't?!

Steven   On my oath! He was sick as a dog afterwards.

Anthony   Tck-tck!

Steven   But rum cured him. He drank two bottles of it at a gulp and was fit as a fiddle.

Anthony   Well, well!

Steven   Oh yes, it's other people's turn now to help me.

Anthony   Your mother will have pity on you when she sees you.

Steven   Of course she will, of course she will, she's sure to. And another Englishman betted he would eat nothing but sugar for a whole year.

Anthony   And did he win?

Steven (*laughs*)   No, he popped it two days before the year was up! Of course she will. But no joke, I can tell you, on the march, through this village and that, on to the next town and the next, stopping here, now there, for official types to come out and make speeches: how the country was having the devil of a time of it, how her brave sons had to stand up and be counted – bringing tears to their own eyes! Chains of office round their fat necks: politicians, government contractors, receivers, mayors, profiteers – all scoundrels. I don't know how a country survives them, do you?

Anthony   Your mother did all right by the war.

Steven   Oh God yes, no denying that! My mother is a clever woman. I respect my mother, that's the chief thing. Why, she came down from that mountain (over there) – barefoot, some say, shoes slung round her neck by the laces – and married my old man and, why, we weren't a lot better off than yourself, Anthony, at the time. What an amount she's added! 'Arina'. (*The last with a wide gesture.*)

Anthony   You'll all be well off when she pops it.

Steven   We won't: she has no plans for that. The only way she'll go will be if my brother Peter makes an end to her, somehow. 'Mama, Mama, dear friend Mama.' Jesus Christ, why they didn't throw away the key when they had that man in the seminary, I don't know.

Anthony   Your other brother?

Steven   Paul? You wouldn't know what goes on in Paul's head – if anything! But d'you know what I think? I've made a lifelong study of drinking men and there's a certain type that never staggers, never gets sick, never starts singing, dancing, shouting, roaring, fighting or cursing, and I often wonder is our Paul a member of that select and chosen brotherhood. (*He looks out into the gathering dusk:*) Of course she will, of course she will, she's sure to.

Anthony   Should we start knocking another few of miles off the road, sir?

As they finish eating and collect their bits and pieces in their packs:

Steven   Anthony, my kind friend and host, if I was rich, first thing I'd do is see you all right.

Anthony   I'm content – no small thanks to your mother.

Steven   I'd make you commander-in-chief of her empire.

Anthony   What was it like at the front?

Steven   All over before we got there. But I saw *action*. Came to this place: there was a service going on in the church and I went in to have a look. And I see this girl there. She's shifting her feet, she's looking around, couldn't stand still, and I gave her the wink.

Anthony   She didn't go with you!

Steven   What's money for?! I offered her three.

They go off into the night.

Anthony (*off*)   Three – yes?

Steven (*off*)   She wanted five.

Anthony (*off*)   Did you have it?

Steven (*off*)   The little vixen!

Anthony (*off*)   Did you have the five? . . .

Scene Three

Victor, *in his nightshirt, and* **Steven**, *both drinking, revelling in the Barkov poem – as in* **Victor***'s bedroom. As said in Scene One,* **Victor** *is frail of frame. He isn't at all well. (Emphysemic?) They seem to revel in themselves and in each other; though, behind the revelry, each is concerned for the other, father and son, as in premonition.*

Victor
   A traveller overta'en by night
   Spent it an at old crone's quarter,
   Inside he found the warmth all right –

Steven
   The crone she had a lovely daughter!

Victor   No! No! Inside he found the warmth all right, full stop! (*Meaning 'full stop' after 'all right'. Then:*)

> The crone she had a lovely daughter,
> A girl much younger than he oughter,
> A girl quite handsome –

Steven *and* **Victor** (*together*)
> A girl quite winsome!

Victor*'s breathlessness and coughing;* **Steven** *coughs in sympathy – as to help (ease)* **Victor***'s coughing. They laugh and cough.* **Arina** *has appeared, as in another part of the house, nightdress, candle.*

Arina   Is the house to be kept awake all night?! Quiet, wretches! Go to sleep!

Steven *and* **Victor** (*whispering*)
> The knobstick in his breeches stirred,
> As soon as he beheld the girl,
> Praise be, what luck! A one-night whirl . . .

They hold on each other, smiling at each other, containing the coughs and laughter as best they can. Then **Steven** *steals away. We stay on* **Victor***, smiling at his own attempts to breathe.*

Scene Four

Arina *is seated, proppping her chin with her fist. Manservant,* **Kiry***, passes through, carrying what looks like medicine on a tray.* **Peter** *and* **Paul** *arrive.* **Ulita** *and* **Vera** *take their coats.* **Ulita** *always tends to* **Peter***.*

Arina   . . . Your father won't get out of bed any more. He believes he is unwell . . . No comment?

Peter   Tsssssss!

Arina   And your brother's been here for two weeks. (*'No comment'.*) He arrived quite pleased with himself, as though he'd just done a good thing. (*Makes a soldier's salute.*) 'Reporting for duty, Field Marshal' (*he said to her*). The dead of night, the dog barking, the watchman sounding the clapper, the whole house woken up. 'I can play the goat for as much and for as long as I like, my old fool of a mother will always be here for me.' I don't understand it. I had him educated, tried to make something out of him, I got him a position, when he lost that I got him another, and another, until: 'What can I do with him?' Maybe if he has a house, some money, he'll sober down. He runs up debts – drink! – the bank possesses the house I bought him and sells it for twenty-two thousand. That was a nice thing to happen? I paid twenty-nine for it. That house, managed, could have brought in fifteen per cent a year and appreciated.

Peter   Tsssssss!

Arina (*testily to* **Peter**)   What does that mean?

Peter   That is no way to deal with a mother's blessing.

Arina   He runs off and joins the army, a private soldier. Well, thank Christ, maybe that's the last we'll see of him. (*To* **Paul**.) Are you interested at all in any of this?

Paul *gestures, shrugs, that he doesn't see that the matter has anything whatsoever to do with him.*

Peter   You did everything for him, Mama.

Arina   How much longer can I stand it? Now he's back to sponge on me again.

Peter   If an undeserving child cannot appreciate a mother's love, then look to the one who can.

Arina   It wasn't by going 'on the razzle' that I made out. Where was I born? Nearly on the top of the mountain! What was there when I married that windmill upstairs? And *he* won't even get out of bed any more! What was there when I married him? Now everyone refers to the whole district as 'Arina'! My name. Is that *failure*?

Peter (*cueing her*)   The first big purchase of land. (*And he claps his hands, once, silently, as in anticipation.*)

Arina   Yes. (We were) Living on the farm, the side of the mountain, rocks, an inhospitable place. Then Rill's came on the market, good fertile land, mostly a plain, nearly all of it adjoining what we had, only Townsend's in between – *still* in between. What age was I, how much money had I? With what I had put by, I got rid of the land on the far side of the mountain, fast, to the sheepman for eleven thousand. I had thirty thousand. No joke this! (*Though she is growing in inner excitement.*) I had a mass said. When the priest asked 'What for?', 'For a purpose,' I said: I wouldn't even publish my business with God! Sleepless nights: the waiting! I visited Our Lady's shrine. I wept there. Then (in) the horse and cart, I went to town to try my hand at the auction. The men there were shouting this sum and that, wrangling like children playing a game, until the auctioneer said, 'Let us be serious, gentlemen.' 'Thirty thousand,' I said. It was marvellous. You could hear a pin drop. It was as if Our Lady had seen my tears. The auction was over. Then the auctioneer came down and shook my hand and I didn't understand a word he was saying. I stood there like a post.

Peter (*claps his hands, silently*)   Mama!

Arina   And I still think of the Lord's mercy – sleepless nights still: what if someone had sensed out my distracted state and shouted – out of trickery, mischief? – 'Thirty-five thousand!' What would I have done? Lost the place which was the beginning of all this? Or would I have called 'Forty!', 'Fifty!' and where would I have come by it? What would have happened?

Peter   Sleepless nights.

Arina   And that dolt thinks – and you think, maybe – that what I have done cost me nothing, *means* nothing?

Peter   'You can't have a pimple on your nose for nothing.'

Arina (*to* **Paul**)   Mind you don't bite me with that face.

Paul   I heard it all before!

Peter   Tsssssss!

Paul (*to himself*)   The horse and cart.

Arina   Well, here's something you haven't heard before: I want you now to judge between your brother Steven and me, your mother.

This is, indeed, something they haven't heard before. And it's most strange.

Peter   Judge, Mama?

Arina   Judge, rule, decide between us – that's why I called you here. And whatever you decide will be right. Find me guilty, say that everything I did in my life was wrong, a mistake, say that property doesn't matter, say that I shouldn't complain ever again about anything, let alone about money being flung on a dung heap. Find against him, then his way of life is wrong, and you'll tell me what to do with him.

Peter   If you'll allow me, Mama, to express an opinion.

Arina   I just asked for it.

Peter   Then, in two words: children belong entirely to their parents, parents may therefore judge their children, but children their parents? Never. That's all.

Arina   That's all?

Peter   Even if it were true that parents wronged their children, it would never be lawful for children to meet parents with the like.

Arina   What're you saying behind what you're saying?

Peter   Mama! Children must obey their parents, must follow their guidance without question and take care of them in their old age.

Arina   All right, you won't judge me – judge him then and rule in my favour.

Peter   We can't do that either, we daren't: you are our mother.

Arina (*grimly*)   Settle your troubles for yourself, Mama, as always.

Peter   But –

Arina (*flips*)   I'm tired! What is it all about? I don't know why or what or who I've been doing it all for!

Peter   . . . To make decisions, Mama, a person would first have to be in a position of authority.

Arina (*to* **Paul**)   You! What do you say?

Paul   Nothing.

Arina   Stupid!

Paul   So should it matter what I say?

Peter   Without first being in a position of authority, a –

Arina   I heard you the first time. It's a bit too soon to bury me.

Paul   Shoot him – He's guilty – And it's all settled!

Arina   That's disrespectful.

Peter   Tsssssss!

Paul (*at* **Peter**)   Tsssssss! (*He doesn't like his brother. To* **Arina**.) What is disrespectful in saying nothing?

Arina   Mind, be careful – both of you – I have grandchildren! (*Under her breath.*) (For) Christ's sake! . . . All right: I'll try kindness again. The Valley, that parcel of land that came from your father's sister: I'll give him that. If he applies himself, he'll get some kind of keep from it, and he's out of my sight. So there we are, the matter's settled. (*And she waits.*)

Peter   . . . That is more than kind.

She nods; waits.

It's generous.

She nods; waits.

It's very generous . . . When one thinks of the shameful way he's treated you. Nice Valley. And you forgive and forget.

She nods.

Peter (*appeals to* **Paul**)   Paul?

Paul *is helping no one.*

Peter   But dear friend, Mama, excuse me.

Arina   Yes?

Peter   I wouldn't do it.

Arina   You wouldn't do it.

Peter   I wouldn't.

Arina   Why not?

Peter   I don't know.

Arina   You don't know.

Peter   I don't. Paul?

Paul (*to himself*, *mimicking* **Peter**)   Tssssss!

Peter   I just keep thinking, my brother Steven appears to be naturally depraved – I didn't like saying that – and what if he treats this gift the same as everything else you've done for him?

Arina   The Valley has remained solely in your father's name. Sooner or later your brother would have to come into his share of it.

Peter   I understand that, but –

Arina   Understand then, too, he will have a legal claim to a share of all the *rest* (*of her 'empire'*). Before settling the Valley on him, he can be made to sign a declaration that he has a claim on nothing whatsoever else – patrimony, matrimony – that he is content with the Valley, and that that's that, forever.

Peter   But shouldn't you have done that when you bought the house for him?

Arina   Did you say that to me at the time?

Peter   He'll squander it and he'll be back to you again.

Arina   He won't be back to me again, not for a crust of bread, a drop of water! He's been nothing but a disgrace and an embarrassment. His life mocks me!

Peter   Mama, Mama –

Arina   *Your* lives mock me!

Peter   You are so angry!

Arina   I should dance a jig?

Peter   So angry, beautiful Mama, and I thought you were a good girl. And what does the Gospel counsel? Possess your soul in patience. Do you suppose God doesn't see us here now, planning this, planning that, while up there He's made up His mind already? Up there, He's said, 'I think I'll send Arina a little trial.'

Arina   How d'you know that? Tell me, straight out, what you're thinking! Don't keep throwing dust in my eyes. Do you want me to keep him here, saddle me with him forever?

Peter   If that's what you've decided on! And make him sign away his claim to everything else for keeping him here.

Arina   . . . All right. He'll stay here. But-not-in-this-house. Enough cripples in this house. We'll find a place for him in the yard. He won't starve, he won't get fat either.

Peter   The return home of our poor prodigal Steven: thanks be to God! Allow me, Mama, to have a word with him and give him some advice. I'm happiest serving a poor person, the rich don't need it, bless them. Do you recall what Our Saviour said about the poor?

Arina   At the moment, no. (*As she walks out.*)

Scene Five

Night. An exterior.

*A woman slowly crossing this empty space, coat/shawl around her, head
bowed, subdued as a woman troubled in herself, taking a meditative
walk in the dark. A shadow is following her: it has something of*
Victor's *shape, if we are not mistaken. The woman is* **Arina**.

Scene Six

Steven Roll up, roll up for an imperfect enjoyment! Come
on in, ladies and gentlemen and see the naked goddess of
desire! Over there, my friends, take your places! . . . Now
hush, and observe.

Night. **Steven** *is about to perform and declaim a poem, 'The Imperfect
Enjoyment' by John Wilmot, Earl of Rochester, for the servants who are
assembling in his room in the yard. A spare place.* **Ulita** *and other
maids (as available).* **Vera**, *the young maid, arrives and puts a plate of
something and a mug of something on the simple table and takes her place
with the others. Manservant (**Kiry**) is present.* **Anthony** *and* **Ivan**
come in. A nod from **Ivan** *at some point and* **Anthony** *produces a
bottle of vodka and places it somewhere for* **Steven**. *The suggestion
is that* **Steven** *puts on a show, clowns for the servants, and they bring
him drink.*

Unlike the others who are wrapped up against the cold, **Steven** *is
scantily clad. For all his clowning, he is a sick man, and when he falls or
keels over, and though he may laugh too, it isn't meant to be part of the act.*

The servants are highly entertained at everything he says and does; **Ivan**
is the exception, the solemn one.

Steven
    Naked she lies, a goddess of desire –

He reclines on the table, perhaps –

    With arms, legs, lips close clinging in embrace,
    She clasps me to her breast, and sucks me to her face.

Her nimble tongue, Love's lesser lightning, played
Within my mouth, and to my thoughts conveyed
Swift orders that I should prepare to throw
The all-dissolving Thunderbolt below –
Roll up, roll up!
But whilst her busy hand would guide that part,
In liquid raptures I dissolve all o'er,
Melt into sperm, and spend at every pore.
A touch from any part of her had done't:
Her hand, her foot, her very look's a . . . ?

What delights has she sent me this evening? (*To the table to sniff at the plate and mug and to make faces.*) And plenty of fresh provisions in the storerooms which she will not have touched till all this putrid stuff is eaten up, by which time fresh provisions are – what?! – putrid! What a lot of stuff she's let go to waste! What a waste of life! Devilishly clever woman, but is that the way to run things?

Anthony   Still, you should eat it, sir.

Steven   Anthony, my brother, you are ruining youself with tea – Who is drinking with me tonight? Not Ulita: Ulita serves only one male 'member' of my family – and it's not mine. Ah-hah-hah-hah-hah, that's all you ladies think about! And what did thought do for the lady? She stuck a feather in her garden and thought she'd grow a cock! (*To* **Vera**.) Has anyone – for instance my ex-seminarian, now very civil-servant brother – given *you* a rub of a holy relic yet? I've made a lifelong study of celibates and they are very fond of good-looking women – specially if they're big. (Your) Face, Ivan! Who died recently, apart from my daddy? 'Inside he found the warmth all right'! 'The crone she had a lovely daughter; a girl much younger than he oughter'. Miss?

He has two mugs and he has poured vodka into both. Now he's offering one of the mugs to **Vera**. *A brief nod from* **Ivan** *tells* **Vera** *she may accept the mug.* **Vera** *simply holds the mug throughout the scene – she doesn't drink from it.*

During the above, outside, the subdued-looking woman – **Arina** *– returning, pausing only for a moment, as though absently registering the sound of* **Steven***'s show, before going off, head bowed. The shadow follows her (*Victor*).*

Ivan   And, Steven, and that has to be the end of it.

Steven   End of what d'you mean?

Anthony   We can't get any more drink for you, sir.

Steven   Money? (*Meaning 'if it's only a matter of money'.*)

Ivan   You haven't had anything in money since your father passed away.

Steven   Where's this been coming from then? She hardly buys it for me.

Anthony   We do.

Ivan   (We) Can't afford it any more.

Anthony   Even if we could and she found out?

Steven   What're we going to do with the witch? And what's she worth? And what's she do with it all? Swallows it all up, I dare say. I swallow drink, she swallows money – D'you see what I mean?

Ivan (*nods to the others 'it's time to go'*)   We'd better be getting along.

Steven (*a plea; there's terror in it*)   Ah no, don't go, please! (*He nearly falls over. Then, a bark:*) Ivan, Anthony! Sit! Who's master here?!*

Ivan (*sighs, sits / stays*)   And the temperature's dropped: you should put on that robe.

Steven   Dressing gown: Papa's. And his slippers. (*Now he recites a piece of Pushkin.*)

And suddenly, behold, we'll die.
There is no happiness, but peace and freedom.

> For long an enviable fate has been my dream,
> For long a . . .

Did you ask her for boots, a sheepskin coat for me?

Ivan's *face suggests he did, to no avail.*

Steven (*now laughing*)   Tell us, what did she say again when you asked for candles? Ah, Ivan! You tell us, Anthony.

Anthony   'He can pace just as easily up and down in the dark.'

Which he finds hilarious. And his audience, exceeding themselves, are now finding everything he says hilarious, their hilarity driving him to excesses – though he might just as well be crying.

Steven (*finds it hilarious*)   'He can pace just as'! (*A bout of coughing. Then:*) You have to admire her, you simply have to! That's the chief thing. And when she calls me – she *will* call me! – 'Come, beloved son! Everybody,' she will say, 'this is my beloved son who was dead! Everybody, this is my beloved son who was lost and is found! Come, my beloved son, back to the fold, back to my bosom, back into the house!' And I shall kiss her hands – I shall kiss her feet, wash her feet – 'Forgive me, Mama, for all my sins!' – and we shall sit down to table and eat – veal. It's perfectly true.

He staggers, recovers, then falls or keels over. The others look fearful for a moment – he could be dead. But, relief, he starts coughing. **Ivan** *tells the others to leave as he helps* **Steven** *up.*

Steven   And I have a remedy – Brothers, sisters, listen! A man told me: you take a living frog, (and at) dead of night place it on (an) anthill. Morning: ants will have eaten it all up, down to one small bone. And so long as you carry that bone with you, you may ask whatever you like of any woman. Whatsoever is your fancy, Anthony? (*And a warning finger at the maids.*) Ladies?!

Anthony   Well, we could go about doing that straightaway, sir.

Steven   Ah! Ah-hah-hah-hah-hah! Thing is: you must first lay a curse on yourself. Y'see! (*And he's coughing, or doubles up.*)

Ivan (*dismissing the others*)   You shouldn't be here at all! (*To* **Vera**.) See will he eat anything of that before you take away the plate. (*He leaves.*)

Anthony   Goodnight, sir. (*And follows the others.*)

Steven (*recovering*)   Had it not been for the putting-a-curse-on-myself part, I'd have the witch down on that floor now, crawling before me. (*He registers that his company have gone.*) . . . Goodnight, brothers, sisters . . . (*He has now become very gentle.*) It is night, isn't it?

Vera *nods.*

Steven   Might as well be day . . . Do you watch the clouds? All day, hanging there, the same place, grey, no change, colour or shape . . . I watch them through that window . . . Would you like me to sit beside you, Miss? (*He sits beside her.*) . . . Do you watch the dots in the distance, moving? Moving dots, people. Going about some business or other: I can't think what. What might they have to defend, or want? . . . Just going for a walk maybe.

He rises and is pacing again, slowly. He has possibly forgotten **Vera***'s presence. He stops to look in the direction of what is meant to be the door as if vaguely considering going out.*

Steven
    It's time, my friend, time: the heart begs peace . . .
    For long an enviable fate has been my dream,
    For long, a weary slave, I've planned to flee
    To a far-off home of work and chaste delights . . .

But it's perfectly true.

Scene Seven

Vera *is assisting* **Anna** *out of her things – black coat, hat, etc.*

Vera   Up to a few weeks ago he was laughing and joking. Then when Anthony found the slipper in the mud in the yard in the morning – What! To run away on such a night, such weather. She sent us all out searching. I thought he's drowned in the river for sure. We searched the forest. Where could he have gone? Then, towards evening, two men came with a horse and cart, Mister Steven lying in the back. If you had seen him! Cuts, bruises – What! His face swollen blue. Nigh insensible. He'd been found in a ditch fifteen miles away. He'd walked fifteen miles that night!

Anna *has grown, and so, too, has* **Vera**. *Having the place to themselves and affecting daring,* **Anna** *pours them two glasses of vodka.*

Anna (*a toast*)   Here goes!

Vera   This to happen and the master not three months in his grave. (*A daring toast.*) Here goes! (*And drinks.*) When he woke up – he slept for twenty-four hours – she sent me to fetch him. I think she was thinking, behind her eyes, of having him back in the house. 'You silly, silly boy, Steven! Running away from your mother? What made you do a thing like that? You caused me great anxiety.' Doesn't sound like her, does it? And she'd say 'What?' 'What?' She wanted him to say something, but he just sat there, staring at nothing. And you could see she wanted to lose her temper, but she'd control herself. 'You're bored?' she'd say. 'But there's nothing for it, my dear. Work is the only thing there is. It's the only way a person can get by. Is there another way? Tell me, for I would like to know.' She offered him a drink. 'Have a glass – have two, bless you!' And I think, you know, she was hoping he might kiss her hand. She doesn't let on but she likes that sort of thing. No. Then, and I don't think he was talking to anyone, he said, 'What a waste of life.'

They put away their glasses and adjust themselves: others are arriving.

Priest, **Paul**, **Peter**, **Ulita**, **Manservant**, **Arina**. *And* **Steven**, *his ghost, following* **Arina**.

Priest   And he had been full of life the evening before, madam?

Peter   Full of life, Father.

Priest   Taken his supper, madam?

Peter   Taken his supper, Father.

Priest   Isn't that the way, sir? We sit down suspecting nothing.

Peter   While the man up there has other ideas.

Priest   Planning for tomorrow, madam?

Peter   Planning, planning, planning, Father!

Priest   In the midst of life we are in . . . madam?

Arina *leaves the room.*

Peter   What grieves the maternal heart most of all is that he departed this world of vanity for that unknown realm without the last rites.

Priest   Well, he has now received all the honours due to the departed that the Church can offer. You would wish that masses and requiem services continue on what basis?

Peter   A daily basis for one month, thereafter a monthly basis for three months, then a three-monthly basis for a further three services.

Priest   That should do it . . . Where did she get that beautiful red velvet pall?

Peter   Something I had in keeping for myself. I like to feel I'm ready for His call at any moment.

Priest   Please God you'll find another one like it, sir.

Paul (*as though to himself*)   How ready if it's Satan – tssssssss! – does the calling?

Arina *is returning.*

Priest   Ah, madam, how doubly sad when a child predeceases a parent – Oh no, no, no, no, no!

Her hand is outstretched and she continues, and unsmiling, until he takes the money it contains.

You continue to be the Church's staunchest support, an adornment.

Arina   We're not sitting down to a funeral breakfast on this occasion, but if you go to the kitchen they'll look after you there. (*To* **Ulita**.) Show him where he's to go.

Priest (*backing out of the room*)   We know not the time or the place? No living man can flee death, madam? Life is a mere – preliminary?

Peter   My warm friend!

Priest   So fleeting is our time here below. (*He's gone.*)

Arina   All this fuss for the sake of a wastrel, a fool. Tea?

Peter   Tea, Mama.

Anna   Yes, please.

Paul   Vodka.

Arina (*to servants*)   Give them what they want.

Anna   Well, perhaps I'll also have . . . (*A glance from* **Arina**.) Tea, please.

Arina   Why again could your sister not travel to attend her uncle's funeral?

Anna   There's flu in the convent, Grandma, and she –

Arina   She isn't well, we don't need details.

Peter   I am stricken with grief for him, dear companion of my childhood.

Arina   He couldn't bring himself to speak to his mother. 'What a waste of life' was all he could say. He wasn't slow, though, or ashamed, to play the clown and appear in rags and cadge money from the people I do business with in town.

Peter   Oh you bad, bad brother!

Arina   Or kick up a row or put out his hand for charity to my servants.

Peter   Strange: he cared nothing for the sacredness of his name.

Arina   He could easily have done something worthwhile. He wasn't stupid.

Paul *laughs 'No', and nods to himself at this: stupidity is meant to be his domain.*

Peter   Tsssssss!

Arina   The plans I had for him.

Peter   And my grief is all the greater at this fresh cross that has been laid upon you.

Anna   Was Uncle Steven very unhappy?

Arina   Was he starved? What do I give myself? – Was he made to work? He did nothing but slouch up and down the room I gave him out there and look out the window.

Peter   My name means everything to me.

Arina   Another man would have thanked his mother enough.

Peter   Thanked his mother.

Arina   'Was he very unhappy?' (*And she rounds, fiercely, on* **Anna**.) And the plans I had for your mother! Instead, she had to run away in the night, she and her soldier boy, to marry, just like dogs, without a priest's blessing or a parent's consent. (*She turns away but then rounds back on* **Anna** *again.*) And when she died, as shamefully as she lived, I inherit the fruit of it all, you and your sister!

Peter   . . . Mama, you are —

Arina (*glaring at her sons*)   *Where* are my grandchildren?!

Vodka has been served to **Paul** *or he has helped himself. Now tea is ready and is served by* **Vera** *and* **Ulita**.

Peter   What's her name?

Ulita   Vera.

Peter (*to himself*)   Vera. Mama, you're chilled to the bone from standing in the graveyard. Will you have a little something in your tea?

Arina (*nods. Then:*)   'What a waste of a life.' *Whose* life was a waste?

Peter   Vera, pour a little brandy in the mistress's tea. Nothing in mine. (*He refuses anything in his own tea.*) The back on that girl, bless it! Vera.

Arina   He never showed me the slightest affection.

Peter   You are carrying burdens beyond your strength for your unworthy children: is there some way we might begin to lighten the load for you? Or, at least, discuss it?

Silence. They sip their drinks.

Arina (*to* **Paul**)   I'd prefer it, my dear, if you said something than have you just sit there sticking pins in me.

Paul   Sticking pins?

Arina   Oh, at least, a parrot!

Paul   All right then. ('*I'll say something.*') I hope the Lord God Almighty gives our Steven a mansion in that unknown realm up there but – Who knows? – of that matter we must continue uncertain.

Peter   Tsssssss!

Arina   I wanted to send him to the Valley, out of my sight and God bless him, instead I had to go whistling for him in the wood. The Valley didn't suit you.

Peter   Mama –

Arina   You wouldn't support the idea –

Peter   No –

Arina   You talked me out of it –

Peter   You had already decided –

Arina   I hadn't –

Peter   You had already decided where he should live –

Arina   You talked me out of it –

Peter   Before you called that meeting.

Arina   I hadn't! (*To* **Paul**.) Had I?

Paul   You always decide matters in advance for other people.

Peter (*playfully*)   . . . And what, darling Mama, have you decided in advance for us today? There's 'something'!

Arina   Are you making fun of me?

Silence. **Paul** *has another vodka.*

Arina   Ah, I think I'll give it all up while there's still a little time.

Peter *and* **Paul** *hold their breath.*

Anna (*innocently*)   And do what, Grandma?

Arina   And do nothing – buy a motor car. Go places, visit the village where I was born, look at my father's grave – start enjoying myself.

Peter   Who will look after the estates?

Arina   God will.

A sudden brusque hand movement tells the servants to get out. They obey. **Peter** *and* **Paul** *are leaning forward in an anticipatory way.*

Arina (*leans towards them as in challenge or defiance and repeats*) God will! . . . (*Now, false gaiety.*) There ought to be some way of taking it all to the grave, but it can't be done!

She laughs and, just as suddenly, she is in tears. Tears embarrass her, so she tries to hide them. **Anna** *takes her hand.* **Arina** *pulls her hand away. After a moment* **Arina** *resubmits her hand for* **Anna***'s attention. In the background – wherever the 'ghost' of* **Steven** *is – a second 'ghost' is emerging:* **Victor**. **Arina** *continues to weep.*

Arina   And I'd like to visit St Bartholomew's Shrine. I was very devoted to St Bartholomew when I was a little girl.

Anna   Dearest Grandma! (*She, too, is weeping.*)

Arina   . . . (It was) A day close to the end for Victor – for the windmill: I was sitting in my bedroom. He wouldn't have wanted me near him, anyway. And I heard a voice, someone in the room, whispering. 'Go to the saint.' 'Go to the saint, go to the saint.' Three times. I looked around. I was completely alone. There was no one there. (*She's now trying to turn her weeping into laughing.*) And the room was full of fragrance. There was no one there! I was completely alone.

Peter (*sheds a tear*)   Dear friend Mama!

Arina   And these days if you say a word to one of the maids they have two back at you!

Peter   God is merciful.

Arina   He was once, while we were good, but – Well, there it is! (*She has pulled herself together.*) I've told our solicitors to be here on Monday. I have three estates. This one, which now has our famous Valley annexed to it, will be yours (**Peter***'s*). The outlying farm on the mountain slopes, separated from here by Townsend's place – it's not the most hospitable of places but you are young, and it's worth money – that will be made over in trust to you (**Anna**) and your sister. And Newbridge, not to be considered a ha'pworth less in value or acreage than here, will be signed over to you (**Paul**).

Anna   Thank you, Grandma, but we don't want anything.

Arina (*to* **Peter** *and* **Paul**)   You've nothing to say?

Peter *gestures that he is overcome with emotion and goes behind her to put his hand on her shoulder and think.*

Anna   What about you, Grandma?

Arina   I have capital.

Paul   Where will you live, Mother?

Arina   Wherever I like.

Paul (*pays his obeisance*)   Ma'am.

Arina   Let Steven's death be a lesson to us all. The manner of his passing was lonely, premature and without the sacraments. That springs from neglecting family obligations and not honouring one's parents always. I regret my son's death but I mustn't go on grieving, nor should you, for – who knows? – his soul, maybe, is having a happy time on high.

*She leaves. And ghosts – **Steven** and **Victor** – follow.*

Paul   Exactly what I said: 'Who knows? Of that matter we must continue uncertain!'

He has another drink in celebration; **Peter***, deep in his own thoughts, also needs a drink; and* **Anna***, who is weeping for everyone and, seeing that her uncles are preoccupied, has a little drink too.*

Thus ends what we can regard as Act One.

Act Two

Scene One

A yard. **Anthony** *and a* **Servant** *carry luggage, as to a carriage off, across the yard (and they will repeat their business with luggage, witnessing and skirting the following scene).* **Anna**, *her sister* **Lena** *and* **Vera**, *the maid, come in. They are dressed for travelling and they carry pieces of luggage. They are now young women.* **Anna** *is upset (and later she will start weeping);* **Lena**, *the darker personality is (understandably) of a sullen disposition.*

Now comes **Arina**, *dressed for leaving. She's aged.*

Arina   On, out, we're leaving. (*Shooing on the others.*)

But she's in a rage and she turns back to shout abuse at the house, where **Peter** *is concealing himself, forward again, shooing on the others, and back again to shout further abuse at the house.*

Arina   I gave my life for this place, creating it, increasing it – what for?! I ran myself into the ground managing it! I gave life to you, to a family – for what?! To be told what to do?!

She makes to leave, returns.

I do not account for myself to anyone, I do not take orders. Nobody tells me what I can, what I can't do! I *give* orders! (*She makes to leave again, shooing the others, 'Out, we're leaving!' – but she's back again:*) Who gave you this place? And added to it since then – Townsend's – bought out of the capital assets I had for the support of myself! And you are mismanaging everything! (*To herself.*) Disastrously. It's *unbearable*. I gave my life for here. (*She starts shouting again:*) I gave you all this and it's not enough without my blood?! . . . I have another son.

She leaves, **Anna**, **Lena** *and* **Vera** *preceding / trailing her.* **Anthony / Servant** *watch her go,* **Anthony**'s *hand raised in a farewell.* **Ivan**, *is somewhere, looking unhappy.*

Scene Two

Newbridge: **Paul**'s *estate.*

A table, chairs, decanter, glasses. **Arina***, standing, waiting;* **Anna** *and* **Lena***, too.*

Kiry*, elderly, comes in.* (*He was the manservant in earlier scenes.*) *She half recognises him. He smiles and winks at her prior to sitting at the table and pouring a drink for himself. Then:*

Kiry   Kiry: I was footman to your late husband one time. Oh! (*'Oh!' as he pulls himself up to offer a drink to* **Arina**.) Ma'am?

She shakes her head, 'no'. This, though, is strange behaviour from a servant.

He sips his drink slowly, contentedly.

Arina   . . . My son knows I'm here?

Kiry   He knows you're here . . . He'll be down soon . . . The rain is coming down now out there. And the rye has come into flower . . . A bad summer.

He replenishes his glass and pours a drink into another glass for **Paul** *who is about to come in.* **Paul** *is an altered man. He's leaning on a stick and on* **Ulita** (*one of* **Arina**'s *servant maids in the old days*).

Paul   Mother! (*A suggestion of cynicism.*)

Arina   My son?! (*As much a 'What is the matter?' as a greeting.*)

He dismisses or ignores the implied question. **Ulita** *seats him beside* **Kiry** *and she takes the chair on the other side of him.* **Kiry** *slides the drink to* **Paul** *and then, 'Ulita?', asking* **Ulita** *would she like a drink.* **Ulita** *declines. And* **Kiry** *again offers to pour a drink for* **Arina**.

Kiry   Are you sure?

Arina   Yes, I'm sure.

Paul   But you'll sit with us?

She sits across the table from them.

(This is) A surprise call, Mother.

Arina   Oh!

Paul   And how is the son who adores you, my brother?

Arina (*decides to play it brightly, airily*)   New business methods! Endless calculations over trifles! Nonsensical sums! Pestering everyone about him to death to fill in forms which he draws up himself! Inventories – he wants to know the exact number of raspberry bushes on the estate. Raspberries! The birds of the air seed raspberries going about their business! To the neglect of the real concerns: crops, grain, timber, cattle, tenants. Waste of time!

Paul   And prayers?

Arina Supplications!

Paul   Well, prayers and form-filling: after the seminary you put him into the Civil Service.

Arina   Pettifogging – he'd go to court over a blade of grass. Needlessly making enemies! Meanness, 'piety' – the air is poisoned with piety – and his hypocrisy: it's useless to him, getting him nowhere! And his . . . and the rest of it. (*She has reined herself back.*)

Paul   More than flesh and blood can stand. 'Love is not where most it is professed'?

She laughs (without knowing why).

You are speaking, Mother, of your favourite child.

Arina   Nobody's smarm and fawning ever took me in.

Paul   What did?

Arina   'What did'?

Paul   You gave him that beautiful estate.

Arina   And I gave you here.

Paul   Here and there don't quite equate. And three years ago – land fever caught up with you in your retirement – you bought Townsend's.

Arina   It came on the market at last.

Paul   Paid out big money for it, your own money.

Arina   Where's the sin in buying Townsend's?

Paul   Added it to his estate.

Arina   The continuity of that place now. One tract, the sweep of it, from the river to the first slopes of the mountain. Marvellous! The range of it, nearly as far as the eye can see, to the farm I gave the orphans, and even to the rocks beyond that.

Paul   Marvellous. And now you are here, in your horse-drawn transport, with 'the orphans', my nieces, and – anybody else?

Ulita *whispers to him.*

Paul   Coachman and maid. Why? A social call? To enquire about my health?

Arina   I didn't know you were unwell.

Paul   So it's simply a social call.

Arina   It's not . . . I've come to stay.

Paul   Have you, Mother? (*He pushes his glass to* **Kiry** *for a refill and, only when that business is effected, he says:*) You're welcome.

Though humiliated, perceptively she's relieved and relaxes, somewhat. **Kiry** *has another drink.*

Kiry   How it's coming down out there!

Paul   It was raining when you left my brother's place this morning?

Arina   No.

Kiry   Half-rotten hay for the cattle this winter, the rye only just in flower.

Arina   Well, sitting around in the afternoon drinking won't help matters.

Paul (*flashpoint*)   And what would you have me do about it? Shift the rain from here to the bloodsucker's place? Would that suit you?

Arina   I –

Paul   Did it never occur to you that some people might like to live their lives other than the particular way you would like them lived?

And as he mutters to himself 'Sitting around in the afternoon', **Ulita** *whispers in his ear something about 'her maid', and:*

Paul   Where's your maid?

Arina   She –

Paul   Where's your maid?

Arina   I sent her to the kitchen. When we arrived and nobody came to meet us I had a look around. In the kitchen I saw the staff sitting there, shovelling food down themselves and throwing what they didn't want under the table, so I sent Vera, my maid –

Paul   She (**Ulita**) is housekeeper here!

Arina   She was my scullery maid.

Paul   He (**Kiry**) manages the estate!

Arina   He was –

Paul   You cannot retire and continue to be in charge: some one person gives the orders in a place. It isn't my idea: it's the rule, everyone acts on it. I know my orders are stupid, yours are clever. You are so clever, Mother, your favourite child has turned you out of your home.

Arina   He didn't turn me out of –

Paul   He's made a beggar of you! You want to stay here – so too your 'orphans', maid, coachman, anybody else – you're welcome, but you give orders to no one, you have no say whatsoever in the running of my household or estate and you do not come near my rooms.

He indicates that he wishes to leave and that the decanter should follow him. **Ulita** *assists him and* **Kiry** *follows them off with the decanter and glasses.*

Arina *sits there ('What have I done?')* **Anna** *is in tears again.* **Lena** *looks disdainful of* **Arina** *and her uncle* **Paul** *is even lower in her estimation.*

Lena   *He* looks like death.

Scene Three

The ghosts have returned, bridging this scene with Scene Two. **Steven** *and* **Victor**, *revelling in a Heine poem – revelling in their coughing and laughter – as if in mockery of* **Arina***'s state.*

Steven *and* **Victor** *(recite, sing, swap and deliver lines simultaneously)*

> *Nach Frankreich zogen zwei Grenadier',*
> *Die waren in Russland gefangen.*
> *Und als sie kamen ins deutsche Quartier,*
> *Sie liessen die Köpfe hangen.*

> *Da hörten sie beide die traurige Mähr:*
> *Dass Frankreich verloren gegangen,*
> *Besiegt und zerschlagen das grosse Heer,*
> *Und der Kaiser, der Kaiser gefangen.*

During which, activity builds in the house as in an emergency. **Ulita** *carrying a basin and towels as from a sick room; other servants actively engaged.* **Arina**, *worried, hanging her head, has to keep out of it. A* **Doctor**, *as from a sick room, taking a break.* **Kiry** *bringing a drink to* **Doctor***;* **Vera** *bringing a shawl to* **Arina***.* **Ulita** *off to sick room again, and* **Arina** *takes the opportunity of approaching* **Doctor***.*

Arina   How is he? He's getting better, isn't he?

Doctor   God is merciful.

Arina   What does that mean?

Doctor   He's dying.

Arina   But you've been treating him for so long – the other doctors – poultices, medication!

Doctor   *I* wasn't called in time. Had he been drained sooner.

Arina (*is desperate*)   I gave him this place! – Did you mention me to him?

Doctor   I did, as you asked.

Arina   Did you mention his nieces? Did you raise the matter of a –

Doctor   Put the idea out of your mind of his making a will. It wouldn't stand up. I don't know if he can even sign his name. Believe me, you would be in trouble with the law. Believe me, your other son would see to that.

Ulita (*returns*)   Doctor, he's calling for you. (*She continues near them.*)

Doctor (*to* **Arina**)   Go and see him.

Arina   He doesn't want to see me.

Doctor   Go and see him. And send for his nieces. I'm sure it won't be necessary to inform his brother. I'm sure his brother is kept advised of the situation. (*The last is knowing – to do with* **Ulita**. *He goes off, followed by* **Ulita**.)

Activity continues on the house; ghosts, **Steven** *and* **Victor**, *resume / repeat their Heine poem and follow* **Anna** *off.*

Scene Four

Anteroom and bedroom.

Ulita *and* **Kiry**, *both watchful, are in the anteroom.* **Kiry** *may have an expression of some concern for* **Paul**, **Ulita** *has none. Towards the end of the following, she has a whispered word with* **Kiry** *('Go and tell Peter that the situation here is critical') and* **Kiry** *leaves, purposefully.*

The bedroom, where **Paul** *lies in bed, is murky, airless, with a greenish light. A lamp burns in front of a holy picture and throws shadows. At the moment,* **Paul** *is looking in the direction of the lamp and holy picture, suspiciously, craftily. He's rambling, talking to phantoms, laughing to himself, shouting angrily . . .*

Paul   . . . There! See him! Kneeling – he thinks I'm dying – praying to the holy picture: 'By the immaculate grace of the Sacred Heart, I think my brother Paul is dying.' (*He laughs into himself.*) Well, I'll have you know – are you listening?! – there's good as well as bad in people, there's more to life than prayers. There's more to it than money, property, or prayers! I'll have you know there are other things. Some believe in God, some trust in horses too . . . Good people out there, well intentioned, yes, playing music . . . Singing? Yes . . . People in the circus, trying to fly! People out there using their time, writing unintelligible poetry, putting sounds together . . . using all their time, without interest in a penny of return . . . (But) when they lose their sense of awe people turn to property . . . and religion . . . Well, I'll have you know there's good as well as bad. Man took up a cow's horn, a simple cow's horn, saw that it was good, saw that it was amazing when he blew into it, and from that simple sound what've you got? So, y'see! . . . (*Whispering.*) There! See him! Kneeling – he thinks I'm dying – praying to the . . .

Lights dissolving – passage of time.

Scene Five

Anteroom and bedroom.

Women **Servants** *whispering what one imagines are prayers in the anteroom.* **Arina** *is entering,* **Vera** *following. And* **Ulita**, *watchful, follows them.* **Vera** *stays in the anteroom.*

Arina *continues into the bedroom to engage in what she knows is a losing battle but fear and desperation driving her on.* **Paul** *is silent in bed. The lamp burns in front of the holy picture, throwing shadows.*

Arina   . . . How are you, Paul? . . . How are you feeling today?

Paul   Not too bad.

Arina   Oh, that's good! That's good!

Paul   Not too bad. Was there a doctor here?

Arina   He's been seeing you every day. He'll be back again tomorrow.

Paul   Poultices.

Arina   Yes. He's a good doctor, better than the others, much better. He'll make you better, you'll see. It's important that you get better. You have to get better.

Paul (*to himself*)   He's a good doctor.

Arina   Yes. And d'you know who's coming to see you?

Paul   Did *she* have affection for anyone?

Arina (*a whisper*)   What?

Paul   For Papa? . . . She hated Steven.

Arina (*a whisper*)   No.

Paul   And maybe, tsssssss – the – bloodsucker too. (Well) Whatever the soft spot there, if there was one, you know I think she was deeply ashamed of him. (Well) I was.

Arina   Do you know who's coming to see you?

Paul   And as for what she thought of me: (Well) I never knew of a stupid man that came entirely of clever people. (*He laughs.*)

Arina   Your nieces, Anna and Lena, are coming to see you – Paul.

Paul   The 'orphans'. (*And a laugh into himself.*)

Arina   I sent for them. They love seeing you. And I sent for His Grace, Bishop Henry.

Paul   And my brother.

Arina   No, he hasn't been sent for.

Paul   There! The pervert!

Arina   What?

Paul   There! Bloodsucker! (*He's pointing.*)

Arina   That's your dressing gown.

Paul   There! Praying – see – now – to the holy picture: 'By the immaculate grace of the Sacred Heart, I think my brother Paul is dying and I come into his estate.' (*He's laughing.*)

Arina   . . . Well, you haven't made a will, have you? And as the law stands, it's true, he is the legitimate heir. And in your present condition you can't do anything about it. That's why you have to get better – you have to get better: To enable you to make other arrangements: to enable you to make a will . . . Paul?

Paul   Are you here for my funeral?

Arina   No. No!

Paul   Are you not?

Arina   I assure you, assure you. So long as you live, so long as you live, there really isn't much, really isn't, to trouble an old woman like me. Really isn't much. You are ill, very ill, that's true, and it's true everyone has to die, but I'm not here for your funeral.

Paul   And you?

Arina   And I?

Paul   Will you die?

Arina   There's a limit to everyone's life.

Paul   Then *wait* for it.

She feels the barb. A reaction in the anteroom as to the arrival of someone downstairs, and **Vera** *goes off.*

Arina   What I'm saying is: it is the custom – for us all – while waiting for the life to come to make provision for our relatives.

Paul   Is that the custom?

Arina   Yes.

Paul   Is it?

Arina   That's the custom.

Paul (*to himself*)   That's the custom . . . Do you still hear voices?

She doesn't understand.

'Go to the saint, go to the saint.'

Arina (*sighs and then starts to laugh*)   Yes, I believe I do still hear voices.

Paul   'There is a humour that treads the brink of tears,' Arina?

And though she perhaps doesn't quite understand it, it fuels her, somehow, to further laughter, and he starts to laugh with her – a dying man and a desperate old woman. Until tiredness/pain stops him.

Arina   And I never went to visit his shrine.

Vera *returns to the anteroom;* **Anna** *and* **Lena**, *still in their travelling coats, are with her.* **Arina** *beckons them to come in and they greet one another. Then:*

Arina   Say hello to him, talk to him.

Anna   How are you, Uncle Paul!

Paul   Not too bad.

Anna   Oh, that's good!

Arina   Kiss him, kiss him.

Anna *kisses* **Paul**. **Lena** *merely touches him with her fingertips and nods at him.*

Paul   Not too bad.

Anna   His arms are so thin, Grandma.

Lena (*a sullen rebuke to* **Arina**)   Have you nothing left at all, no money?

Arina   Sit by him, talk to him.

Anna   We finish school forever, Uncle Paul, in three weeks' time, then we're going to look for work. In the arts.

Arina   Bless us, do you hear that?

Lena   Are we now going to have to live on a mountainside?

Arina   You own it. Talk to him.

Anna   We are going to devote ourselves to holy art.

Paul (*whispers, pointing*)   There!

Anna   We are! (Going to devote ourselves to art.)

Paul   See him – be careful! The pervert – praying to the holy picture! 'By the immaculate grace of the Sacred Heart, I think my brother Paul is dying and I come into his . . . ' (*He's laughing again, which moves into a moan of pain.*)

Arina (*to no one*)   It is too late for any will. (*To* **Anna**, *who is crying.*) Shush! (*New tone, loudly.*) Well, that's all right, let your brother have the house and land, what about the movable property: capital, effects, assets? Paul! It's perfectly lawful to give away those matters in your own lifetime without having recourse to legal documents and without having to be accountable to anyone, for they are things that may be gained or lost, here today, gone the next. They can be let go to your brother Peter, who you keep referring to as the Bloodsucker – and other names. Or they can – in front of an upstanding witness, Bishop Henry, whom I've sent for – be given to your nieces who love you, whose only inheritance is an inhospitable scalp of rock halfway up a mountain. Or they can be given to me, your mother, who made you, who gave you everything in the first place . . .Paul!

Lena (*another rebuke*)   Why are you bothering? When Uncle Peter arrives, ask him straight out for this place. Shame him. Put it to him in public.

Arina   I should shame myself by asking? I'll – run – my – course.

Paul   Property, land, money. That's all she ever thought of. She sold her soul. But, at least – are you listening? – she did not emasculate her son with self-pity. I'll have you know she did not. With a mother's self-pity, no – alas! She had other weapons . . . She could easily have done something worthwhile with her life.

Arina   What could I have done, other than what I did?

Paul   But a tyrant can't be wrong.

Arina   What ought I to have done? For I'd like to know.

Paul   She doesn't know me, never did, but I know her. Watching me back then in case I'd smile. Was everything serious as that? Now watching, *waiting* for a smile. I know her. She put all her money on the black and it came up red.

There has been a stir in the anteroom in reaction to the arrival of someone downstairs. **Ulita** *says 'The new master', which we hear, and goes off.* **Arina** *is looking about distractedly.*

Anna (*cued by a whisper from* **Lena**)   Grandma, the air is so heavy here, may we go downstairs?

Arina (*nods 'yes'; absently*)   Say goodbye to him.

Anna   Goodbye for now, Uncle Paul!

Lena (*to* **Arina**)   This is doing no good. This is stupid.

Arina (*to no one*)   I fear for my sanity! – (*To* **Lena**.) You bastard imp! – (*To herself*.) Deliver me from evil! (*She knows that* **Peter** *has arrived.*)

Peter *has arrived in the anteroom.* **Ulita** *is with him, whispering to him. He shepherds* **Anna** *(weeping again) and* **Lena***, who were about to leave, back into the bedroom, his eyes are on* **Arina***'s back.*

Peter   Tsssssss!

He approaches her from behind, puts his hands on her waist, his chin on her shoulder:

Mama, Mama! So this is how it is, so this is how it is! And you are my good friend, aren't you?

Arina   This is how it is.

Peter   And it's much too soon, much too soon. And you are downcast, I can tell, very downcast.

Arina   Not too bad!

Peter   Oh, don't say that, oh, I can see you are! But it's wrong, wrong, very wrong, to go sorrowing and repining against the Almighty! Questioning the Creator. You in tears too, grasshoppers! (*Takes their hands.*) What would God say to this? Tsssssss! Smile at once if you please and there's an end to it! (*He takes a few steps to have a quiet peep at* **Paul***.*) Though I too have grieved. Very, very, very much . . . Oh you bad, bad brother to be leaving us! (*He returns.*) And wasn't he exhalted, didn't he have notions? Didn't he, just! All his elevations and superiority are now controverted in a single moment. Mmmm! I called several times over the years to see him and he wouldn't see me. My brother. Is he in pain? There was no reaching out to him, was there – he'd hardly open his mouth to speak to you, Mama, would he? Now the trial date has arrived, he might be only too glad to cover up those sins of pride and haughtiness.

Arina   He isn't dead.

Peter   No, but once sins are written down in the Book of Life they aren't so easily scratched out?

Arina   Repentance isn't accepted?

Peter   I hope it is, I sincerely hope so. I hope he pleads guilty, throws himself on the mercy of the court to avoid the terrible wrath. That would be the best thing for him. He never liked me. I wished him well. You and I had our fallings-out too, Mama, but I wish well to everyone. I wish well, as the Bible teaches, to those who calumniate, hate and injure me and try to cheat me out of what's mine by right. God has good reasons for everything He does. All unseen He chose to shorten the days of my brother Steven. And now Paul. Tsssssss!

Lena   Uncle Peter! If Uncle Paul dies, do you think you'll be able to manage this estate on top of the very big estate you have already? Do you wish it on yourself?

Peter   Grasshopper, it's not what I wish but what the law commands, and I must obey. I value my good name above everything so I do my duty no matter what, even when it's a heavy burden. If a man didn't have a cross to bear, he'd forget himself and fall into sinful ways. And this estate joins my own one: the two belong together. Indeed, since Townsend's became mine, your place, grasshoppers, the mountainside, is the natural extension of the tract in that direction. (*Of* **Paul**.) Does he suffer much?

Arina   Not so very much! In fact the new doctor gives us great hope. (*A lie.*)

Peter   Well, there you are for you then, that's splendid! But, just in case, I'll stay for a few days. It's a family concern, I can maybe advise on certain matters, offer some words of comfort in his ear, and help with the – arrange whatever. You'll allow me that, won't you?

Arina   It's not for me to allow: I'm only a guest here too.

Peter   I'll do my duty. Before I sit with him I'll say a little prayer over here first. (*He tiptoes to the holy picture and kneels before it.*)

Arina (*goes to* **Paul**'s *bedside*)   Paul, if I've done you any wrong, forgive me, for Christ's sake.

Paul (*referring to the kneeling figure of* **Peter**)   See! Do you see him *now?* Satan! (*And he laughs.*)

Anna *is crying, servants are crying and praying,* **Peter** *continues praying.* **Kiry**, **Priest**, **Anthony** *are entering. Ghosts –* **Steven** *and* **Victor** *– appear.* **Paul** *joins them.*

Thus ends Act Two.

Act Three

Scene One

Farmhouse on the mountainside, a rude place. An old peasant **Woman**
*talking to herself, perhaps with knitted hat and a shawl across her
shoulders, is pouring soup from a saucepan into two bowls. She takes up
one of the bowls.*

Woman (*not really distinguishable*)   Take this one in to Her
Ladyship and tell her to get up. (*She stops, pauses. Then:*) Did
something happen?

We come to realise it is **Arina**. *She takes the bowl off. She returns and
takes the second bowl for herself. She pauses again.*

Arina   What has happened? . . . I'm old, is it? . . . No one
ever dared think of me as old . . . It's the last few years of cold
and damp up here. And the curse of being idle has me stupid.
(*She is taking her bowl of soup to a chair. She pauses again, this time to
address the emptiness of the place, reprimand absent ghosts.*) Where are
you now? – Where's your dirty songs? 'Cherrymaid it's time
for fun!' Spouting. Poetry. (*She sits, drinking her soup. The chair
commands a view of the plain below.*) I ruled that place well.
People down there were frightened of me. People like to be
ordered . . . Plenty to do down there. And there's years of
work left in me . . . Do you know I don't know. There's been
a queer decline in activity. It's dying out, is it? That's what it
was all for? Aw, that can't be! . . . (*She looks at what she's eating.*)
Cabbage soup . . . The stores of food I promised myself . . .
soup with goose giblets . . . And you'd sleep safe and sound
down there as you might in Christ's bosom, without fear at
night of thieves, ghosts, that howling outside, without fear of
the candle falling over, the spark from the hearth to burn the
place down . . . Or that *wretch*, devil, waking me up –
whatever he wants of me – knocking, scratching behind the
board in the wall . . . (Well) I'm going back down there. Oh, I
am! Who has more right? Yes! . . . But bowing the head? *Me?*
To a son? *Son* – is that what he is? – 'Tssssssss!' . . . (*Then,*

pathetically:) And God would reward you, my dear, for being kind to your old mother . . . And she would love you, my dear, as now the only child she has left.

She's near tears, resisting tears; she's agitated; and now short little steps, almost at a run, as if to get away from herself (like a dog scurrying from an internal pain), and to put away the bowl.

She recovers herself and now she returns to her vantage point of the plain, shouting, angrily:

I'll go down there and to summon you I'll send messengers flying, and when they drag you before me I'll be standing on the top step of that building, the townland assembled round looking up at me, to hear me denounce you!

Now she is backing away from her vantage point of the plain: someone is approaching in a car.

Anna *comes in, as from a bedroom, barefooted and wearing some kind of nightdress. She is now a grown woman, striking. As always, her gentle nature; now too, though, a marked vulnerability: something is wrong, something has befallen her that she is concealing, that she is unable to reveal.*

Anna   Grandma? I heard you shouting.

Arina   I have another visitor.

The car has arrived. There is a silence. **Arina** *isn't going to be the one to break the silence. Eventually:*

Peter (*off*)   Now! Muhammad had to come to the mountain! . . . Bearing gifts! . . . A few gifts for his dear friend Mama! . . . And we are dear to each other, aren't we? . . .

Arina   We are in need of nothing today!

Peter (*off*)   But wait'll you see!

Anthony *comes in with a sack, puts it down, nods a self-conscious greeting, and goes out again.*

Peter (*off*)   Oh, I'm a bad, bad boy! . . . But you are a bad, bad girl! How we've let time pass! And didn't we promise —

how long ago was that? — to call on each other?! . . . And look what else I brought you! I've a maid for you!

Arina   We have just acquired a maid, thank you! All vacant posts are now filled! (*She winks her control of the situation at* **Anna**.)

Peter (*off*)   But wait'll you see!

Anna *retreats to the bedroom, off. And* **Vera** *comes in. She, too, is now fully grown. She is wearing some kind of loose overcoat. She bows shyly, and whispers:*

Vera   Ma'am.

Arina   . . . Turn around. (*And when* **Vera** *obeys:*) What a back!

Vera   Always on about my back, what has it done on you?

Arina (*takes her hands*)   You've grown. You look well. (*And now a discovery.*) And what is this? Is this something else? What wind brought you this? (**Vera** *is pregnant.*)

Vera   It's nothing to do with me.

Arina   It's what?

Vera   It's as Peter pleases.

Arina   Who?

Vera   The master.

Arina   Well, well!

Peter (*off*)   And it isn't as though a continent divided us!

Arina   This is our Christian monk! (*But something in the situation pleases her.*)

Anthony *comes in, immediately preceding* **Peter**. **Peter**, *obviously, has aged too. He's nervous.* **Arina** *is offering no greetings, so no greetings are exchanged.* **Anthony** *has a chicken, which he holds up.*

Peter   I thought to bring you a turkey.

Arina   Did you?

Peter   But it would be no use to you because of its dimensions and your circumscribed cooking facilities . . . And your modest requirements, now that you live alone.

Arina   Yes.

Peter (*producing items from the sack*)   Cheese. Cucumbers. Apples. You never tasted sweeter.

Arina   I planted the trees.

Peter   Eternal gratitude to you.

She has her back to him: a movement towards her – or he only considers it – to put his hands on her waist, as was his habit.

So this is how it is, this is how it is . . . (*He has baulked at the idea of touching her.*) And longing to kiss my dear mama . . . Not a lot of growth up here, let alone apple trees. But maybe that will change. Well, please God. (*Producing other items from the sack.*) Pickles. Sausage. Vegetables. What's this? Oh yes. Not that we ever indulged in those days, but once in a blue moon there were certain bought articles from the town, one in particular that you liked, wasn't there?

Arina   Rum.

Peter   No.

Arina   Marzipan.

Peter   Marzipan.

Arina   . . . And you are well?

Peter   I'm sad. But allow me to ask, how are the grasshoppers, our young proprietresses? Do you hear from them?

Arina   You didn't notice the hackney car drive across the plain yesterday and come up here? – You didn't *notice* it?

Peter   Was that what that motor car was about? So they're here?

Arina   Anna is here. 'Grandma, may I stay for a while?'
You see: asking my permission! She and her sister own the
place.

Peter (*to* **Anthony**)   Take that idle creature into the kitchen
and do something with it!

Anthony *goes off with the chicken, the 'idle creature'.*

Arina   You see: '*May I* stay for a while'!

Peter   But strange of her to arrive out of the blue like that.

Arina   Oh, they've always kept in touch. Anna writes.

Peter   Looking for money.

Arina   No! I account to them – as I should – for running
the place, and now and again I'd find something to send
them. Then the letters: 'Don't send us any more money' –
They're on the stage. 'Don't send us any more of anything',
they didn't need anything, they were having a great time.
'We're given presents, we're wonderfully happy', parties,
restaurants, champagne, 'And we don't have to pay for
anything.'

Peter   Tsssssss! (*To* **Vera**.) Go out! You might find
something in there too to occupy you.

Vera *goes off to the kitchen.*

Peter   They can't be keeping themselves straight.

Arina   What does that mean?

Peter   Anna was always giddy.

Arina   No! –

Peter   You wouldn't know what –

Arina   No! –

Peter   You wouldn't know what goes on in the other one's
head.

Arina   Anna, yes, is soft, but I'd still have hopes of her.

Peter   She'll hook up with a ne'er-do-well stranger – A soldier? And what will that mean then for this place?

Arina *(which gives her pause; then, angrily)*   What will it mean?

Peter   And what will that mean then for *you*? It bears thinking about, that's all I'm saying. There's no sin for girls that go on the stage. They lose their treasure and – *(he blows a short, tuneless whistle)* – that's all they care about it.

Vera *comes in to select something from the sack or box. She has removed her loose coat and the evidence of her pregnancy is clearly evident; imminent. She goes out again.*

Arina *(as though to no one)*   Oh, nowadays it appears they don't even have to go on the stage.

Peter   Even saints sinned, Mama.

Arina   Did they?

Peter   When driven to it.

Arina   Hard pressed, they say, a magpie will sing like a nightingale. What brought you up here?

Peter   What brought me up?!

Arina   Yes!

Peter   What brought me up here?!

Arina   If it's to do with Vera, you're not leaving her here.

Peter   That never crossed my! – I never thought of! – Tsssssss, I! Vera is my – I made Vera my housekeeper.

Arina   And you made her something else!

Peter   I, tsssssss! Well, you always handled such matters.

Arina   'Such matters'?

Peter   I know nothing about it! It's got nothing to do with me!

Arina   And it's got nothing to do with her!

Peter *(starts to cry)*   I value my name . . . No mud will stick to me.

Arina (*viewing his tearfulness suspiciously; she is, though, working out something. To herself*) 'Such matters' . . . Would such a matter be such a bad thing? Would an heir be such a bad thing? . . . But what could I do about such matters up here? Up here, what can a person do for anyone, that's all *I'm* saying. What?

Peter   The other matter then that we were talking about.

Arina   What other matter then?

Peter   I don't know.

Arina   You don't know.

Peter   The other matter!

Arina (*to herself*)   Christ! (Can he talk straight?!)

Peter   This place then – the other matter we were talking about – this place! You should have control of it. You should have them have a deed of trust drawn up for it in your favour.

Arina   I've one already for running it.

Peter   I know you have for 'running' it, but one for protecting it, for yourself. Or mortgaging it if you wished to? Or stitching it back on to the rest like you had it one time? The latest, it's rumoured: talks of afforestation for places like this from the government. Well, please God. Trees look nice on the mountainside. And there'll be grants going for those able to fill in the forms. It bears thinking about, that's all I'm saying.

Anna *comes in. She has dressed. There is something very vulnerable about her. And there's something touching about her costume: perhaps the innocence of high-heel shoes.* **Peter** *is taken with her – a degree of leery senescence.* **Anthony** *and* **Vera** *return from the kitchen during the following.*

Anna   Hello, Uncle Peter!

Peter   Who is this?

Anna   I'm afraid it's only me, Uncle Peter.

Peter   Who-is-this-big-woman!

Anna   Anna, Uncle Peter.

Peter   Anna-Uncle-Peter!

He kisses her, forehead, cheeks, presses her to him, rubs her back . . .

None of you knows what I'm going to say to you now, do you? People nowadays like to go round a subject because they don't know what they're going to say next, but that's not my way. I'm not like that. I don't like it. It's trying to be too clever, that's what I think it is. And the thing I'm going to say to you now – and the thing that brought me up here is: 'What can a person do for anyone up here?' – I agree with you – so would you consider coming down for a visit, stay for a while? settle those couple of outstanding matters we were talking about while you were about it, stay for as long as you like? forever if you like, including this big grown-up lady here (**Anna**). Would you consider that, Mama?

Arina   I would.

Scene Two

*We are back in the location of Act One, once **Arina**'s now **Peter**'s place. It is night.*

N.B. The following is an optional scene.

Ulita *spreads a baize cloth on a table, sets chairs and a pack of cards.*

Anna *and* **Vera** *come in.* **Anna**'s *sashaying and singing to herself are not what they seem; they are a cover for something she can't face up to or reveal to others. Also, she would like to convince herself that safety lies here in this place.* **Vera**, *never a knowing person, who is quite simple really, has grown brighter: satisfaction in her pregnancy and impending motherhood. She now has her own part of life.*

Anna (*singing*) Ah! Ah! '*Que j'aime, que j'aime! Que j'aime les mili-mili-mili-taires!*' Uncle is a good man, isn't he? Isn't he very understanding? Isn't he a very caring person, Ulita, Vera?

Ulita *leaves.* **Vera**'s *smiling moon face. As in adolescence,* **Anna** *steals a drink for herself and* **Vera**.

Anna   Life – *everything* – is so simple to him! It's – *enviable*. He's funny. (*A toast.*) *À votre bonne santé!* Everything with *chic*, you see!

Vera   Here goes! (*The toast from adolescence.*)

Anna   He's very caring of Grandma. And, after *everything*, she's very happy with him. *She's* funny. She wants the farm back to give to him, I think – I don't care! He wants me to stay, live here.

Vera   He fairly licks his mouth when he looks at you.

Anna (*twirls, laughs*)   But what do you do here, aren't you bored?

Vera   I'm not a lady.

Anna   Does he ever stop talking?

Vera   No. He's getting *worse!* That's the reason, Ivan says, it's so hard to get anyone to work here. But I have a trick. I don't listen.

Anna   Doesn't he notice?

Vera   How can he tell? I keep looking at him while he's talking, but I amn't here.

Anna   Where are you?

Vera   I think a lot about potatoes. Your sister? (*Meaning 'How is she?'*)

Momentarily, a startled look, fear, on **Anna**'s *face.*

Vera (*repeating her question*)   Lena?

Anna   Tell you some other time – (*singing:*) *Que j'aime, que j'aime! Que j'aime, les mili-mili-mili-taires!*

Arina (*off and as she comes in*) '*Que j'aime, que j'aime, que j'aime, que j'aime! Les mili-mili-mili-mili-mili-mili —*' Whatever that means!

Arina, **Priest**, **Peter** *and* **Ivan** *come in.* **Ulita** *is in attendance. Something of a festive spirit – though not from* **Ivan**. **Arina** *seems to have taken* **Vera** *under her wing.*

Peter (*to* **Anna**) Miss Madam! Running away from the dinner table without my permission!

Anna (*giggling*) Sorry, Uncle!

Peter 'Sorry Uncle!'

Arina (*of and aside to* **Vera**) And this Miss Madam! You'd think it might be a prince she's expecting! (*Seating* **Vera**.) Come, my beauty!

Priest So unexpected: Again, so kind of you to have me here?!

Peter *has a whispered word with* **Ulita**, *who leaves; while* **Arina** *continues to* **Vera**, *kindly:*

Arina And maybe it will be a prince! But the place is quiet, Ivan, even during the day? (*Why is that?*)

Ivan (*non-committal*) Oh! (*He's unhappy and he's removing himself.*) Goodnight!

Peter Aren't you going to play cards with us?

Ivan No.

Peter No? *No?* Come over here and sit in this chair beside Vera. (*He would like to set up* **Ivan** *with* **Vera**.)

Ivan No, thank you! There are things to be seen to, and I think a storm is coming on.

Peter And we've just got up from a nice stuffed big roast turkey dinner!

Laughter. He is great fun.

With glazed accompaniments!

Laughter.

Arina   Well, let a storm come on, Ivan!

Peter   Let it! Mama will deal with it for us! We're in here nice and snug, Little Miss Madam, aren't we?

Anna (*giggling*)   Yes, Uncle!

Peter   'Yes Uncle!'

Ivan   Goodnight! (*He leaves.*)

The others call 'Goodnight'. **Peter**, *though, has now become pensive.*

Peter (*as if to himself*)   Ivan. (*And shakes his head.*)

Arina   Ivan is a good worker.

Peter   Oh, we cannot fault a good worker as a worker, but what if that worker's intelligence quotient is lacking?

Arina   Ivan's? Ivan is loyal, Ivan is.

Peter   I once read a book – Excuse me, Mama, while I tell you about the book I once read. It said that the intellect is not to be despised if it be directed by faith. For a man without intelligence soon becomes a plaything of his passions. Wasn't that book in this house, Mama?

Arina   I expect it was if you think it was!

Peter   Would you agree, Father?

Priest   I? (*He doesn't know what answer is expected of him.*)

Peter   Oh, yes!

Arina   Theologians! Are we going to play cards?

Peter   Little Miss Madam, you come over here and sit next to me.

Anna   I'll watch, uncle.

Arina (*to* **Peter**)   Not in that one (*chair*), I don't want you on that side of me.

Priest   Madam? (*Asking her where he should sit.*)

Arina   There!

Priest   Madam (*Thank you.*)

Peter   Mama is the boss, Mama is the dealer.

Arina (*announcing the name of the game and dealing the cards*)
'Fools'!

Priest   Again so kind, Sir, the invitation, unexpected.

The cards are being dealt. The rhythm of the speeches often come from how the cards are dealt out, gathered, sorted, played. **Anna**, *whether hovering in the background, approaching or withdrawing from the table is a study in herself. The serenity of* **Vera**'s *trust, too, is marked.*

Anna   May I, uncle, have a glass of this?

Peter   Order what you like, Miss! We haven't seen this lady in years, suddenly she arrives out of the blue, the farm, (on) the mountainside: 'Oh, Grandma, may I stay for a little?' Next she's down here, can't put up with us past a week: 'Oh, uncle, I must go, it's so dull here.'

Anna   Well, let's see how it goes!

Peter   But I'm going to make her my prisoner.

Arina   And we haven't talked about your sister.

Peter   The sullen Lena.

Arina   How is she?

Anna   Yes, well, she's! (*A private moment of fear and confusion for her.*)

Arina   She was prone to colds and flus, as I remember it.

Anna (*Singing to herself*)   'Que j'aime, que j'aime, que j'aime les mili-mili-mili-taires!'

Arina (*to herself*)   'Mili-mili-mili-militaires'.

Peter (*as to himself*)   Mama always handled things. Settled everything for the best.

Arina   I'll take care of things, my good son . . . The things that happened here. Love intrigues? No end of them. They'd try to carry them off, hide the results of their jiggery-pokery, but there was no taking me in. Every time I tracked them down and dealt with them. Better than in a book.

Peter (*cueing her*)   'Those weren't meant to know?'

Arina   Those who weren't meant to know were kept in the dark.

Peter   Never a hint of scandal.

Arina   And it wasn't always to do with the servants. My sister-in-law came running.

Peter   'Arina, Arina' – listen to this, Father.

Arina   'Arina, Arina, help me, save me.' I did. With the Church at my elbow. And I never liked her. Got herself into trouble while her husband was away. I was present at the birth. A healthy baby boy. Her husband in the next room. Never knew a thing about it for as long as he lived. Now! Men! 'Fools'!

She laughs. She's won the first game.

Peter   She's too clever for us, Father!

Priest   Madam! (*Which is his applause.*)

Vera   She's too clever for us!

Arina (*to* **Vera**)   Deal. (*Meaning 'Deal the cards.' To herself.*) I didn't always do the right thing. A healthy baby boy.

Peter   Always settled everything for the best, Father, the Church at her elbow, assisting and making all the necessary arrangements.

Vera (*paused in dealing the cards, listening to the storm; and whispers in her superstitious manner*)   Ivan was right about the storm.

They listen to the storm for a moment or two.

Peter   Ivan, tsssssss! No, we can't fault a worker for his good work, no more than we can fault a beast of burden for carrying a good load. But we can fault that worker for other things, can't we, Father?

Priest   I?

Peter   If the intelligence quotient is lacking?

Priest   I don't quite follow where you're going, Sir.

Peter   I like to speak my mind. No shilly-shallying. Beasts nor reptiles nor fish have intelligence. Nor birds. Hens? They have temptations but no one expects them to resist them. Hens don't take vows, do they? Everything is natural to them. But we? Supposing you, Father, were to feel a bodily temptation, now, this minute, what would you call on for help?

Priest   My faith.

Peter   No, your intelligence. We were given intelligence, not for probing the unknown, but to refrain from sin including bodily passions. So a servant may be loyal – like Ivan – but if intelligence isn't that servant's strong point? Now you follow?

Priest   Yes!

Peter   Mama?

Arina   (*ordering her hand of cards*) Yes! Hens! They have to answer to no one, neither God nor the authorities. They have only one superior. And who is that? Who is that? The cock! (*And she laughs.*) The cock, the cock! 'Fools'! He's like the Turkish sultan to them!

She's won the second game. **Vera** *laughs, and there are complimentary sounds from the others; though* **Peter** *is disapproving of* **Arina***'s risqué remarks; he's annoyed.*

Ulita *comes in with a tray of savouries – small strawberry jam tarts – which she hands round.* **Peter** *moves away from the table to take* *a jam tart to* **Anna** *and/or to replenish her glass. An intermission in the card-playing.*

Arina   Jam tarts!

Peter   And if we want a little savoury we can have it, so we can! Can't we, Miss Madam?

Anna (*giggling*)   Yes, uncle.

Peter   'Yes uncle'!

Arina   Strawbery jam (*She's relishing her tart.*) And when I was carrying – which one of them was it? – I couldn't abide strawberries or anything to do with the blessed things. The minute a strawberry came into the house, I could smell it was there, 'Take the damn thing away, fling it out!' Blackcurrants? I couldn't get enough of them. Now, whose deal is it?

Priest (*caught with his mouth full*)   My – my – my-

Arina   Yours! (*Calling to* **Peter** *to return to the table.*) Attend! (*Approvingly, aside to* **Vera**.) I saw you forking down your whack of spuds and pint of milk , earlier. (*To no one.*) I'll take care of things.

Priest *is dealing the cards.* **Peter** *is returning to the table.*

Peter   A man must always behave so that his life can be seen from all sides like a candle in a lantern. (*To* **Priest**.) Men must be on their guard against sins of the flesh

Arina   And it's hard on them.

Peter   Hard or soft!

Arina (*finds this very funny*)   Hard or soft!

Peter (*is annoyed and would deny the ribald innuendo*)   Hard or soft! But such a man will be at peace with his conscience, no mud will stick to that man.

Arina   And hard or soft on intelligent men, women pay the bill.

Vera   Still, I wouldn't like to be caught out in that (*weather*).

Peter (*sudden anger, taking his annoyance out on* **Vera**)   Well, maybe that's where you belong, *Miss*! Maybe that's where you should be, Miss!

Arina   Everything is going to be fine, my good son.

Peter (*continues angrily to* **Vera**)   Or up on the side of the mountain! Would you like that, *Miss*? Instead of being down here in my house, safe and snug and fed . . . (*But in the next, he's back to his considerate, kind self.*) Where we'd all be maybe, if it weren't for the King of Heaven: out there, creatures, like the poor, cold, broken clogs on our feet, wet through and hungry.

Vera   Clogs indeed on gentle folk!

Peter   Do you know why we are gentle folk?

Vera   King of Heaven.

Peter   If it hadn't been for Him, I'd be a poor man.

Arina   Well, I had a hand in it too?

Peter (*ignores her remark*)   If it hadn't been for Him, I'd be living in a hut without a chimney now.

Vera (*laughing*)   Oh no, no, no, no, no!

Peter   I'd be mending one of your broken clogs, my eyes streaming from the smoke in the hut! Ow! Ow! (*He has hit his thumb with his imaginary hammer, mending an imaginary clog. He's quite a comedian.*)

Vera (*laughing*)   Oh no, no, no, you wouldn't!

Arina   No doubt God is good to us, but –

Peter   It's all His doing – Everything!

Vera   He gives us firewood!

Peter   We fancy we do things of ourselves, but do we?

Vera   We don't!

Peter   Do we?

Priest   We don't.

Peter   We don't!

Anna (*laughing, calls*)   We don't!

Vera   But my uncle was very pious. He was always praying. But one night he was caught out in a storm and he froze to death just the same.

Peter   What?

Vera   You'd think God would've done something.

Peter   That's just it! You can pray all you like, but if God wills it a man will freeze to death, and if He doesn't that man will stay alive. Isn't that true?

Vera   That's true!

Peter   Isn't that true, Father?

Priest   That's true, sir!

Peter   But isn't that true?

Anna   That's true, uncle! (*She's laughing too much.*)

Peter   (You can) Pray all you like, but God is wiser. You ask God for butter and he gives you onions.

Vera (*who is quite excited*)   You ask Him for – for –

Peter   That's just it!

Vera   For honey!

Peter   And He simply won't have it!

Vera   Or He'll – He'll give you a sting!

Laughter is dying down. **Arina** *has been quiet for some time.*

Peter   Mama is tired.

Arina   No. (*She's not tired.*)

A final sorting of her cards and, as against the earlier trumping of her successes and calling 'Fools', this time she simply holds up the winning hand of cards and places it on the table.

Vera   She's too clever for us.

Arina   My good son, I know what you've been expecting of me, but have you though what this means for us? New life here.

Peter   What?

Arina   Continuity, a baby.

Peter   Excuse me, Mama, while I finish about prayer.

Arina   And though everything isn't all as it should be, it's the real thing just the same.

Peter   Mama, allow me, excuse me –

Arina   It's holy, you know.

Peter   Acceptable prayers reach their destination, the not acceptable ones are as good as nothing.

Arina   And it all won't have been for nothing!

Peter   Mama! –

Anna *(calling)*   Uncle Peter, Uncle Peter! –

Peter   Anna! –

Arina   We won't just die out!

Anna   Uncle Peter! –

Peter   Mama! – Anna! –

Anna   Can I be godmother?!

Arina   Marvellous!

Peter   We'll put away the cards.

He takes the pack of cards and leaves the table. The others rise. **Anna** *(laughing) slips away.* **Priest** *will join* **Peter**. **Vera** *assists*

Arina *out of her chair – or vice versa.* **Ulita** *will clear up when they have all gone.*

Arina   My good son. (*Talking to herself.*) He's worried, and frightened. That's how men are at a time like this. But it's going to be all right. He'll see. Yes, because love intrigues? No end of them here. And who did they begin with? They began with myself and the young windmill – (*Calls to* **Peter**.) Your father! (*Talking to herself again:*) And that Miss Madam (Vera) came down from the very same village up there as me. (*She's moving to leave, stops, calls:*) And tomorrow, we'll sit down – you, me and Anna and settle the business of the farm for you! (*Going out, followed by* **Vera**:) Come, my mountain beauty, now you're in for it! You enjoyed the sowing, now try the harvesting.

Peter (*to* **Priest**)   I cannot fault her as a house-keeper. She's a good worker. But in that other department? Intelligence? That's how it happens that they fall into sin. But I shouldn't like to institutionalise her. I'll keep her on. (*Sighs.*) It. doesn't look good, though, to see a strange child in a house. The example? When the time comes, you'll do the baptism – everything's to be done properly – and make the other arrangements. Dear friend Mama's grown old: We all grow old, Father? But Ulita will be here to assist in whatever (*He has left with the* **Priest**.)

Scene Three

Arina *waits expectantly. She starts to laugh to herself. She is remembering* **Victor**, *who now appears, declaiming an ode of his own composition. Without necessarily looking at him, she is listening to and enjoying his words. The words reflect something of her present, good and expectant, mood.*

Victor   'Ode to a Newborn Son'.

O potent organ,
Respectful to orders in the dead of night –

Germinal, generous cock –
Stiff awaking, and on defiant rocks of fire,
You arise and go
To Venus' thickly wooded Mount
Above the generative cavern,
The font of love below.

The mouth soft yields and inside poked,
Attentive in courtesy and to acknowledge
The antechamber's fond wet welcoming
Reception and embrace,
Clito's swelling node of pleasure's stroked.

But courtliness observed, the welcome paid,
Not to further linger in the hall –
Inmost, the serious work is to be done –
Plunging on the guarded sanctum to attain
And charge what lies within that holy pantheon.

And suddenly the cock can drive no more –
It's there! Rammed to the balls
The noble fucker stops, at the inner door.
And waits. For what?
The shuddering. The proud head then explodes
And as from (a) cunning Trojan Horse
A million soldiers storm the walls.
Determinedly, in attack, they rush, scramble,
Concentrated in intent, swim,
Up and on, to meet the moon-ship coming down.

One soldier only gains the craft –
But one will do! –
And sails it into womb's safe keep.
That warrior, my son, is you!

In the background, a newborn baby cries. **Victor** *disappears.* **Vera**,
in nightdress, emerges from the darkness holding a baby. **Arina** *goes to*
Vera *and they meet in a soft embrace, sharing the baby between them.*

Scene Four

The small hours. **Anna** *is sitting alone. There is a glass in her hand, held out, which she appears to have forgotten. She appears, too, to be unaware that she is crying, weeping silently, with, at the same time, a gentle smile on her lips in a memory of some deep private grief. When, later, she moves about, it is as if her movements are not connected to her brain. As the phrase has it, she appears to be 'out of it'.*

Peter, *dressing gown hanging open, comes in cautiously – like someone who has been watching her for some time.*

Peter   I thought everyone was long asleep.

Anna *(could be talking to herself)*   I think I'd like to stay here.

Peter   . . . You're crying.

Anna *(as before)*   I think I'd like to stay here.

Peter   Would you? . . . Would you?

She nods in a vague way.

Do you like being an actress? . . . What is it like being an actress?

Anna *(sings quietly to herself)*
I want to come under the colonel,
The colonel, the colonel . . .

Peter   Is it true that men can touch actresses whenever they like?

Anna *(still weeping and her smile, as in a memory)*
I want to come under the colonel,
I'll only come under him . . .

She claps her hands over her head, silently, as if introducing someone on stage, and:

Lena!

And, as if she is **Lena**, *she starts to perform the vaudeville number 'An Old-fashioned Colonel', moving about, circling. For all her consciousness of* **Peter**, *he might not even be there. The song becomes fragmented; the movement is continuous and suggestive, though strangely innocent.*

Anna

> When I first saw the regiment's colonel
> All silvery-headed and slim,
> My feelings were – Oh! – so maternal:
> I want to look after the colonel,
> I want to cater for him!
>
> A ramrod-stiff old-fashioned colonel
> . . . I'll only be dressed down by him!
> . . . I want to serve under him!
>
> His seat is firm in the saddle
> . . . For his age he is lissom of limb
> . . . And his eye is more than paternal . . .
> . . . And I know that he'll never skedaddle!

Peter *reaches out a hand, tentatively; and again, this time his fingers touching her. She does not appear to notice. He touches her again. She continues her performance.*

Anna

> . . . I'll only take stick from the colonel,
> I'll only go riding with him!
> . . . I want to be drilled by the colonel,
> I'll only be dressed down by him!
> . . . I want to come under the colonel,
> I want to go down with him!

Here, perhaps, **Arina** *comes in in her dressing gown; perhaps smiling; something woke her up. Now she sees* **Peter** *touching* **Anna**. **Peter** *sees* **Arina***: he smiles/says the word 'Mama' at her, but no authority of hers is going to deter him in his pursuit of* **Anna***, whose dance takes them off in the following.*

Anna

> I want to come under the colonel,
> The colonel, the colonel,
> I want to come under the colonel,
> I'll only come under him . . .

Arina, *aghast, impotent, stands there. Her ghosts –* **Victor**, **Steven**, **Paul** *– emerge from the darkness around her.*

Scene Five

Night. Silence. **Arina** *somewhere in the darkness of the house, watching, listening for a sound, secretly. The silence is ominous.*

Ulita *comes in through the patches of night light and shade; stealthily, though rather swiftly, a glance behind her as she comes. She waits. She has a bundle, half concealed, under her topcoat, which she rocks gently.*

Peter enters, emerges from the deep shadows to say something to her, give her something (money), to raise his hand, ambivalently, over the bundle that she holds – blessing, farewell, to scratch his chin? And Ulita steals away.
After a moment, Peter draws back, retreats to the deep shadows, because someone is coming.
And Vera comes in, slowly at first, in her nightdress, the question on her face becoming worry, becoming fear, terror dawning on her, panic as she moves here, there, searching for her baby; and, off, frantic, to search further.
Peter emerging again, cautiously, only to draw back again into the deep shadows: Vera is returning, wide-eyed, distraught, to scream, silently and move off.
Now Arina, the silent witness, emerges from her place of hiding, blighted, hopeless; and to muster what strength she has, to call into the deep shadows:
Arina   I curse you!

End of Act Three.

Act Four

Scene One

Ulita *spreads a cloth on the table. That done she starts setting crockery.*

Upstage, ignored, forgotten, **Arina** *sits alone, dull eyes on the scene, immobile.*

Vera *comes in with something for the table. She is being deliberately slovenly. In private moments,* **Ulita**'s *face says 'Vera has a cheek'.* **Vera**'s *remarks appear to be directed at nothing but the air in front of her mouth. But there is despair, rage, latent violence in her.*

Vera   I wish I could have a look at how some people live, I wish I could have a good look. (*She deposits whatever she has brought in on the table.*) I wish I could have a look at Mickelson's place across the river, I wish I could have a look at that place. Mickelson's housekeeper has a fine time of it. She . . . (*She has gone out again.*)

Peter *comes in, with* **Ivan** *following.* **Peter** *has a document which he will leave on the table.* **Ivan** *has his ledger and some receipts, which he would like* **Peter** *to inspect.* **Peter** *is hardly interested.*

Ivan   Receipts. They aren't very –

Peter (*to* **Ulita**)   Miss Anna isn't down?

Ivan   Peter, they aren't very good, they're bad. And –

Peter (*to* **Ulita**)   When you're done there, call Miss Anna. Tell her the paper is ready that she's to take with her. (*He glances at a receipt.*)

Ivan   And the tenants – those of them that remain, that is –

Peter   Well, let me do a calculation for you. (*He starts writing figures on the back of a receipt.*)

Vera (*coming in*)   The Mickelsons across the river know how to treat people. Their housekeeper – (*To* **Ulita**, *dangerously, who is going out.*) You! Don't use a look like that on your face looking at me! Mickelson's housekeeper doesn't have to go to the cattle sheds or the cellars. (*She dumps a handful of cutlery on the table.*) Their housekeeper wears silk. No one forces her to do anything.

Peter   Now that will do!

Vera (*as before, to no one; going out again*)   Now that will *what*? Now that will *what*?

Ivan   . . . Your tenants are withholding the rent. They're saying it's your responsibility to see that the houses are maintained, the land fertilised. It's only the beginning of something bigger from them.

Peter (*pompously*)   What revenue, Ivan, do you think, would the estate achieve from milk if there were, say, no other cows in the area but mine – (they were) poisoned by that weed, (or) confined outbreaks of a bovine disease, which my herd escapes – and my herd produces twice as much milk as before, and the price of milk goes up by twelve and a half per cent?

In answer to the blank look on **Ivan**'s face, **Peter** *gives him the paper on which are his calculations and answer.*

Ivan   What do you want me to do about the tenant situation?

Peter   I'll think about it.

Ivan   But –

Peter (*crankily*)   Talk to your old friend my mother about it!

Vera (*coming in*)   Mickelson's housekeeper wears one dress today, another tomorrow, special ones for holidays.

Peter   Bless her!

Vera   What her?!

Peter   Are you in rags? (*He goes out.*)

Vera (*calling after him, violence in the sounds*)   Silk! Silk! If the master wishes to see her, she receives him! She and the master drive to church together on Sundays with the child she bore him in the back seat! The priest rings the bell when he sees them coming!

Peter (*returning*)   What kind of woman of your class wears silk?

Vera   Tell me, then I'll know! But of course some women are fools, they do it for a cotton dress – for nothing at all! Or, 'Eat as many apples as you like!'

Peter   This is shocking!

Vera   It's what – this is *what*? You got burnt knees on the floor saying prayers with me, is it?

Peter   You have an evil tongue! This has been going on for weeks. Stop your tricks! Get along with you, shame on you, shame on you, how dare you!

Vera *is suddenly in tears.* **Ulita** *returns with* **Anna**. **Anna** *hangs back, reluctant about entering the scene as yet. She is, though, collected; she's in control of herself.*

Vera (*in tears*)   Oh Lord God, Our Saviour, what am I to do?

Peter   Shame on you, shame on you! The child is in good hands and will grow up a good servant of God.

Vera (*a wail*)   Oh Jesus, help me!

Peter   Do you know how God punishes ingratitude?

Vera   Oh Mother Queen of Heaven!

Peter   He punishes ingratitude by –

Vera (*still in tears*)   No, no, no, I'm not a child, you won't wear me down or bully me with your talk or bringing God into it! Do you know what he (**Ivan**) says about you? He says your words would rot a person.

Anna *joins the scene. She avoids eye contact with* **Peter**.

Anna (*to* **Ulita**)   I'll just have a cup of tea. (*To* **Ivan** *and*
Vera.) Good morning, good morning!

Vera *retires*.

Peter   And no 'good morning' for me? (*He kisses her*.)

Anna   Always kissing.

Peter   You aren't a stranger.

Anna   I'm your niece.

Ivan (*discards his ledger and whatever else*)   I don't think I'm
needed here any more.

On his way out he sees **Arina** *and he stops for a moment to shake his
head at her* ('*You shouldn't have handed over your property*'), *then a bow:*

Ivan   Ma'am. (*And he's gone*.)

Peter   Ah, dear friend Mama! (*To* **Ulita**.) Take morning
tea to the mistress. Little Miss Madam thinks she's leaving us
today! In such a hurry to be off, and what is haste for?

Anna (*mock airily, lightly*)   Lent is over, the theatres are
opening up again!

Peter   Haste is for catching fleas. The trouble I take for
people, to arrange things so that they'll be snug. In bed last
night I was praying, asking God what we should do about our
Anna, and kind God said, 'Take your Anna by her plump
little waist and hold her to your heart!' And further, kind God
said – I wrote it down. (*He takes a note from his pocket and gives it
to her*.) Here, Miss, read it.

She looks at it. He watches her recoil from it.

And haste is what's needed if there's a fire in the house . . .
I've been meaning to say to you, Anna, your grandmother
and I don't like the way you live.

Anna (*mock airily*)   Not enough, Grandma, Uncle, to say you
don't like it, you must point a way out for me. That's why I
came home!

Peter   Live here.

Anna (*wryly*)   Don't tempt me.

Vera *rejoins the scene through the following.*

Peter   It's soldiers she wants. We're not good enough for her. She prefers going round from fair to fair with her guitar.

Anna   What're you talking about?

Peter   Or is it a tambourine? With your sullen sister. Play-acting for soldier boys and other riff-raff, having them look at you.

Anna   (I) Don't want to say anything unpleasant now.

Peter   Having them touch you.

Anna   You're ridiculous!

Peter   Oh?

Anna   You talk terrible nonsense – have always done! – and insist on it too.

Peter   She doesn't like what I say!

Anna   I don't!

And she yields to a perverse compulsion to laugh at him. Which is followed by a harsh, coarse laughing sound – a rattle – from **Vera** *at* **Peter**, *a complement to* **Anna**'s *laugh.*

Peter   The truth isn't to your taste!

Another coarse laughing sound from **Vera**. *He would enlist* **Arina**'s *assistance.*

Peter   Mama? (*No help from* **Arina**. *To* **Anna**.) Well then, you must forgive me but I am a plain-spoken man. I tell the truth and I expect to hear it back from others.

Anna (*under the above*)   'Que j'aime, que j'aime, que j'aime!'

Peter   If I'm asked to speak what isn't true, I may feel sorry for you but I have to refuse.

Anna   Do you really pretend to mean that?

Peter   I never have to think things over. It's my training –
the seminary, and what I've understood and learned at my
mother's knee.

Anna   Fine: we won't say another word about it. (*She directs
the next to* **Arina**.) There's a paper, papers, a deed here for the
farm – the *mountain* – that you want me to sign. Is this it? (*She
picks it up and a pen.*)

Peter   And be so kind as to take it with you and have your
sister sign it.

Anna (*to herself*)   My sullen sister . . . Grandma, Uncle, that
won't be necessary. One less annoyance for you, worry for
you, nuisance, one less burden, one less hungry mouth to
feed, one less vile useless creature, spawn of a shameful
mother and a soldier boy. Bastard imp? (*She signs the document.
She's quite dispassionate in the following. She has grown up.*) Life for
actresses touring the provinces *is* tricky. Specially if they are
untrained, and especially if they have no sense of self-worth.
And, hang it all, Uncle, Grandma, life really has to be about
more than a struggle to protect one's treasure. And men can
be liberal, depending on the goods. So! ('*So!*' *meaning, 'We had
a royal good time.'*) But it all can go wrong. So astray, out of
hand, that it got to the point where it became clear that I and
my sister ought to die. And my sullen sister said, 'Let's get on
with it then, let's give it a hand.' I said, 'Let's go home.' No.
She hated here, now more than ever. And though she did,
she had, I knew, a longing, somewhere in her heart, to live
in the place that she detested. We are young ladies, I told
her, we have property, family graves. No, she kept on
remembering that she was useless and that she was vile. She
knew about phosphorus, the stuff they put on the tips of
matches. I agreed. And we got all these matches and we got
the phosphorus off the tips. She made a solution. I agreed.
She inhaled the stuff, then she drank it. I hesitated with mine.
She had drunk the stuff, I still hesitated, and she was dying.

Drink it, drink it, you fucking bitch. I couldn't. I couldn't. She's buried by the roadside as is the custom.

Peter   And I don't like the way you talk to your elders.

Anna   Do you *really* mean to say you understand *nothing*?

Peter   . . . Mama?

Arina (*laughs into herself*)   Why am I still alive? . . . (*Another fatalistic laugh into herself.*) There's something more to come?

Anna *is putting on a coat.* **Vera** *would join her grievance to* **Anna***'s, but it comes out as a whimper.*

Vera   Curse of hell on them, Miss Anna.

Anna   I shall never come here again. It's terrifying to be near you. There's nothing I'll have any regrets for here. (*She leaves.*)

Peter (*calls after her*)   Silly! Silly! There she goes! Dull, dull, 'It's so dull here' and she can't say why! (*He has followed her off.*) She could have lived here with her uncle and old granny, but she has a mind of her own and that's what a mind of her own has brought her to . . .

Vera (*to* **Arina**)   Better that my father had cut my throat there and then than send me down here to work for you.

From the time of **Anna***'s leaving,* **Vera** *is again in tears. The emptiness of the place makes her more forlorn. And now a low wail:*

Vera   Oh Lord God Our Saviour . . . Oh Jesus, what am I to do . . . Mother Queen of Heaven . . . Oh Jesus . . .

Absently or through habit, she has started to clear and tidy the table. **Ulita** *is coming in to assist in this work, her face again showing its disapproval of* **Vera***'s behaviour, and a 'Tck!' And* **Vera** *holds up a knife as a warning of what she is capable of, and* **Ulita***, knowing what's best for her, retreats.*

Vera *sits down carelessly.*

Arina, *at a remove watches, waits, with a kind of fascination / expectation of what's next.*

Vera *(to no one)*   Mickelson's housekeeper sits with her hands folded. She hardly has to do a tap of work. The master never flings a bad word her way. Nor she at him. He has her all dressed up. He doesn't keep reminding her of what he gives her father. Bag of flour, bag oats, bag potatoes, bag, bag. He doesn't pester her.

Peter *(off, overlapping the last)*   Truth isn't to her liking! She has a mind of her own! She – *(He has come in. He sees* **Vera**.*)* You whore! This won't do! You whore! Is this the plan Jesus has for your life? Is it any use talking to you? Get along with you and get on with your work! I don't know where you've learned these tricks but they must stop at –

Vera   Silk! Silk!

When she says the last, he is almost at her side, standing just behind her. She doesn't look back, her action is like that of someone putting away a nuisance article: two backward thrusts of her hand, which still holds the knife she picked up earlier, stabbing him. He collapses. She continues talking, and leaves slowly through her speech.

He does nothing to annoy her. My dear, my darling, to each other I suppose. I wish I could have a good look at how sweethearts spend their time. Arm in arm I suppose, they walk through the house, into this room and that. And stopping to admire each other, look into each other's eyes . . .

Arina *has witnessed it all and sensed the emergence of her ghosts through the above.* **Lena** *now, too, has joined* **Victor**, **Steven** *and* **Paul**. *Now they have come forward; they are restive and vocally fitful. A cacophony.* **Victor**, *declaiming the Lermontov poem below, overlaps* **Vera***'s last speech.* **Paul** *breaks into his 'rambling' speeches, as in Act Two, Scene Five: 'Property, land . . . She sold her soul . . . She could easily have done something worthwhile with her life.'* **Lena** *does her version of 'Ah! Ah! Que j'aime', or something from 'An Old-Fashioned Colonel'. And* **Steven** *says 'What a waste of life', and tells the story below. All are the product of a disordered mind:* **Arina***'s.*

Victor
    A lonely sail shows white
    Out in the blue mist of the sea!
    What does he seek so far away?
    Why has he left his own country?'

Steven   And another man told me of a man that knew a
magic word. And if that man asked his mother for money and
she refused, he'd say the magic word. (Then) Her eyes would
bulge, arms, legs, go shooting out, her whole body into
spasms of the most violent convulsions that would not stop,
nor abate, until she'd forked out to him.

Victor
    Alas, he seeks not fortune,
    Nor leaves he happiness behind!
    But rebelliously he seeks out storms
    As though in storms his peace to find!

Steven   It's perfectly true.

Arina *has made her slow, tired way out through them. Now, joined by*
Peter, *they follow her.*

Scene Two

Arina *is coming in.*

Arina   If anyone's expecting me to cry, expect again!

As in Scene One, it's a cavernous place, only that it now appears to be
an exterior. Day. As in Scene One, **Arina** *looks self-possessed, able,*
erect and, if anything, younger. This image of her former self also comes
from her disordered mind. She is dying but she will not see herself on a
deathbed. She thinks she's going home, walking to the mountain and
climbing it.

She thought only about money, property, sold her soul,
became a tyrant, cared nothing about her children – Enough
insults, stupidity! She restored the fortunes of the family she
married into, doubled them, changed the names of the lands

she conquered – 'Arina' – and that's failure, that's a waste of
life! (*She nods in the direction ahead of her.*) Up there I'm going.
(*She wipes her forehead.*) Now they're plastering her with oil,
sprinkling cold water on her face, 'Oh my God I'm heartily
sorry', in her ear, 'Confess, repent, that you may receive
salvation', pestering her to death! I'm going home. Like I've
been for so long promising myself. And she doesn't want
anyone hunting her!

The last as she checks behind her for pursuers. Then on again.

It wasn't by lickerishness that anyone from up here made out.
Or by going on the razzle either. What age was she when she
came down to work for the windmill's family? Her father'd
done a deal with them for her. Thirteen, fourteen?
Thereabouts. Did she cry then, whinge? That family'd lost
most of what they had one time by that time, were losing
more and no doubt in time would lose the lot. No greed left
in them, which is a thing difficult to revere. And they thought
she was a fool, because she let them.

She checks behind her again.

Then the young windmill started to waylay her. She never
knew when he'd pounce, or where: Till, mind you, times, her
heart'd be in her mouth waiting for the ambush. Which led of
course to a change in her figure.

In all, she had four children, five miscarriages. Two
grandchildren. Three.

But where is the understanding of empty-headed drunkards?
I'd like to know. What was she to do? Things were out of
hand. Let things go from bad to worse? – To nothing?
Someone had to take over, full control. She took over. Full
control. And I hate uselessness. And when the time came, she
took on the bigger world. What was she to do? Watch
chances rot, leave openings to the invader? She took on –
seized – the bigger world, man's world, of trading, business,
dealing. No laughing matter, the excitement of it was

frightening, the delight of being on a knife edge: Lord, Christ, Marvellous, Yes!

There is nobody can or is able to stop me! There is nothing I can't do!

(I was) Tough? D'you think innocence stands a chance? And, do you, for a woman? Show your feelings and you'll soon discover what softness can expect of male or any other kind of gallantry.

What something otherwise should she, could she, ought she, so worthwhile, so easily have done with her life? I'd still like to know about that one too.

She is checking behind her again. The absence of pursuers, her family, contrary to what she protests, now seems to be agitating her, disappointing her, making her angry and emotional.

And she cared nothing about her children? She saw that you were schooled, educated in what, yes, she thought would best suit each of you! Decisions. If she had doubts, who to share them with? She led by and set them an example of what could be done. What did the tyrant want in return? What was the deal? To be told she'd sold her soul? To see her determination used as the excuse for *your* weakness?! . . . I showed you as much love as was safe! Love is love, goes without saying, it doesn't need frills – frills put a lie to it – love is deciding to take your next breath, love is life . . . (*A lull.*) And she'd love to grow old . . . She was watchful, feared for them – showed them as much of that too as she dared, lest fear, any defect in her be handed down. What did she want in return for herself? (*She is shouting.*) Each one of you to be better than me! . . . And maybe I'd be at peace. And I'd need envy no one. And I'd want nothing. And I'd need fear nothing . . . And don't.

The last in reaction to becoming aware of her complete isolation and that it does not frighten her. The light is closing in around her.

. . . And don't . . . What a waste of life? I don't think so . . . Repent, confess, oh my God I'm heartily sorry? I don't think

so . . . In any case, that deal is to come. Between me and
Him . . . It's not that I'm going to enforce a claim on salvation.
I won't. Maybe I don't even deserve it. But I'll get it.

And she's gone.

Methuen Drama Student Editions

Jean Anouilh *Antigone* • John Arden *Serjeant Musgrave's Dance* Alan Ayckbourn *Confusions* • Aphra Behn *The Rover* • Edward Bond *Lear* • *Saved* • Bertolt Brecht *The Caucasian Chalk Circle* • *Fear and Misery in the Third Reich* • *The Good Person of Szechwan* • *Life of Galileo* • *Mother Courage and her Children* • *The Resistible Rise of Arturo Ui* • *The Threepenny Opera* • Anton Chekhov *The Cherry Orchard* • *The Seagull* • *Three Sisters* • *Uncle Vanya* • Caryl Churchill *Serious Money* • *Top Girls* • Shelagh Delaney *A Taste of Honey* • Euripides *Elektra* • *Medea* • Dario Fo *Accidental Death of an Anarchist* • Michael Frayn *Copenhagen* • John Galsworthy *Strife* • Nikolai Gogol *The Government Inspector* • Robert Holman *Across Oka* • Henrik Ibsen *A Doll's House* • *Ghosts* • *Hedda Gabler* • Charlotte Keatley *My Mother Said I Never Should* • Bernard Kops *Dreams of Anne Frank* • Federico García Lorca *Blood Wedding* • *Doña Rosita the Spinster* (bilingual edition) • *The House of Bernarda Alba* • (bilingual edition) • *Yerma* (bilingual edition) • David Mamet *Glengarry Glen Ross* • *Oleanna* • Patrick Marber *Closer* • John Marston *Malcontent* • Martin McDonagh *The Lieutenant of Inishmore* • Joe Orton *Loot* • Luigi Pirandello *Six Characters in Search of an Author* • Mark Ravenhill *Shopping and F***ing* • Willy Russell *Blood Brothers* • *Educating Rita* • Sophocles *Antigone* • *Oedipus the King* • Wole Soyinka *Death and the King's Horseman* • Shelagh Stephenson *The Memory of Water* • August Strindberg *Miss Julie* • J. M. Synge *The Playboy of the Western World* • Theatre Workshop *Oh What a Lovely War* Timberlake Wertenbaker *Our Country's Good* • Arnold Wesker *The Merchant* • Oscar Wilde *The Importance of Being Earnest* • Tennessee Williams *A Streetcar Named Desire* • *The Glass Menagerie*

Methuen Drama Modern Plays
include work by

Edward Albee
Jean Anouilh
John Arden
Margaretta D'Arcy
Peter Barnes
Sebastian Barry
Brendan Behan
Dermot Bolger
Edward Bond
Bertolt Brecht
Howard Brenton
Anthony Burgess
Simon Burke
Jim Cartwright
Caryl Churchill
Noël Coward
Lucinda Coxon
Sarah Daniels
Nick Darke
Nick Dear
Shelagh Delaney
David Edgar
David Eldridge
Dario Fo
Michael Frayn
John Godber
Paul Godfrey
David Greig
John Guare
Peter Handke
David Harrower
Jonathan Harvey
Iain Heggie
Declan Hughes
Terry Johnson
Sarah Kane
Charlotte Keatley
Barrie Keeffe
Howard Korder

Robert Lepage
Doug Lucie
Martin McDonagh
John McGrath
Terrence McNally
David Mamet
Patrick Marber
Arthur Miller
Mtwa, Ngema & Simon
Tom Murphy
Phyllis Nagy
Peter Nichols
Sean O'Brien
Joseph O'Connor
Joe Orton
Louise Page
Joe Penhall
Luigi Pirandello
Stephen Poliakoff
Franca Rame
Mark Ravenhill
Philip Ridley
Reginald Rose
Willy Russell
Jean-Paul Sartre
Sam Shepard
Wole Soyinka
Simon Stephens
Shelagh Stephenson
Peter Straughan
C. P. Taylor
Theatre de Complicite
Theatre Workshop
Sue Townsend
Judy Upton
Timberlake Wertenbaker
Roy Williams
Snoo Wilson
Victoria Wood

Methuen Drama Contemporary Dramatists
include

John Arden (two volumes)
Arden & D'Arcy
Peter Barnes (three volumes)
Sebastian Barry
Dermot Bolger
Edward Bond (eight volumes)
Howard Brenton
  (two volumes)
Richard Cameron
Jim Cartwright
Caryl Churchill (two volumes)
Sarah Daniels (two volumes)
Nick Darke
David Edgar (three volumes)
David Eldridge
Ben Elton
Dario Fo (two volumes)
Michael Frayn (three volumes)
David Greig
John Godber (four volumes)
Paul Godfrey
John Guare
Lee Hall (two volumes)
Peter Handke
Jonathan Harvey
  (two volumes)
Declan Hughes
Terry Johnson (three volumes)
Sarah Kane
Barrie Keeffe
Bernard-Marie Koltès
  (two volumes)
Franz Xaver Kroetz
David Lan
Bryony Lavery
Deborah Levy
Doug Lucie

David Mamet (four volumes)
Martin McDonagh
Duncan McLean
Anthony Minghella
  (two volumes)
Tom Murphy (six volumes)
Phyllis Nagy
Anthony Neilsen (two volumes)
Philip Osment
Gary Owen
Louise Page
Stewart Parker (two volumes)
Joe Penhall (two volumes)
Stephen Poliakoff
  (three volumes)
David Rabe (two volumes)
Mark Ravenhill (two volumes)
Christina Reid
Philip Ridley
Willy Russell
Eric-Emmanuel Schmitt
Ntozake Shange
Sam Shepard (two volumes)
Wole Soyinka (two volumes)
Simon Stephens (two volumes)
Shelagh Stephenson
David Storey (three volumes)
Sue Townsend
Judy Upton
Michel Vinaver
  (two volumes)
Arnold Wesker (two volumes)
Michael Wilcox
Roy Williams (three volumes)
Snoo Wilson (two volumes)
David Wood (two volumes)
Victoria Wood

Methuen Drama World Classics

include

Jean Anouilh (two volumes)
Brendan Behan
Aphra Behn
Bertolt Brecht (eight volumes)
Büchner
Bulgakov
Calderón
Čapek
Anton Chekhov
Noël Coward (eight volumes)
Feydeau
Eduardo De Filippo
Max Frisch
John Galsworthy
Gogol
Gorky (two volumes)
Harley Granville Barker
   (two volumes)
Victor Hugo
Henrik Ibsen (six volumes)
Jarry

Lorca (three volumes)
Marivaux
Mustapha Matura
David Mercer (two volumes)
Arthur Miller (five volumes)
Molière
Musset
Peter Nichols (two volumes)
Joe Orton
A. W. Pinero
Luigi Pirandello
Terence Rattigan
   (two volumes)
W. Somerset Maugham
   (two volumes)
August Strindberg
   (three volumes)
J. M. Synge
Ramón del Valle-Inclan
Frank Wedekind
Oscar Wilde

For a complete catalogue
of Methuen Drama titles
write to:

Methuen Drama
36 Soho Square
London W1D 3QY

or you can visit our website at:

www.methuendrama.com

Lightning Source UK Ltd.
Milton Keynes UK
01 May 2010